Culture and Demography in Organizations

Culture and Demography in Organizations

J. Richard Harrison and
Glenn R. Carroll

PRINCETON UNIVERSITY PRESS   PRINCETON AND OXFORD

Published by Princeton University Press,
41 William Street, Princeton, New Jersey 08540
In the United Kingdom: Princeton University Press, 3 Market Place, Woodstock,
  Oxfordshire OX20 1SY

Library of Congress Cataloging-in-Publication Data

Harrison, J. Richard.
    Culture and demography in organizations / J. Richard Harrison and Glenn R. Carroll.
      p. cm.
    Includes bibliographical references and index.
    ISBN-10: 0-691-12481-7 (cloth : alk. paper)
    ISBN-13: 978-0-691-12481-0 (cloth : alk. paper)
    ISBN-10: 0-691-12482-5 (paper : alk. paper)
    ISBN-15: 978-0-691-12482-7 (paper : alk. paper)
    1. Corporate culture. 2. Organizational change. 3. Strategic planning.
    4. Employees—Recruiting. 5. Labor turnover. 6. Social sciences—Computer
    simulation. I. Carroll, Glenn. II. Title.

    HD58.7.H3696 2006
    302.3'5—dc22

                                                          2005049251

British Library Cataloging-in-Publication Data is available

This book has been composed in Sabon
Printed on acid-free paper. ∞
pup.princeton.edu
Printed in the United States of America

10 9 8 7 6 5 4 3 2 1

To the memory of his father, Charles A. Harrison, from JRH

To the lovely Lihua Olivia Wang, from GRC

Contents

x • Contents

Figures

Tables

Preface

A long-noted observation about organizations concerns the strong persistence of their cultures over time. By many analysts' views, organizational cultures change slowly, if at all, and often require great effort if they are to change in certain intended directions.

Yet the apparent stability of organizational cultures remains something of a mystery. The individuals who enter an organization often know little or nothing of the culture a priori, and they may vary radically in terms of their personalities and social characteristics. Moreover, in many organizations, individuals enter and leave rapidly and in great numbers. These possibilities suggest that the degree of cultural persistence likely varies systematically across organizations; persistence would also be perplexing if observed under some conditions commonly encountered in the organizational world.

Understanding how and when organizations maintain cultures potentially involves many processes. Obviously, the ways individuals get chosen for membership in an organization and socialized initially play a role. It is also apparent that the rates at which individuals retain internalized cultural material may be important. But there are also crucial collective dimensions to cultural stability: patterns of interaction among members, perhaps shaped by their social characteristics, common experiences, and the structure of the organization; and management attempts to design and control the culture, reinforced by various sanctions as well as recruiting and dismissal practices. Finally, the level and stability of demographic flows of members of the organization potentially constrain the organization in a severe manner. Indeed, the substantial demographic turnover of a typical organization turns cultural maintenance into a problem of cultural transmission across generations of individuals.

In this book, we describe a research program we have conducted over the last fifteen years or so on the maintenance and transmission of culture in formal organizations. Despite the volumes written about organizational culture, little other theory or research has examined specifically the dynamics of cultural maintenance or transmission over time in organizations, especially when demographic considerations are given their due. Instead, social scientists almost always focus on what we call the *content of culture*. By content, we refer to the substance of the culture—the actual sets of ideas, beliefs, values, behaviors, symbols, rituals, and the like that characterize the culture. Research organized around content typically tries to discover or identify the important elements of cultural content, to understand how members of the culture interpret these elements, and to explain how content shapes behavior. Yet most content-based research presupposes a certain degree of cultural stability and does not recognize the potentially problematic nature of such an assumption. Accordingly, we integrate the content-based approach with another approach, the distributive approach to culture. This approach to culture views content, especially interpretations, as varying across individuals, locations in the social structure, and time. Synthesizing these two approaches leads us to conceptualize organizational culture as comprising the distribution of managerially preferred cultural content across individuals within the organization and across time. Analyzing organizational culture in this way provides a general method for understanding the dynamics and morphology of cultural systems.

At the core of our research program is a demographically based formal (mathematical) model of cultural transmission in organizations. This book motivates and describes the model, its assumptions, its mechanisms, its extensions, and its behavior in a series of studies. In our different studies, we extend various parts of the model at times and collapse some parts at other times, depending on the substantive focus. Nonetheless, our primary interest throughout lies in the effects of various factors and conditions on the maintenance and variation of organizational culture over time, especially as it concerns demographic activity. Specifically, we examine how organizational demography affects the extent to which an organization embodies management's cultural ideals, as exemplified by the mean level of enculturation among its constituent members and by the dispersion of enculturation across members. We believe that analyzing the cultural transmission process of organizations in this way leads to new insights about many aspects of organizational culture, some of which call into question commonly held beliefs.

Our primary analytical exercises with the model use computer simulations, where we systematically vary many of the model's components and examine cultural outcomes. We use simulation methods for two main reasons. First, simulations allow us to study the cultural system of an organization as composed of three simple, interdependent processes (of individual entry, socialization, and exit) where the joint outcomes are far from obvious, especially over time. By using simulation, we are not forced to make unrealistic assumptions in the model to ensure analytical tractability; we also can move from the individual to organizational levels of analysis with ease. Second, simulations let us sidestep the many measurement controversies that surround the study of organizational culture, not to mention the practical problem of collecting cultural measures for a sample of organizations longitudinally. Moreover, we are able to do so without specifying the actual content of the culture or the number of associated cultural dimensions (although we also show how our model can be directly interpreted in these terms in chapter 3).

The use of simulation in organization theory goes back to work from the early 1960s, especially that of James G. March. Despite the importance of this early work, few simulation-based studies had much impact on mainstream theory and research until the 1990s. Now simulation research on organizations appears in top journals with some regularity, and its usage appears to be picking up momentum as new (mainly young) simulators enter the field. While we would be delighted if this book contributed to the renewal of interest in simulating organizational processes, our main audience is not the simulation modeling crowd per se but the many researchers and students interested in organizations generally. That is, we seek primarily to contribute to the development of organizational theory and specifically to the development of theory about culture. For us, simulation provides a valuable methodological tool for doing theoretical analysis. Accordingly, the book does not emphasize technical details any more than a typical scientific monograph: we give details of the models and methods so as to facilitate detailed evaluation and possible replication, but we pay primary attention to the theoretical ideas considered and their implications.

Simulation methodology allows us to demonstrate the value of a sustained focus on a single basic formal model and its applications to sets of related problems. There are, of course, plenty of other books that take such a focused approach to modeling, including books about organizational culture. What (partially) differentiates our research program is a sort of disciplined flexibility, whereby in tackling various research questions we retain the model's basic structure but adapt certain elements of it to address the specific issues raised by each question. Often these model adaptations are "hierarchical" in that we relax certain simplifying assumptions or explore complications (as when we look at structured influence networks in chapter 8). At other times, we alter the model slightly to fit the context (as when we study top management teams in chapter 7) or use it in a totally different way (as when we examine cultural integration in mergers in chapter 10). Simulation methodology enables this approach because it does not tightly constrain the direction in which the model might be developed.

Even though the model undergoes a series of transformations in the process, we believe that a research program based on disciplined flexibility can generate cumulative knowledge. From a distance, this may be hard to see, since each model adaptation appears in publications as a separate entity addressing a particular question. The book format allows us to put all the pieces of the program together better, to explain the basic model and its assumptions, to justify the various model adaptations, and to emphasize the connections among the adaptions. As a result, the book does contain some previously published findings and other material; however, it also contains significant amounts of new, previously unpublished material (including whole chapters), as well as a good deal of new integrative text. We think that the book provides a fuller and deeper insight into our research program and its contributions.

Notes on Style

A scientific monograph always contains a good deal of technical material, and this one is no different. We have tried, however, to make the book as readable as possible by eliminating nonessential technical material (for instance, standard errors of regression estimates are dropped, although significance levels are indicated either by marking or by omission, as each table explains) and by presenting models and findings in summary or graphical form whenever possible. Our goal was to make the monograph readable without losing its scientific integrity, recognizing that the result will remain directed mainly to an audience of professional social scientists. Accordingly, we attempted to reproduce enough of the details so that readers can follow our reasoning and even draw their own conclusions from much of the evidence; however, we have likely not provided enough technical evidence for those who wish to go off in entirely different directions. For those wishing to explore issues in greater depth, we refer (in most cases) to published technical articles that can usually be obtained in a research setting without great effort.

A few words on notation. We use the term log to refer to the natural logarithm. We use a time subscript t to indicate that we are referring to the value of a time-varying variable at time t, whether or not it is an explicit function of time; and we use commas before the time subscript (e.g., $_{i,t-1}$) for clarity because cases of subscripts like $_{it-1}$ do not make sense. The notation used in our models, which varies somewhat as the basic model is extended or adapted in later chapters, is summarized for convenient reference in appendix A.

We have also used some terms interchangeably even though others sometimes draw important distinctions between them. Again, our motivation is to enhance readability. For persons within organizations, we use the terms *individual, member, participant, employee,* and *worker.* For organizations themselves, we use the term *organization* as well as *firm, formal organization,* and *social entity.* The context makes clear those instances where the meaning is intended to follow the more restrictive definition.

Acknowledgments

This project has come a long way since its inception in Dallas and Las Vegas in the late 1980s. Along the route it has received much support—intellectual, emotional, and financial—without which it would have withered up and disappeared long ago. It is impractical for us to thank here individually all those persons and institutions that have contributed to the project in many, many ways. But we certainly remember who they are, and deeply appreciate every one of them for helping us to develop this research program and book. Thanks.

A few colleagues made contributions that were so important and direct that we would be remiss not to acknowledge their efforts explicitly. They include especially Charles O'Reilly, who from the beginning saw the potential value of this line of research and then encouraged us time and time again. For reading messy early drafts of chapters of the book and helping us see how to put it together in sensible fashion through detailed comments, we thank Jennifer Chatman, Jerker Denrell, Michael Hannan, Dave McKendrick, Jesper Sørensen, and Toby Stuart. For research assistance at various points in time, we appreciate the help of Jason Davis and Lucia Tsai.

As is obvious from the list of joint publications that follows, our collaboration has been a long and productive one. Indeed, we have grappled together with issues about cultural maintenance for so long that it makes little sense to us to try and separate individual priority or credit for various parts of the project. The book is truly a collective work, and we each bear equal responsibility. We decided the order of the names on the title page by tossing a coin.

The book is dedicated to two special people. From Richard, the dedication to the memory of his father pays tribute to his father's steadfast belief in the value of higher education and lifelong encouragement and support for Richard's academic pursuits. From Glenn, the dedication to Lihua reflects his inestimable love for her, as well as his gratitude for her patience in putting up with his many imperfections, including occasional obsessive bouts with finishing a book (not an easy thing to live with).

Finally, we would like to thank the following publishers for permission to adapt and excerpt portions of the following copyrighted materials:

Harrison, J. Richard, and Glenn R. Carroll. 1991. "Keeping the Faith: A Model of Cultural Transmission in Formal Organizations." *Administrative*

PART I

Cultural Analysis

The two chapters in this part of the book discuss cultural analysis and our unique ways of conducting it. Chapter 1 provides a brief overview of social science's experience with culture generally and with organizational culture specifically. It draws out a major distinction between theories of culture based on content and those based on the distribution of content. The chapter describes how the research in the book relies on a partial synthesis of these two approaches, and explains the attractions of this synthesis for studying organizational culture. Chapter 2 discusses our methodology—computer simulation of formal models. It describes how this methodology differs from more traditional approaches and what its implications are for cultural analysis.

CHAPTER 1

Culture in Organizations

1.1 INTRODUCTION

Consider the culture of the organization that currently employs you. Jot down a few words or phrases to describe its essential features. In doing this exercise, ask yourself about the specific beliefs embodied in the culture, and about the particular practices and behaviors regarded as appropriate and inappropriate in the organization.

Now think about how the culture was yesterday, how it was last week, how it was last month, how it was last year, and how it was five years ago, if you know. Odds are, if your organization is typical, that while some parts of the culture may have changed over the longer periods, the cultural essence of the organization has shifted little, if at all. Yet many other things about the organization likely did change: employees came and went, jobs changed hands with regularity, top managers moved around, suppliers were shifted, customers left and new ones were cultivated, competitors emerged and fell by the wayside, and the economy exerted itself in different ways.

Cultural stability in organizations, even over very long periods of time, is a fact of social life. It may not be a universal fact, as we can all point to particular organizations where significant cultural change has occurred. But it is a highly prevalent fact, and an amazing one at that. Given the vast amount of demographic and other change that occurs in the typical organization, it seems reasonable to expect some kind of cultural drift or erosion as the normal state of affairs—after all, culture resides in and gets reproduced by the specific persons present, and when they come and go regularly, it would seem that cultural elements might too. Instead, most social scientists would contend that organizational cultural usually persists over time with great force, even in the midst of strong pressures apparently to the contrary. The famous phrase of nineteenth-century French novelist Alphonse Karr (1849), "The more things change, the more they remain the same," seems an apt way to describe the cultures of many modern organizations.

This book investigates the amazing social fact of cultural persistence. We aim to understand when cultures persist and when they change. We pay special attention to dynamics, especially the demographic dynamics of personnel. This is an unusual approach to the study of organizational culture, and its potential value may not be immediately obvious. Accordingly, we start in this first chapter by painting the backdrop to our research program and its theoretical orientation, by explaining how it connects with the extant literature on culture and what we think it has to offer.

The chapter begins with a short observation about the state of cultural analysis in social science and then moves quickly to a brief overview of the more contemporary literature on culture in organizations. Following that, in the next two sections, we draw a distinction between two general approaches to cultural analysis, the popular content-based approach that focuses on the actual substance of cultural symbols and practices, and the lesser-known distributive approach that concentrates on the variability of cultural interpretation across the members of a population. We then explain how we use aspects of both approaches to develop a limited synthetic approach to study and model organizational culture. In our approach, we conceptualize organizational culture as comprising the distribution of managerially preferred cultural content across individuals within the organization and across time. Viewing organizational culture in this way gives us a general model for analyzing the dynamics and morphology of cultural systems. Next, we hint at the power of our approach by offering summary glimpses of some of the findings presented in the book. Finally, we conclude with an overview of the book and some suggestions for how to read it.

1.2 Culture in Social Science

Although probably controversial, a case could be made that the scientific study of the social world began with early investigations of culture. It would start by making clear, if it is not so already, that ethnography qualifies as a scientific method. It would proceed by claiming that the dispassionate narrative accounts of premodern societies found in the journals of explorers and natural historians constitute a kind of early ethnography. The case would then be finalized by showing that these kinds of activities were earlier and more widespread in the literature than the statistical analysis of human mortality conducted by John Graunt (1662), commonly cited as marking the origins of social science.

Whatever the lineage of social science, professional accounts of cultures can be found in the journals of geography and natural history from at least the early nineteenth century. For instance, early issues of the *Journal of the Royal Geographic Society of London* contain numerous descriptive accounts of adventurers' and naturalists' explorations, including descriptions of native customs, religious practices, laws, polity, organization, and behavior. Heavily descriptive and often narrative, these reports typically have the tone of objective and systematic exposition, even when making moralistic judgments. At times, they are even somewhat analytical, as in the ethnographic article of J. C. Prichard (1839, 200) on "high Asia" which focuses on language differences and their origins:

> On comparing the Mongolian, the Mandschu and Turkish languages, in relation to their grammatical structure, a series of remarkable analogies is discovered. The resemblance of the Mongolian and the Mandschu is much closer than between either of them and the western dialects of the Turkish language. These dialects, especially that of the Osmanli, have been subjected to a foreign influence and culture, the result of intercourse with Persians and Arabians, and the introduction of Mohammedan literature among the Turks.

Discussion of culture can be found in the early journals and books of each of the modern social science disciplines, including economics, sociology, and political science. But, of course, nowhere is culture's early prominence greater than in anthropology, where the discipline essentially constituted itself around the concept. From its foundation, anthropology's concern with premodern societies showed a special fascination with cultural phenomena (Tylor, 1871).

Given such early interest, it might seem natural to expect that modern social science would have either reached a consensus about how to regard culture scientifically or eschewed use of the concept altogether. But neither characterization accurately describes the current situation. Remarkably, ample dissensus still exists in many quarters over what culture is, what it means to social life, and how to analyze it (see Brumann, 1999, and associated commentary).

Despite disagreement about such fundamental questions, culture maintains a grand presence on the stage of contemporary social science. Indeed, the last decade or so has witnessed a resurgent, and perhaps deeper, interest in culture (often dubbed "the cultural turn"), initiated by a widespread belief about its importance in explaining social life (see Lie, 1997; Mohr, 1998; Perrow, 2000). Current fascination with culture as an explanation of behavior is so widespread across areas and disciplines that some social scientists wonder if anthropology has any distinctive approach left for analyzing the social world.

1.3 CULTURE IN ORGANIZATION THEORY

Cultural studies in the field of organization theory show several notable parallels with its more general development. As with the basic disciplines, one can find cultural issues raised and discussed seriously in some foundational texts.

For instance, the pre-paradigmatic classic book of Barnard (1938) does not use the word *culture*, but it is replete with references to informal organization and cooperation.[1] Later, as the nascent field of organization theory began to develop, the eminent sociologist Talcott Parsons (1956: 67) wrote in the first issue of *Administrative Science Quarterly*:

> Like any social system, an organization is conceived as having a describable social structure. This can be described and analyzed from two points of view, both of which are essential to completeness. The first is the cultural-institutional point of view which uses the values of the system and their institutionalization in different functional contexts as its point of departure; the second is the group or role point of view which takes suborganizations and the roles of individuals participating in the functioning of the organization as its point of departure. . . . primary attention will be given to the former.

Although early organizational theorists (most notably the human relations and institutional schools) developed ideas about informal structures, as suggested by Barnard, Parsons, and others, a specific focus on organizational culture did not come until around 1980.[2] During this period, large Japanese firms rose rapidly in prominence in many world markets, making analysts acutely aware of their apparently homogeneous cultures. A flurry of studies attributed the rise of Japanese corporations to their peculiar cultural designs, touting the potential performance benefits of homogeneous cultures and offering recipes for cultural management in organizations (Ouchi, 1981; Deal and Kennedy, 1982; Peters and Waterman, 1982).

The surge of interest in organizational culture rapidly developed to include more tempered scholarly analyses. Among other things, studies of culture pointed to the potential liabilities of cultural homogeneity (e.g., inertia, discrimination, and the suppression of creativity), the difficulties of analyzing culture (e.g., its multidimensionality, ambiguity in interpretation, and incomparability), and the subtle complexities of attempting to manage a culture (e.g., the reactive nature of human behavior and the development of subversive subcultures). Studies also

---

[1]Scott (2003: 68) claims that "many of the themes initiated by Barnard have become highly fashionable in recent decades as students of organizations rediscover the importance of *organizational cultures* shaped by zealous managers supplying strongly held values to their members." He goes on to say that "Barnard is the godfather of contemporary business gurus . . . who advocate the cultivation of 'strong cultures.'"

[2]An earlier literature about the concept of organizational climate is sometimes linked to the study of culture.

demonstrated, however, that cultures vary across organizations and that these differences affect behavioral outcomes (Hofstede, 1980). Moreover, few, if any, analysts argued that culture was irrelevant or could be ignored in organizational analyses.

Given the short but intense history of theory and research on organizational culture, an outside observer might anticipate that analysts would have either settled basic questions about organizational culture or dismissed it as a nonviable path for investigation. Again, as with culture in anthropology and the basic disciplines, this view would be wrong. Theories, methods, and even conceptual approaches to the issue reflect stark and often inconsistent differences. Dissensus is so strong that Martin (2002) refers to intellectual exchanges in the area as "culture wars."

Yet almost no one denies the potential importance of organizational culture. Social scientists may argue about many aspects of organizational culture. But there is little disagreement about its potential ability to control behavior or its role in assisting members to interpret and derive meaning from their experiences while inside particular organizations. Analyses of culture can be found today in most issues of the leading academic journals on organizations and in every major textbook used in organizational courses throughout the world. Culture receives credit for the spectacular long-term success of companies such as Nordstrom, Southwest Airlines, and Hewlett-Packard (Tushman and O'Reilly, 1997) and blame for tragedies such as the *Columbia* space shuttle accident at the National Aeronautics and Space Administration (NASA; Columbia Accident Investigation Board, 2003). Most experienced managers will also tell you that culture is one of the great intangibles in managing a business or complex organization, especially the modern multinational corporation that spans different businesses and countries. For example, CEO Lou Gerstner (2002: 182) of IBM writes that "culture isn't just one aspect of the game—it *is* the game."

1.4 THE CONTENT APPROACH TO CULTURE

Despite the many different approaches to culture, social scientists typically maintain a strong focus on what we call the *content of culture*. By *content*, we refer to the substance of the culture—the actual sets of ideas, beliefs, values, behaviors, symbols, rituals, and the like that characterize the culture. In various studies, content might be described in terms of specific cultural features, such as *teknonymy*, the practice whereby individuals are referred to not by their personal names but as derived from their offspring's names (e.g., Lishan's mother).[3] Or, content might be characterized in more general terms, such as collectivist or individualistic (Hofstede, 1980).

Research organized around cultural content typically tries to discover or identify the important elements of the culture. It then attempts to understand how members of the culture interpret these elements and to explain how content shapes social interaction and behavior. The usual study also assumes that for a cultural element to be important, it must be more or less shared, a coherent collective phenomenon. Cultural analysis thus tends to concentrate on the shared content, an approach consistent with social science's general orientation of analyzing relationships between the means of variables.

Much theoretical debate over culture involves disputes about what exactly constitutes the important general elements of cultural content, the specific ways that they control or guide behavior, and their interrelationships with each other.[4] Perhaps the most fundamental difference lies in the distinction between the materialist view of cultures as adaptive systems and the ideational view of cultures as cognitive, structural, or symbolic systems (see Keesing, 1974). In the materialist conception, cultures are viewed broadly as "systems (of socially transmitted behavior patterns) that serve to relate human communities to their ecological settings. These ways-of-life communities include technologies and modes of economic organization, settlement patterns, modes of social grouping and political organization, religious beliefs and practices and so on" (Keesing, 1974: 75). By this view, the material conditions of life constrain and shape the form of culture that develops and adapts as conditions change. In the ideational view, ideas define the content: "A society's culture consists of whatever it is one has to know or believe in order to operate in a manner acceptable to its members. . . . culture is not a material phenomenon, it does not consist of things, people, behavior or emotions. . . . it is the forms of things that people have in their mind, their models for perceiving, relating and otherwise interpreting them" [Goodenough (1957: 167)]. An attempt to elaborate the ideational elements of content yielded the following phenomena: forms, propositions, beliefs, rules, values, recipes, routines, customs, meaning, and function (Goodenough, 1981).

Contemporary debate over cultural content has shifted somewhat, with the materialist view receiving far less attention. According to Hannerz (1992), current studies of culture primarily address one of two general dimensions of content: (1) ideas and modes of thought, or

---

[3]Teknonymy is common among the Balinese, as well as other groups. Geertz and Geertz (1964) interpret it to mean that the Balinese de-emphasize individuality.

[4]Of course, considerable debate also exists over methods for studying culture.

(2) forms of externalization. He considers the first to be primary in anthropological study:

> Understanding structures of knowledge, belief, experience, and feeling in all their subtlety, and in their entire range of variations at home and abroad, is reasonably enough the core of cultural analysis. Secondarily, perhaps, anthropologists have occupied themselves with . . . the way meaning finds expression in a somewhat limited range of manifest forms—speech, music, graphic arts, or certain other communication modes. (Hannerz, 1992: 9–10)

Criticisms of the culture concept commonly consist of criticisms of the content approach, especially its emphasis on shared content. In summarizing the critiques, Brumann (1999: S1) notes that "the major concern of the sceptical discourse on culture is that the concept suggests boundedness, homogeneity, coherence, stability, and structure whereas social reality is characterized by variablity, inconsistencies, conflict, change and individual agency." Rodseth (1998: 55) sees the critics as claiming that culture "is tainted by essentialism, by holism, by ahistoricity; the concept inevitably suggests that human variation comes packaged in neatly bounded systems of changing forms: primordial, homogeneous and overly coherent."

Organizational Cultural Content

Content issues also dominate theory and research on organizational culture. Consider, for instance, definitions of culture from three sets of organizational researchers with different disciplinary backgrounds:

- "Culture: a pattern of basic assumptions—invented, discovered, or developed by a given group as it learns to cope with its problems of external adaptation and internal integration—that has worked well enough to be considered valid and, therefore, to be taught to new members as the correct way to perceive, think and feel in relation to those problems" (social psychologist Edgar Schein, 1985: 9).

- "We define culture as a system of shared values (that define what is important) and norms that define appropriate attitudes and behaviors for organizational members (how to feel and behave)" (psychologically oriented management theorists Charles O'Reilly and Jennifer Chatman, 1996: 160).

- "Culture refers to the commonly held values and beliefs of individuals within the organization and, accordingly, the evaluative criteria used to make both large and small decisions" (economists Garth Saloner and Andrea Shepard and sociologist Joel Podolny, 2001: 76).

While differing in the particular cultural elements highlighted (basic assumptions, shared values and norms, or commonly held beliefs), each of these definitions directs us to look at the patterns of more or less shared content found in an organization. Typical aspects of cultural content would include beliefs, values, norms, special languages, and mental maps that make sense of the organization.

As with culture generally, theory and research on organizational culture vary greatly in terms of the specific content emphasized. For example, Schein (1992) identifies three levels of cultural content: (1) basic assumptions, (2) values, and (3) artifacts and creations, including technology, art, and visible and audible behavior patterns. Likewise, Trice and Beyer (1993) demarcate two general types of content: (1) ideologies, abstractions composed of belief, norms, and values; and (2) forms, concrete cultural manifestations composed of symbols, languages, narratives, and practices. Moreover, dissensus prevails about what to highlight. In her review of the field, Martin (1992: 53) notes that prominent studies[5] of organizational culture "disagree about what exactly is being shared," including beliefs, values, patterns of meaning and expectations, understandings, basic assumptions, and communication rules.

Designing Cultural Content

A major difference in views of organizational culture revolves around the question of design—the extent to which culture can be engineered to look like one wants. Of course, most social scientists believe that culture is a naturally occurring phenomenon that every formal organization possesses. For instance, political theorist James Q. Wilson (1989: 91) states, "Every organization has a culture. . . . Culture is to an organization what personality is to an individual."

Compared with societies, formal organizations differ in several ways that plausibly affect cultural design. First, formal organizations possess much greater specificity in goals or purposes (Parsons, 1956). Second, formal organizations typically exhibit relatively smaller scales. Third, formal organizations find it relatively easy to control their boundaries with the outside. Fourth, formal organizations usually do not encompass all their members' lives but only some part of them. All except the last factor would seem to make cultural design highly salient, and even partiality of membership might make design easier to implement, since individuals will be less invested in the culture.

Nonetheless, opinions differ about the extent to which the content of the organization's culture can be designed and controlled effectively, especially by top management. At one end of the spectrum, management theorists such as Michael Tushman and Charles O'Reilly (1997: 35)

---

[5]She calls these "integration approaches."

claim that "great managers effectively manage the short-term demands for . . . bolstering today's culture and the periodic need to transform their organization and re-create their unit's culture." At the other end are those who believe that culture is too amorphous and too reactive to be designed and managed in ways that produce precise intended outcomes. Failure in implementing a cultural design might emanate from any number of managerial or other factors,[6] but morphologically it takes either of two forms: (1) a discrepancy in content between the design and enacted culture, such that values, beliefs, and norms of the two differ radically even to the point of opposition; or (2) a wide variation in cultural content within the organization, such that the design's values, beliefs, and norms are only one small set among a much broader range represented and widely held in the organization. In either case, the culture winds up differing from the intended design and quite possibly interfering with it.

The issue rarely comes up in analysis of societal culture, which is usually assumed (at least implicitly) to be naturally evolving according to its own logic, and not easily influenced by individual actors, let alone designed, except perhaps in small and dense societies with a strong central government such as Singapore or under extraordinary political circumstances such as the Cultural Revolution under Mao Tse-tung. But it seems natural that it should be an issue for formal organizations, given their goal specificity and their smaller scales (Parsons, 1956; Scott, 2003).

In the business world, the executives of many companies and organizations unquestionably believe that they can design and implement a culture to good effect. Many of them try to put in place a culture that embraces the values and norms they believe will make their organization better, as a competitor or as a place to work. Few, however, think that they can do so quickly or without considerable attention, effort, or money.

A GLIMPSE OF TWO DESIGNED CULTURES

A stereotype of designed organizational culture holds that it consists of content primarily of a caring or worker-friendly nature. While this is true of many designed cultures, warmheartedness is hardly ubiquitous. The contents of the cultures that executives and employees design and implement in their companies range wildly, from the secretive and spartan coldness of candy maker Mars, Inc. (Brenner, 1999), to the exclusive gentility of investment bank Goldman Sachs (Endlich, 1999), to the hippie egalitarianism of ice cream manufacturer Ben & Jerry's (Lager, 1994).

---

[6]For instance, cultural design is constrained by the broader social context of the organization (Hofstede, 1980). An organization's culture is superimposed on the society's culture and must maintain a level of consistency with it; this consistency constraint also holds for any attempt to change the culture of the organization.

A vivid illustration of such differences and their implications for individual behavior can be seen in two companies we are familiar with, Dreyer's Grand Ice Cream and Cypress Semiconductor. Both companies grew at fast paces in the 1980s and 1990s. Dreyer's went from a small shop to a dominant national business with more than 4,500 employees and sales of over 1 billion dollars. Cypress went from a start-up to a multinational corporation with over 4,100 employees and revenues that have passed 1 billion dollars. Both companies were still actively led in the year 2000 (the date of information we use here) by the executives responsible for designing their cultures.[7]

Dreyer's Grand Ice Cream. Gary Rogers and Rick Cronk initiated the modern incarnation of Dreyer's in 1977 when they bought a local ice cream shop in Berkeley, California.[8] As the company grew and expanded geographically to Los Angeles, they realized that different values, norms, and behaviors were developing in the various locations. They sought to unify the culture by articulating their values and beliefs. In 1988, they put together a pamphlet describing their philosophy, which they had been practicing since 1981. They named it the "I Can Make a Difference" philosophy:

> At Dreyer's Grand Ice Cream, we believe in the individual. . . . In return for committing their energy and enthusiasm to their jobs and identifying personally with their company's goals and challenges, employees today expect that company to value and respect their hearts and souls as well as their minds and bodies. . . . People today also want to be trusted. . . . People want their company to just assume that they will come to work on time, work hard . . . without needing time clocks, stop watches, forms, and rigid procedures to ensure this behavior. . . . Finally, the days when employees were blindly willing to do what they were told and follow their bosses' instructions or their company's policies without question are gone forever. Today, most people have an opinion on almost everything and want a major voice in how their work environment functions. (Chang, Chatman, and Carroll, 2001: 11)

Rogers and Cronk expressed the philosophy more concretely in ten tenets, or "Grooves," which were the company's values, its culture, and the "way we do things around here."[9] The essentials of the Grooves are

---

[7]Dreyer's was subsequently acquired by Nestlé, and Rick Cronk has retired.

[8]Portions of this section are adapted from Chang, Chatman, and Carroll (2001).

[9]The term *Grooves* came from Peters and Waterman's (1982) concept of employees being "in the groove" or having a clear company culture that enabled them to know intuitively what an appropriate company or individual response would be to any situation they faced.

TABLE 1.1
The "Grooves" at Dreyer's

Management Is People

Hire Smart

Respect for the Individual

People Involvement

Ownership

Hoopla

Train, Train, Train

Face-to-Face Communication

Upside Down Organization

Ready-Fire-Aim

Source: Chang, Chatman, and Carroll (2001). Copyright © 2001 by the Trustees of Leland Stanford Junior University. Used by permission.

shown in table 1.1.[10] Rogers stated that the overall goal of the Grooves was to maintain a "day one attitude in its employees. . . . an employee has a perfect attitude on day one, wanting to progress in his or her career, enthusiastic, committed. . . . our job is not to change this."

Cypress Semiconductor. T. J. Rodgers and six partners founded Cypress Semiconductor of San Jose, California, in 1982. For many years a niche producer, making high-end innovative chips, the company eventually ramped up scale to become a large producer as well.

Cypress prides itself on its aggressiveness in markets, including the labor market. The company proactively recruits top-notch engineers and gives them great responsibility, provided they can demonstrate worthiness to their colleagues. Employees are attracted to the company in part because they see it as highly meritocratic and devoid of organizational politics. Table 1.2 gives the stated core values that underlie the culture at Cypress.[11]

Obviously, many of the values, norms, and behaviors endorsed by these two cultural designs differ radically. In a nutshell, Dreyer's

---

[10]For further information, see Chang, Chatman, and Carroll (2001). Quotations are from Chang, Chatman, and Carroll (2001: 11–13).

[11]For further information, see O'Reilly and Caldwell (1998). Quotations are from O'Reilly and Caldwell (1998: 22).

TABLE 1.2
Core values at Cypress

Cypress is about winning

Cypress people are "only the best"

We do what's right for Cypress

We make our numbers

We invent state-of-the-art products

Source: O'Reilly and Caldwell (1998). Copyright © 1998 by the Trustees of Leland Stanford Junior University. Used by permission.

embraces many of the "feel-good" principles of the human potential movement, including self-determination and mutual respect as manifested in civility of exchange. People treat each other nicely at Dreyer's, even when they are being frank about less-than-pleasant realities. The culture makes members feel as though they are in a warm and caring family. Employees at Cypress feel they are part of a very different kind of family—one with a tough, uncompromising paternal leader. Cypress people pride themselves on their hard edges, their stark views of reality, and their acceptance of adversity as a great motivator. Feeling good and being nice are not valued nearly so dearly as winning.[12] Despite these dramatic differences in content, both companies attribute at least part of their success to their cultures.

As noted earlier, a designed culture can be superfluous and not reflected in the actual culture of an organization. Although we do not possess hard evidence for these two cases, it is our observation about Dreyer's and Cypress in 2000, based on casual and occasionally systematic fieldwork by ourselves and colleagues, that these designs reflect a great deal about the actual cultures in place. This is not to say that every employee had likely internalized, accepted, or even knew all aspects of each cultural design. But we venture with some confidence that a sound empirical study, ethnographic or otherwise, undertaken at either place would have turned up cultural accounts and behaviors mainly consistent with these articulated values, norms, and behaviors. If so, then these examples suggest that questions about designed culture should be not so

---

[12]After reviewing these materials, it may come as no surprise to learn that Rogers and Cronk lived in Berkeley during the late 1960s, when personal liberation became a social movement, and that Rodgers is an ex-marine.

much about its possibility as about its degree. For any given cultural design, it makes sense to assess the extent to which the enacted culture of the organization agrees with it or not.

Content Alignment

As a constraint on action, the cultural content of an organization matters for how it behaves compared with other organizations, and how life is experienced by its individual members. Moreover, in the eyes of many scholars and executives, cultural content also ultimately affects how the organization performs. Why?

Analysts generally agree that the key content issue concerns alignment or congruence between the culture, on one hand, and the organization's competitive strategy, on the other. For instance, Tushman and O'Reilly (1997: 101, 128) proclaim: "To manage organizational culture effectively, managers must be clear in their own minds about the type of culture and the specific norms and values that will help the organization reach its strategic goals. . . . The overarching search is either for needed norms that are not aligned or for norms that are currently valued which need to be eliminated or downplayed in the future." Alignment of cultural content with other dimensions of an organization's design may also be an issue. Particularly important in many analysts' frameworks is the organization's formal structure, including the way it groups activities and people, as well as its compensation scheme.

Textbooks commonly prescribe a high level of overall alignment among an organization's strategy, cultural content, and formal structure because of the purported effects on organizational performance. With high or strong alignment, analysts regard an organization as well designed. Lack of alignment leads to deficient or at least substandard performance and could be corrected by realignment of one or several dimensions (Saloner, Shepard, and Podolny, 2001).

For example, a tight-button-downed, control-oriented cultural content, such as that found at Cypress Semiconductor, is typically not thought to be well aligned with a strategy of technical innovation, where slack resources and independence are usually associated with success. As O'Reilly and Pfeffer (2000: 229) surmise:

> Cypress says it wants the best, but the company has created an environment that is, in many ways, unlikely to attract some of the talented, creative entrepreneurial people it claims to be seeking. Cypress has built a culture that does attract people who work hard, like to compete, and want to win— all potentially important ingredients for its primary strategy of short-term

incremental innovation. But the values that promote this capability may also run counter to those needed for its secondary strategy of breakthrough technical innovation.

Because innovation is typically fostered in loose, carefree cultures, this observation claims an inconsistency or lack of alignment or congruence between Cypress's cultural content and its business strategy of innovation.

With Dreyer's, a milder criticism can be made, namely, that the cultural content fostered by the Grooves bears no direct relationship to the strategy but stands apart from it. That is, the Grooves do not apparently have much to do—positively or negatively—with how the company competes in the ice cream market. As a result, to some the Grooves may represent an indulgence rather than an inconsistency; the cost is in the missed opportunity for aligning the culture rather than any inherent contradiction or tension.

Despite the intuitive appeal of such analysis, we should note that in our view no scientific theory of cultural content addresses questions of alignment in a precise enough way, giving definitive judgments about dimensions of content relative to each other. This means that there exist no strong scientific criteria by which one can assess a priori the objective compatibility or incompatibility of a given culture and a particular strategy. In other words, ad hoc arguments supporting any judgment about content congruence or alignment can be advanced in a compelling manner.

1.5 THE DISTRIBUTIVE APPROACH TO CULTURE

Although historically less popular, the *distributive approach* to culture represents a conceptual alternative to the content approach. It starts from the view that there is more cultural variation within a society (or other unit of analysis) than advocates of the content approach commonly recognize.[13] By the distributive approach, this variation should not be ignored or de-emphasized but rather recognized as an inherent part of the phenomenon. As Rodseth (1998: 55) explains, this recognition

---

[13]The roots of the distributive approach lie in psychological anthropology, where individual variablity and cultural contention often caused analysts to react strongly against the assumption of uniform and homogeneous culture driving individual behavior (see Sapir, 1932; Schwartz, 1978a, 1992). Rodseth (1998) argues that the approach may experience a resurgence of interest because of its intellectual compatibility with postmodernism, which voices many of the same critiques against the content approach.

leads to a very different depiction of culture, one that does not necessarily reflect a coherent or integrated system:

> [The distributive approach] construes culture not as integrated system or text and not as a mere aggregation of traits or behaviors but as a semantic population—a population of meanings. These meanings have definite material embodiments. They may be stored in human brains, expressed in speech and other forms of action, or transmitted in writing and other artifacts, but they are always things in the world, rather than mere abstractions. From this perspective, meanings exist not in formal or idealized systems but in spatiotemporal distributions, which may or may not be orderly, coherent or stable.

A distributive analysis of culture first identifies patterns of cultural variation across time and space. It then seeks to account for them. Because the variation occurs within a society or organization, the approach finds differences within the society or group valuable for explanation. For instance, Sperber (1996) emphasizes the distributive approach's ability to deal with cultural change, especially as a function of lower-level (micro) processes. Using the word "representation" (rather than Rodseth's *meaning*), he claims that in the distributive model of culture

> the causal explanation of cultural facts amounts, therefore, to a kind of *epidemiology of representations*. An epidemiology of representations will attempt to explain cultural macro-phenomena as the cumulative effect of two types of micro-mechanisms: individual mechanisms that bring about the formation and transformation of mental representations that, through alterations of the environment, bring about the transmission of representations . . . in the epidemiological perspective, the explanation of a cultural fact—that is, of the distribution of representation—is to be sought not in some global macro-mechanism, but in the combined effect of countless micro-mechanisms.

Hannerz (1992: 8) takes the approach a step further, arguing that cultural distributions serve to structure and shape future meanings and representations. He claims that "complexity in [cultural] distribution and in externalization has a large part in breeding complexity in the order of meaning."

Perhaps the most influential practitioner of the distributive approach is anthropologist Fredrik Barth. In his study of Inner New Guinea, Barth (1987: 1) analyzes the cosmological knowledge and rituals of the population. When he does, he looks at "the (variety of) ideas that it contains, and how they are expressed; the pattern of their distribution, within and between communities; the processes of (re)production in this tradition of knowledge, and how they may explain its content and pattern of distribution; and thus, the processes of creativity, transmission and change."

He goes on to explain that such an approach is not simply about cultural diffusion because "it seeks to identify the developments, departures, and dogmatisms of each of the small local centres *within* a tradition of knowledge, to discover the patterns of variation and thereby the underlying *processes* of thought innovation and stimulus at work within it" (pp. 19–20).

Barth advocates a naturalistic research strategy, whereby "analytical operations . . . should model or mirror significant, identifiable processes that can be shown to take place among the phenomena they seek to depict" (Barth, 1987: 8). Some other distributive theorists show more of an inclination to abstraction. Schwartz (1978), for example, notes that between the extremes of total homogeneity and total heterogeneity, there is a structure of commonality. It "consists of all of the intersects among idioverses [implicit cultural constructs of individuals]—among all pairs, all triads, etc.—all subsets of the total set of idioverses of members of a society" (Schwartz, 1978b: 428). And, for any given common social function, Schwartz sees a social structure of commonality.

A difficulty with the distributive approach to culture involves its tractability in actual analysis. Consider, for instance, that Schwartz (1978b) defines culture as the union of all individuals' sets of cultural constructs (what he calls "idioverses"). Goodenough (1981) regards the shared content (the intersection of the idioverses) as the culture but still requires us to consider the "cultural pool" (the union of the idioverses). The two models are "extensively similar" in Schwartz's view because they both involve looking at the diversity and the commonality in content simultaneously. But if there are no exclusionary criteria on content (or the criteria are loose), then just about any and all content held by an individual might be legitimately considered cultural. Moreover, in the case of extreme heterogeneity, where each individual's set shows little or no overlap with others, there seems to be a danger of losing the intuitive sense that something commonly regarded as cultural might be operating.

Even with a precise criterion for relevant content, the distributive approach often has trouble demarcating the population's boundaries. As Schwartz notes, the difficulty arises where individuals' networks of interaction are overlapping, non-discrete and inclusive, implying that similar content will be widely distributed. At the extreme, "we may find that the maximal extension of a given society ramifies widely and indefinitely through the networks of its individuals, until such interlacing and overlapping networks include all of the geographically accessible populations of an area in chains of relatedness" (Schwartz, 1978a: 222). In these cases, the analytical solution involves using some arbitrary threshold to decide what degree of interaction or shared cultural content constitutes the boundaries (Brumann, 1999).

Organizational Cultural Distribution

Perhaps unwittingly, a common type of cultural analysis in organizational theory is appropriately classified as using the distributive approach. Organizational theorists and practitioners express a strong interest in what they call "strong-culture" or "high-commitment" organizations. They typically define a strong-culture organization in purely morphological terms as one where wide consensus exists about the content and where participants believe in the importance of the content (O'Reilly, 1989). Content consensus implies homogeneity of beliefs, norms, and values—a high degree of shared understanding among the members of the organization. Importance of content means that participants take it seriously as the appropriate way to behave, internalize the content as something personal rather than something imposed, and act to enforce the content by sanctioning others when they do not conform (Baron, Burton, and Hannan, 1996).

Cultural strength in organizations is especially important because social control may be exercised informally through the culture rather than formally through a bureaucratic system. Strong culture also provides a common focus, generates intrinsic motivation, and engages peers in monitoring and evaluation. As a result, a widespread tacit understanding of the organization's goals develops that helps to generate consistent actions in novel situations and serves to lower conflict. In general, a strong culture economizes on administrative structure and even management, making it a potentially powerful and very attractive way to run an organization.[14] That is, irrespective of content details, homogeneity of content may affect organizational performance as well as its variability over time (Sørenson, 2002a).

Surprisingly to some, cultural content also does not seem to matter much in generating a strong culture. Indeed, O'Reilly and Chatman (1986: 179) provocatively compare designs and processes of cults, corporations, and other organizations. They argue that "religious organizations, self-help organizations, cults and strong culture firms use participation as means for generating commitment, symbolic action to convey a sense of purpose, consistent information to shape interpretations and extensive reward and recognition systems to shape behavior. . . . the underlying psychology of social control is fundamentally the same across these types of behavior." Organizational practice shows clearly that, by putting in place certain structural (architectural) design features, it is possible to create and maintain a strong-culture organization.

---

[14]On the flip side, strong culture may also reduce creativity and increase unwanted discrimination on the basis of social characteristics.

O'Reilly (1989) points to the following design features as key: (1) a rigorous selection of members based on cultural criteria; (2) an intensive period of socialization; (3) a social system with high levels of broad participation entailing numerous incremental commitments; (4) a comprehensive reward and recognition system, including especially intrinsic rewards; and (5) the use of symbolic actions and language to reinforce the content of the culture. This explains why, despite radically different contents, our example companies of Dreyer's and Cypress can both develop and maintain strong cultures.

Demography and Cultural Distribution

Demography concerns the composition of a population and its change over time. The distributive approach to culture sensitizes analysts to demographic fluctuations, as these may radically affect the distribution of content in sparse pockets of a population. Moreover, in comparison to societies and large ethnic groups, the distribution of cultural content in formal organizations heightens the salience of three major demographic issues.

First, the overall distribution of cultural content is driven at least in part, and we suspect heavily, by organizational structure and over time by organizational demography. In modern societies, people belong to many organizations, and most of these memberships last for only a short period compared with their lives or careers. Examine almost any organization over time and you will see a sizable churning of new members replacing old ones, as well as transfer and relocation among the remaining members. Unless cultural content automatically and instantaneously derives from location within the organization, these shifts of personnel must affect the distribution of cultural content.

Second, inertia and change of an organization's culture over time—its dynamics—likely vary by the form and pace of demographic activity. It appears obvious that culture will persist in an organization like the old Jesuit order of clergy, where overall growth is slow, socialization is intense, and turnover is ordinarily low because members intendedly join for life. But what about an organization with fast growth, weak socialization, and high rates of lumpy (uneven spurts of) turnover? It should be possible to map differences in demographic regimes onto cultural stability.

Third, much of the demography of an organization is directly under management control. This means that management potentially affects strongly the distribution of cultural content: it can define the type of content considered ideal, and it controls many of the levers driving the internal demographic system. In particular, management typically decides (or decides to delegate) how many persons will be hired at any time, how selective (from a cultural viewpoint) the hiring process will be, and who is hired. Management also often designs and operates its own socialization process through mechanisms such as orientation and training, as well as placing constraints on the ease with which peer socialization processes operate through mechanisms such as grouping design, job rotation, and incentives. Finally, management sets limits on how culturally tolerant the system will be, and those who deviate culturally beyond the permissible limits will be likely to leave or to experience termination. So, in explaining the distribution of cultural content in formal organizations, it is important to analyze managerial preferences and the policies designed to implement them.

1.6 A LIMITED SYNTHETIC APPROACH
TO ORGANIZATIONAL CULTURE

As our review suggests, the content and distributive approaches to culture have both proved insightful but also limited in fundamental ways. It is, however, encouraging that advocates of both approaches recognize the value of the other. For instance, content theorist Schein (1990: 271) notes, "Revolution, restructuring and massive replacement of people may occur, and possibly a new cultural paradigm may occur." Likewise, distributive theorist Goodenough (1981: v) states that "whatever its other characteristics, [culture] has content and organization." And psycholinguist Sperber (1996: 35) proclaims that the "study of cultural representations cannot ignore their contents."

What seems to be called for is a synthesis. Of course, the difficulty of any full synthesis entails combining the attractive features of approaches while dispensing with, or at least minimizing, their deficiencies. We make no pretense of being able to accomplish this formidable task in a general way. But we do believe that the organizational context provides a natural setting whereby a specific limited type of synthesis becomes possible and proves extremely valuable.

Indeed, a particular synthesis motivates and sustains the efforts in this book to understand and model organizational culture. It initially entails representing cultural content in terms of an individual's propensity to embrace the values and norms of a particular organizational culture by a single measure indicating the degree to which an individual organizational member fits management's cultural ideal. We refer to this measure of cultural fitness as the individual's *enculturation* level; it represents a very specific conception of organizational cultural content, a certain fitness measure of an individual to a given culture. With this enculturation score in hand for each individual, we are then able to examine the distribution of cultural content across the entire organization and the structure of this distribution across different parts of the organization. By looking at the mean level of enculturation, we can also examine the overall degree to which the culture jibes with management's preferences.

Of course, this representation does not, in and of itself, yield a model of organizational culture or its transmission. To create that, the representation needs to be embedded in a set of social processes (e.g., socialization) that reflect some particular way(s) that culture plausibly operates among individuals within an organization. We construct such a model in chapter 4. For present purposes, a key aspect of the representation is that it can be used in conjunction with modeling the organization's demography—allowing individuals to enter the organization, to interact with each other as they experience management enculturation efforts while in the organization, and to leave the organization. Within the organization, individual enculturation scores—as well as their distributions—can change or remain stable, according to the effects of specified mechanisms such as socialization, or social influence, and decay. Demographic considerations thus allow us to tie together distributive-based notions such as cultural heterogeneity with a managerially based content formulation.

Why does this limited or partial synthesis make sense? Generally speaking, the reason has to do with the ways particular characteristics of formal organizations allow us to overcome, or at least bypass, certain troubling limitations of both approaches to culture. Recall that one major problem with the content approach concerns figuring out which elements of content should be singled out for study; different elements of content might give different views, and different persons might share different elements. There is also no precise scientific theory of cultural content. But collapsing content on to an overall abstract preference ordering is justified in this context because some individuals in this context (specifically, those in top management) are endowed with the authority to pursue the limited specific goals of the organization, or to change them. That is, this construct lets the cultural content of the organization potentially be any or all of the elements noted earlier, depending on managerial preferences. The justification for placing the ordering in top management's hands resides in the theoretical definition of a formal organization as a limited-purpose entity with relatively specific goals. Note that this would not be the case with a family, tribe, ethnic group, or society, where goals are more diffuse and rights to change them less clear-cut. Also, it is important to recognize that the preference-ordering construct leads to little loss in content generality, as we show in chapter 3. Recall, too, that the chief limitation of the distributive approach involves its inherent unboundedness of both content and persons. The preference ordering construct again takes care of the content issue. As for the boundedness of persons, the natural membership boundaries of a formal organization provide a clear point of delineation. Although there have been occasional debates, for the most part organizational boundaries are clearly circumscribed and identifiable. Not only do these boundaries coincide with the general limits of managerial control and discretion, but most demographic activity occurring across and within them also falls under the purview of top management. Both factors reinforce the content construct used in the limited synthesis.

With this conceptual synthesis as our background, we are able to construct a model of cultural transmission. We use it here to explore the dynamics of culture in formal organizational settings. We believe that the research program we report in this book represents the most systematic and sustained study ever conducted on the demographic foundations of cultural transmission. In our view, it yields much insight and leads to many new observations about organizational culture. For example:

- Cultural systems in organizations apparently equilibrate under very different demographic regimes. However, the time required to reach equilibrium and the managerial preferredness and homogeneity of culture obtained at equilibrium do vary by demographic activity. These differences underly some fundamentally different organizational types such as bureaucracy and entrepreneurial organizations (see chapter 5 for details).

- Very rapid organizational growth sometimes facilitates rather than impedes cultural stability, when stability is viewed as the quickness with which the system reaches equilibrium or rebounds to it after perturbation. Moreover, some previously observed cultural patterns ascribed to behavioral processes might be accounted for entirely by demographic processes. Cultural intensity, for example, is greater in declining organizations because of the dynamics of attrition, not necessarily because of some psychological reaction to the decline (see chapter 6).

- Common substantive interpretations about heterogeneity in tenure found in the organizational demography literature are potentially spurious. Specifically, an aggregated set of independent individuals with negative duration dependence in the rate of departure generates a statistical—but not behavioral—relationship between heterogeneity in tenure (length-of-service) distributions among members of an organization and the likelihood of a departure. In addition, the strength of the linkage between demography and culture varies by organizational conditions, potentially explaining the inconsistent findings of a large and popular research program in organizational demography (see chapter 7).

- Social influence networks may affect cultural variability in surprising ways. For instance, greater overall inequality of influence in the network lowers cultural variability within the organization. However, when a single individual has very high influence, cultural variability increases after controlling for the overall structure of influence (see chapter 8).

- While some governmental actions can weaken terrorist networks and their cultures, they still retain significant capabilities. Terrorist networks show a high degree of resilience and are not easily destroyed. However, the culture of a typical terrorist network appears to be more vulnerable to the incremental removal of terrorists rather than the elimination of full cells. Also, when facing governmental policy directed toward inhibiting replacement of vacancies in the network, the more viable strategy appears to be delaying replacement of cell vacancies rather than forcing the terrorist organization to skimp on the selection and training of replacements (see chapter 9).

- Post-merger cultural integration increases more quickly in some organizational situations than in others. Organizations with relatively larger acquirers, higher hiring selectivity, stronger management socialization processes, and more severe sanctions for cultural misfits (what we call an *alienation effect*) facilitate faster integration. Surprisingly, only small effects can be attributed to the layoff policies of the acquirer, the degree of cultural inertia in the acquiree, and the level of turnover and growth. Moreover, in a substantial number of cases, an unexpected pattern occurs: cultural heterogeneity rises in the short term, even when the mean level of enculturation is increasing in the merged organization. A strong alienation effect can overcome this pattern and produce consistent integration patterns (see chapter 10).

- Cultural heterogeneity can play a significant role in organizational mortality processes often linked to organizational aging and known as the *liability of newness*. Specifically, age dependence in organizational mortality can be accounted for by the effects of small size and cultural heterogeneity. So, observed age dependence in mortality might be a spurious relationship masking an effect of cultural heterogeneity. Organizations that grow without developing homogeneous cultures continue to experience higher risks of failure than those that do. Overall, it appears that cultural heterogeneity mediates size and growth effects on organizational mortality. This general finding suggests that classic arguments about the liability of newness imply a complex relationship between organizational growth, size, and culture— a relationship that is not obvious from purely age-based considerations (see chapter 11).

1.7 READER'S GUIDE

This book might be read in a number of ways, depending on one's background and interest. We have tried to de-emphasize the technical aspects of the theory and research, but a certain amount of this material is necessary to ensure precision and to allow possible replication by others.

Chapter 2 discusses the use of formal models, and especially simulation models, to study social phenomena generally but especially organizational culture. It is somewhat didactic and could be skipped by those with technical training; however, it does at points explain the pragmatic philosophy of science we use in the book. Accordingly, this chapter serves as a guide to some distinctive views implicit in our research strategy.

Chapter 3 describes in some detail our way of representing and modeling organizational culture. Obviously, we adopt a synthetic approach that takes into account both cultural content and the distribution of culture. Specifically, we envision a managerial ideal of culture and then model its distribution over time and over different organizational structures as a function of demography. Chapter 3 analyzes the relationship between this representation and the more conventional method of measuring cultural content on multiple dimensions. This chapter could be skimmed or skipped in an initial reading of the book; however, we believe that any serious attempt to deal with the issues we tackle will need, at some point, to address the fundamental issues and findings there.

Chapter 4 presents our basic model of cultural transmission, the foundation for most of the book. The model contains three core components for the experiences of an individual in the organization: (1) a hiring function, (2) a socialization function, and (3) a departure function. We regard this chapter as essential reading for understanding the research program, the book, and many subsequent chapters. It lays open for inspection the bare skeleton of the model that we dress with different costumes in subsequent chapters.

Chapters 5 and 6 describe much of the basic behavior of the model; they should be read together as a module. Chapter 5 organizes findings by type of organization, relying on seven distinctive configurations of demographic features. Chapter 6 continues the investigation of the basic model in the context of these configurations, looking in detail at growth and decline processes in organizations.

The remaining chapters contain applications of the models and extensions or modifications. With an understanding of the basic model in hand, each of these chapters pretty much stands on its own and can be read in any order, except that chapter 9 builds on the network model developed in chapter 8 and might require some backpedaling as a result.

Chapter 7 looks at heterogeneity in organizational demography, especially the length-of-service distribution. It scrutinizes a key assumption made in the literature on internal organizational demography and makes some suggestions for future research in this area. Chapter 8 elaborates the socialization component of the model by specifying variations in internal organizational networks of influence. Chapter 9 explores the structure of network-based terrorist organizations and their cultural stability over time. Chapter 10 analyzes cultural integration following mergers from a demographic viewpoint. Chapter 11 models the relationship between cultural heterogeneity and organizational growth and mortality. Finally, chapter 12 concludes the book with some brief remarks.

CHAPTER 2

Modeling Culture with Simulation

2.1 INTRODUCTION

Chapter 1 reviewed some of the ways that social scientists disagree about how to think theoretically about culture generally and about organizational culture specifically. Besides these theoretical differences, ample debate exists about the appropriate methods for studying culture.

To oversimplify somewhat, the debate splits into two camps. A qualitative camp of cultural researchers wants to spend more time exploring the rich multidimensional character of organizational culture, typically using ethnographic methods. A quantitative camp insists on moving forward with objective measurement instruments and systematic empirical research. Although not always true, the division between the two camps also often reflects differences about how best to do science. The qualitative camp of cultural researchers advocates an inductive approach, whereby insightful observations are used to advance novel theory or interpretations. The quantitative camp employs a more deductive approach involving the testing of theoretical claims advanced a priori. As a result, cultural studies unfortunately sometimes become consumed by debate about epistemology and measurement rather than about the phenomenon or its integral processes.

The research we report here sidesteps this debate by using computer simulation or computational modeling, a third way of doing science. Computer simulation has a long history in organization theory, dating from Cyert and March's (1963) simulation of firm behavior and Cohen, March, and Olsen's (1972) simulation of garbage can decision processes, but its usage in the intervening decades has been rather limited. As March (2001: x) recounts, despite the great initial promise for organizational studies, "simulation entered a state of intellectual limbo, neither adopted nor discarded. Simulation came to be tolerated but not much emulated."

Although recent developments suggest that the scientific landscape is shifting, many organizational theorists still express a lack of familiarity with simulation, while others hesitate in fully accepting simulation models and findings. These reactions seem especially prevalent in areas of organizational theory—such as organizational culture—dominated by qualitative research, where model building is not widespread. To explain our use of simulation to the larger audience interested in organizational culture, it is therefore perhaps necessary to take up and discuss some basic issues about simulation and formal modeling.

Accordingly, this chapter describes simulation modeling of organizational culture.[1] Our goals are to explain and motivate our use of simulation, as well as to break down some of the obstacles to understanding and accepting simulation. Specifically, we aim to demonstrate the potential utility of simulation analysis in studying social phenomena, and organizational culture in particular. Thus, much of the discussion is didactic. Since we also use this chapter to explain how our approach to simulation differs from some (prevalent) others, it also provides an epistemological guide to the theory and analysis reported in subsequent chapters.

2.2 Forms of scientific inquiry

Historically, scientific progress has been based on two approaches: theoretical analysis or deduction, and empirical analysis or induction. In the deductive form of science, a set of assumptions is formulated and the consequences of those assumptions are deduced. Often the assumptions are stated as mathematical relationships, and their consequences are deduced through mathematical proof or derivation. This strategy has led to some extraordinary successes, particularly in physics; the general theory of relativity is the prime example. A major problem with this approach, however, is that derivation can be mathematically intractable—mathematical techniques may be inadequate to determine the consequences of assumptions analytically. This problem seems to be common in the social sciences, perhaps due to the complexity and stochastic nature of social processes, and has led researchers to choose assumptions (such as perfect rationality, perfect information, and unlimited sources of funds) on the basis of their usefulness for deriving consequences rather than because they correspond to realistic behavior. And even when elegant results can be obtained in the form of mathematical equations, sometimes these equations can be solved only for special cases; for example, while the equations of general relativity can be solved for the case of spherical symmetry, no general solution is known.

The inductive form of science proceeds by obtaining observations or measurements of variables (data) and then examining or analyzing the data to uncover relationships among the variables. This approach has also been highly successful; one example is the development of the

---

[1]Parts of this chapter are adapted or excerpted from Harrison et al. (2007).

periodic table of the elements before atomic structure was understood. A variant of this approach has been used to test the predictions of theoretical analysis. A major problem with empirical work is the availability of data. Variables may be unobservable (e.g., secret agreements) or difficult to measure (e.g., the power of organizational subunits); the problems are compounded by the need for comparable measures across a sample or, in the case of dynamic analysis, across an extended time frame. Consider the prospects for obtaining data on the cultural values of employees across a sample of organizations over a period of decades.

Computer simulation is now recognized as a third way of doing science (Waldrop, 1992; Axelrod, 1997). It renders irrelevant the deductive problem of analytic intractability—mathematical relationships can be handled computationally using numerical methods. It also partially overcomes the empirical problem of data availability—a simulation produces its own data.[2] Because of these features, computer simulation can aid enormously in theory construction. It allows theorists to make realistic assumptions rather than compromise with analytically convenient ones, as is common in deductive theory.

The first well-known computer simulation involved the design of the atomic bomb in the Manhattan Project during World War II. The complex system of equations used in the design process—specifically to model the implosion of the fissionable material after the detonation of the triggering explosions—could not be solved analytically, and human calculation using numerical methods was not practical. Nor was induction feasible; besides the unknown risks of attempting to set off an atomic explosion, not enough fissionable material was available at the time for even one test. This was not, however, a simulation in the modern sense because programmable digital computers were still under development. But it pioneered the method of using electronic machines for computational solutions to problems that could not be solved analytically (Feynman, 1985; Gleick, 1992).

The modern style of simulation began shortly after the war when the first programmable digital computers, ENIAC and MANIAC, became operational (Ulam, 1991; McCartney, 1999). Over the decades following the war, simulation became an accepted and widely used approach in physics, biology, and other natural sciences. But despite the early work of March and colleagues, the use of computer simulation in the social sciences has lagged behind that in the natural sciences (Lomi and Larsen, 2001).

---

[2]Of course, simulation has its own potential problems, several of which are addressed at various points in this chapter.

2.3 WHAT IS A COMPUTER SIMULATION?

A computer simulation begins with a model of the behavior of some system the researcher wishes to investigate. The model consists of a set of equations or transformation rules for the processes through which the system variables change over time. The model is then translated into computer code, and the resulting program is run on the computer for multiple time periods to produce the outcomes of interest.[3]

Simulation Defined

Formally, we define a computer simulation as a computational model of system behavior coupled with an experimental design. The computational model consists of the relevant system components (variables) and the specification of the processes for system behavior (changes in the variables). The equations or rules for these processes specify how the values of variables at time $t + 1$ are determined, given the state of the system at time t. In stochastic models, these functions may depend partly on chance; the equation for the change in a variable's value may include a disturbance term to represent the effects of uncertainty or noise, or a discrete process such as the turnover of an organizational member may be modeled by an equation that gives the probability of turnover. Computationally, these stochastic processes are simulated using numbers produced by random number generators, a technique known as *Monte Carlo simulation*.[4] Random numbers with different statistical distributions can be produced using different generators, and it is crucial to choose generators that yield distributions appropriate for the processes being modeled. For example, a disturbance or noise term may be simulated with a generator that yields numbers that are normally distributed with a mean of zero, and organizational foundings can be simulated with a negative binomial generator to match the empirically observed distribution of foundings.

---

[3]Actually, the model could consist of a single process, although simulations are usually used to study systems in which multiple processes operate simultaneously. Also, one could use a static model—for example, to generate a probability distribution lacking an analytic density function (as in Harrison and March, 1984)—but most simulations in organizational research are dynamic.

[4]The Monte Carlo actually predates the computer. It was initially developed in the 1940s by physicists working on the Manhattan Project. Theory had given a stochastic model of neutron diffusion, and the simulation used a mechanical device to take inputs, make random draws from a distribution, and generate outputs. Within organizational theory, Monte Carlo simulation underlies nearly all simulation work using stochastic models, beginning with Cyert and March (1963) and including much of the modeling reported in this book.

The model's functions typically require the investigator to set some parameters so that computations can be carried out. For example, in the basic model of cultural transmission in organizations described in chapter 4 and used throughout the book, one process consists of the arrival of new members of the organization at time t. These new members arrive at a certain rate (governed by a specified stochastic hazard function) with certain enculturation scores (drawn from a specified distribution). The arrival rate and the mean and standard deviation of the distribution of enculturation scores from which new members are selected are all prespecified parameters of the process.

Experimental Design

The experimental design of a simulation consists of five elements: the initial conditions, the time structure, the outcome determination, iterations, and variations. The computational model specifies how the system changes from time t to time $t + 1$, but not the state of the system at time 0, so initial conditions must be specified. For example, in our cultural transmission simulation model, initial conditions include the number of members in the organization at the beginning of the simulation and their enculturation scores.

The time structure sets the length of each simulation time period and the number of time periods in the simulation run. Once the time period is determined, the number of time periods to be simulated can be set to obtain the desired total duration of the simulation run, or a rule may be established to stop the run once certain conditions (e.g., system equilibrium) are met.

The outcomes of interest are some function of the behavior of the system, and need to be calculated from system variables. In the cultural transmission simulation behind much of this book, the chief outcomes of interest are the mean and standard deviation of the enculturation scores of the organizational members and the number of periods it takes the system to reach equilibrium (meaning that the mean level of enculturation remains stable).

Since most simulation models are stochastic, multiple iterations are necessary to assess system behavior. The results of one simulation run may not be representative of the system behavior because the outcomes will vary somewhat from run to run depending on the random numbers generated. But by repeating the run many times using different random number streams, a distribution of outcomes characterizing the behavior of the model can be obtained (and statistics such as the outcome means and variances can be calculated for the model).

Finally, the entire simulation process described here may be repeated with different variations. Both the parameter values and the initial conditions can be varied. There are at least two reasons for doing this. First, the behavior of the system under different conditions may be of interest; indeed, examining the implications of such differences is often a primary reason for conducting simulations in the first place. In the cultural transmission model developed here, for example, turnover rates of organizational members are often varied to allow examination of the differences in system behavior under conditions of low turnover and high turnover. We regard these variations as experimental manipulations and often refer to them as such. In designing experiments, our approach resembles that of many laboratory experimentalists in that we do not usually attempt to reproduce reality but instead construct manipulations so as to create particular contexts for comparison, including some that occur rarely in the real world but represent boundary conditions on a theory or model.[5]

The second reason for introducing variations is to learn about the sensitivity of the simulation model to the choices of conditions examined. Simulators might conduct such sensitivity analyses across variations in initial conditions and hold other parameters constant in the experimental design to ensure that they are not driving the findings. Sensitivity analysis may also examine the effects of small changes in the values of parameters that vary by design to check for system stability by looking, for example, for discontinuities or other qualitative changes that indicate bifurcation points or other nonlinearities in the model's behavior. In general, by focusing on the robustness of the model's behavior, sensitivity analysis differs from the usually wider-ranging variations included in the experimental design for theoretical reasons.

In practical terms, simulation research is constrained by combinatorial considerations and computer limitations. A full investigation involves design variations, sensitivity variations for each design setting, and multiple iterations of both the design and sensitivity variations to determine how stochastic fluctuations affect the behavior of the model. Despite the power of modern computers, processing speed and memory availability impose limits on what can be done, and trade-offs often need to be made. For example, in designing some runs for parts of this book, we occasionally calculated that a desirable run for a particular topic would take months to complete or would fill up an 80-gigabyte hard drive with output. So we were forced to modify designs to make the process more manageable, even using multiple computers.

---

[5]Of course, a major difference with simulation-based experimentation is that the model or theory is under investigation, not actual human or organizational behavior. The simulation analyst also does not run up against the constraints imposed by a human subjects pool (see, e.g., Kitts, 2004).

In general, since purely stochastic fluctuations will produce a distribution of outcomes, we think that priority should be given to multiple iterations to generate a representative distribution of outcomes for each variation (determining the necessary number of iterations requires some experimentation); otherwise comparing outcomes across variations might lead to specious conclusions. After establishing confidence about the representative distribution, primary attention can turn to variations designed by theoretical considerations to search parameter space (within computational constraints, of course). But the combinations of parameter settings required can be high even in fairly simple models, a practical motivation for parsimonious models (see also discussions of model properties in sections 2.5 and 2.6).

An important consideration has to do with the scientific goals of the project. When, as is usually the case in this book, the goals concern understanding the effects of varying strengths of specified processes (or the effects of alternative processes), then the analyst wants to ensure that random fluctuations are not interfering with the inferences. On the other hand, when the focus is on outcome variability generated by randomness in the process, as is often the case, for example, with theoretical stories about path dependence (see Carroll and Harrison, 1994), then the analyst would want to demonstrate that minor changes in parameters do not appreciably alter findings.

For these reasons, and because of our familiarity with the cultural transmission model under study here, we typically make multiple (as few as 10 and as many as 1,000) runs with a given model to explore stochasticity and to examine two or three (sometimes more, when circumstances warrant) variations for each parameter.[6] Two variations in a parameter suggest a linear directional trend; the third variation in values of a parameter, of course, allows us to check for apparent nonlinearity (including nonmonotonicity) in effects. Despite these restraints, our simulations still typically produce many conditions to investigate. For example, in exploring the cultural integration process following a merger reported in chapter 10, we hold many parameters constant and vary many others only as binary variables (using only high and low values). We still wind up with 5,832 conditions (three values each for six parameters and two each for three parameters)—each simulated for thirty six months and across ten iterations. (And this excludes the sensitivity analysis!) Increasing variations magnifies geometrically the amount of data produced.

Upon completion of simulation runs, the data output often needs to be analyzed further. Simulations can produce a great deal of data for each

---

[6]Appendix B gives the set of parameter values we explore for each chapter. See Kitts and Trowbridge (2003) for another, detailed examination of parts of the model.

variation, including the values of system variables and outcomes for each time period and summary statistics across iterations, as well as the parameter settings and initial condition settings. These data may be analyzed in the same manner as empirical data, although the amount of information provided for analysis can be overwhelming. Inspection of graphical representations typically plays a bigger role in analysis because the large number of observations easily generated makes it possible to investigate directly nonlinear relationships.

A Simple Example

A simple example may be instructive at this point. Suppose you are interested in finding the probability of getting first a head and then a tail in two independent coin tosses, and because your recall of probability theory is sketchy, you turn to simulation. The components of the computational model for this problem are coin tosses. The process consists of determining whether a toss is a head or a tail. Computationally, we can define a parameter p as the probability of a head and set it to some value between 0 and 1 (not necessarily assuming that the coin is fair). The simulation program can then call a uniform random number generator, which will yield any number between 0 and 1 with equal probability, to produce a number. If this number is less than p, the program concludes that the toss was a head, otherwise a tail. (To see why this works, say we have a biased coin with $p = .4$; the probability that the generator will produce a number less than .4 is precisely .4, since all values between 0 and 1 are equally probable.) Obviously, this is a Monte Carlo simulation.

In the experimental design, no initial conditions need be specified, since the outcome of the first toss depends only on the parameter p. The time structure is two periods, one for each toss (although in this example length of the time period does not matter). The program can determine the outcome by examining the results of the run to see if the first toss was a head and the second a tail. The run can be repeated many times with different random numbers supplied by the generator—say for 10,000 iterations—to determine the percentage of head-then-tail outcomes. Finally, variations can be introduced by changing the parameter p and repeating the entire process. Further analysis could consist of plotting the percentage of head-then-tail outcomes for different values of p to produce a graph of the relationship.

Comparison

We can use the coin-tossing example to illustrate the three forms of scientific inquiry. The question can be addressed deductively by using probability theory to derive the answer. It may be addressed empirically by performing a coin-toss experiment with many trials; this procedure is simple for $p = .5$, assuming that a normal coin is fair, but it may be difficult in practice to obtain coins with different p values. Or a simulation can be used to address the question computationally.

Simulation is similar to theoretical derivation in a very fundamental way. Both approaches obtain results from a set of assumptions. The results are the logical and inevitable consequences of the assumptions, barring errors. If one accepts the assumptions, then one must also accept the results; put another way, the results are only as good as the assumptions. Thus, a simulation may be thought of as a numerical proof or derivation.

2.4 WHY USE SIMULATION?

Computer simulations seem to us especially helpful in studying the behavior of complex systems, or systems composed of multiple interdependent processes. In such systems, each of the individual processes may be simple and straightforward, and each may be well understood from previous research or at least well supported theoretically. But the outcomes of the interactions of the processes may be far from obvious, especially over time. Simulation enables the systematic examination of the simultaneous operation of these processes in a specified theoretical model over time.

In our view, the cultural system of an organization fits this description well. Based on current scientific knowledge, a model of cultural transmission in an organization can be fully specified with three basic processes (as we describe in chapter 4 and use throughout the book). New members enter the organization (first process), current organizational members undergo socialization (second), and some members exit the organization (third). Although each process has been investigated thoroughly in isolation, new insights into organizational culture can be gained by studying a dynamic organizational system that includes the simultaneous operation of all three. Simulation makes it possible to do this, including examining how the three basic processes interact to generate the behavior of the organizational system over time. Simulation also allows us to observe many realizations of the organizational system under tightly controlled conditions, often constructed to deviate only slightly from other conditions (thus allowing fine-grained comparisons) or to generate multiple observations of rare conditions or to explore regions of parameter space that occur rarely in the real world, as well as simply to produce observations that may be difficult, or even impossible, empirically.

Our computer-based investigations of organizational culture allow us, at various points in the research, to accomplish several of the general scientific goals noted by simulators Axelrod (1997) and Harrison et al. (2007):

- *Proof.* Axelrod discusses the issue of proof in terms of existence proofs; a simulation can show that it is possible for the modeled processes to produce certain types of behavior. For example, in chapter 5, we show that culture can equilibrate in organizations with very different demographic regimes. This strategy can be used to examine the feasibility of models and to demonstrate that the resulting system behaviors meet certain conditions (such as boundary conditions).[7]

- *Discovery.* Simulations can be used to discover unexpected consequences of a process or the interaction of simple processes. In chapter 7, we report a simulation where we discovered that in the aggregate, a set of independent individuals with negative duration dependence in rate of departure automatically yields a correlation between heterogeneity in length-of-service distributions among members of an organization and the likelihood of a departure (so the "causal" relationship inferred by organizational demographers is spurious).

- *Explanation.* Frequently behaviors are observed, but it is not clear what processes produce the behaviors. Specific underlying processes can be postulated and their consequences examined with a simulation; if the simulation outcomes fit well with the observed behaviors, then the postulated processes are shown to provide a plausible explanation for the behaviors (Mark, 2004). For example, the simulation of organizational mortality in chapter 11 shows that cultural heterogeneity might play an important role in the widely observed liability of newness, as negative age dependence in organizational mortality is known. The explanatory use of simulations is related to the use of simulation as proof but typically goes beyond just showing that it is possible for the model to produce certain outcomes by isolating the conditions under which such outcomes are produced.

- *Critique.* Simulations can be used to examine the theoretical explanations for phenomena proposed by researchers and to explore more parsimonious explanations for these phenomena (Denrell, 2004). This is similar to the explanatory use of simulation, except that in this case simulation is used to assess preexisting explanations and possibly to find simpler explanations. In the simulation of cultural transmission presented in chapter 6, we show that increasing cultural fit among members of declining organizations results naturally from the three basic processes of entry, socialization, and exit, without the need to invoke psychological aspects of decline as researchers in this field have done.

---

[7]For further examples, see Hutchins and Hazlehurst (1991) and Bendor and Swistak (2001).

These kinds of investigations do not square neatly with many social scientists' ideas about cumulative research programs. Many methods textbooks state that successful development of cumulative knowledge about a phenomenon proceeds linearly and sequentially down a path from less structured qualitative approaches to the highly structured approach of formal modeling. The textbook by Ragin (1994), for example, claims that qualitative research methods work best for developing new theoretical ideas and making interpretations of a theory's or a phenomenon's significance; quantitative research is directed toward the "goals of identifying general patterns and making predictions."

By this view, organizational culture should be analyzed with a mixture of qualitative and quantitative methods, perhaps with a nod to the qualitative. As noted in chapter 1, there is little doubt that the phenomenon exists and that it exerts powerful effects, which vary across organizations. Consensus has yet to emerge, however, about which theories are most plausible and merit rigorous study. The qualitative camp of cultural researchers wants to spend more effort exploring the rich multidimensional character of organizational culture, presumably to advance novel theory or because of the problems of systematically assessing cultures whose content dimensions may vary across organizations. The quantitative camp insists on proceeding with systematic empirical research, presumably to sort out the many various theoretical ideas that have already been advanced. Consequently, debates about epistemology and measurement are widespread in the literature on organizational culture.

Our view is that the presumption of a linear sequence of cumulative knowledge development from qualitative (and informal) to quantitative (and formal) may be debilitating. And, in the case of organizational culture, it could be downright counterproductive. Phenomena such as organizational culture are inherently difficult to measure, and (although we admire attempts to do so) we do not believe that theoretical progress needs to wait for breakthroughs in measurement technology. In particular, we see no reason why insights from qualitative and other observations might not be directly translated into formal models. Indeed, we believe that doing so potentially improves theory in many ways and that formalization efforts may in turn help empirical researchers better target their efforts. That is, by using a simulation model, we are able to sidestep the many measurement controversies that surround the study of organizational culture. Moreover, by using our (limited) synthetic approach, we are able to do so without specifying the actual content of the culture or the number of associated cultural dimensions, while retaining a meaningful role for cultural content, as explained in chapter 3.

We also believe that development of theories and models may generate new empirical strategies. This is not to say that modeling organizational culture will help in measuring culture directly—it may or may not. Rather, establishing a formal model of organizational culture holds out the possibility of uncovering systematic connections between previously unconnected observables—a consequence of the logic of the model. In other words, tracing through and understanding the implied connections between variables may show an expected covariation between two or more observable variables that can be used as a hypothesis in systematic empirical research.

2.5 SIMULATION MODELING

Throughout this book, the simulation models we build and use represent operationalizations of mathematical models of culture in organizations. This means that we fully specify equations governing the components of the cultural transmission process, in much the same way any mathematical theory of organizational behavior does.

Noted economist Kreps (1990b: 6–7) states that the main advantages of a formal, mathematical model are the following:

- clarity ("It gives a clear and precise language for communicating insights and contributions.");

- comparability ("It provides us with general categories of assumptions so that insights and intuitions can be transferred from one context to another and can be cross-checked between different contexts.");

- logical power ("It allows us to subject particular insights and intuitions to the test of logical consistency."); and

- transparency ("It helps us to trace back from 'observations' to underlying assumptions; to see what assumptions are really at the heart of particular conclusions.").

The advantages Kreps lists are not inherent properties of any mathematical model but rather standards that provide benefits to good models that can be deductively examined.

For current purposes, it is worthwhile to consider Kreps's standards in the context of a formal, mathematical model examined with computer simulation techniques. In our view, the first three standards still apply fully, and their combined appeal makes a strong case for using a mathematical representation in simulation rather than just a set of computer instructions.

The fourth standard is more complex. Transparency, like deduction, seems to require models that are analytically tractable, in order to trace the sequence of reasoning connecting assumptions with conclusions (whether forward as in deduction, or backward as in Kreps's statements). This is true regardless of whether or not the model is simulated. However, the requirement of analytical tractability in a model sometimes forces theorists to use convenient assumptions rather than realistic ones, as discussed earlier. Simulation is attractive, in part, because the model escapes this constraint: it allows analysts to make realistic assumptions, whether or not they are analytically convenient. Although the deductive theorist attempting to use such realistic assumptions may not be able to get very far, to derive many results, the simulator can still proceed and use the model to generate outcomes.

But freedom from the tractability constraint should not be interpreted as a license to ignore clarity and parsimony. The rub is that, unless the analyst is judicious, realistic assumptions can be more likely than analytically convenient ones to lead to a complicated model. Many scientists think that results from complicated models are of dubious value if the analyst cannot identify precisely what it is in the model that produces variations in outcomes; they are holding the model to Kreps's transparency standard. Others think that the standard, however desirable, is not always necessary for progress, and indeed may not be realistic for (at least some kinds of) complex systems, where outcomes may not always be deducible or traceable from assumptions in a step-by-step way. In these instances, formal simulation models may still be able to illuminate the relationships between model assumptions, model components, and system outcomes; this may be the best one can hope for in such situations.

Equations and Agents

Some recent literature on computational modeling divides simulations into two classes: equation-based and agent-based. The equation-based simulation is said to be one where "the model is a set of equations and execution consists of evaluating them. . . . equation-based modeling begins with a set of equations that express relationships among observables" (Parunak, Savit, and Riolo, 1998: 10). The tradition originates in the system dynamics research of Forrester (1971) and continues today in organization theory (e.g., Repenning, 2001). By contrast, the agent-based simulation "consists of a set of agents that encapsulate the behaviors of the various individuals that make up the system, and execution consists of evaluating these behaviors. . . . agent-based modeling begins, not with equations that relate observables to one another, but with behaviors through which individuals interact with one another" (Parunak, Savit, and Riolo, 1998: 10). Similarly, according to Macy and Willer (2002: 143), agent-based models depict "social life as interactions among adaptive agents who influence one another in reponse to the influences they receive." Agent-based simulation is currently very popular and can be found in much organizational work (see, e.g., Carley and Lin, 1997; Strang and Macy, 2001; Rivkin and Siggelkow, 2003; Chang and Harrington, 2005). Analysts often discuss agent-based models as though they represent an advance over the earlier equation-based modeling framework.

In our opinion, the agent- and equation-based distinction does not prove very helpful. In practice, agent-based models may be formalized in simulations using equations or any other type of computational method. By the definitions cited here, what makes a simulation agent-based is that it involves the modeling of the interactive behaviors of entities within a system, not the form in which such behaviors are specified. The choice of computational method depends on the nature of the processes under study and the preferences of the researcher(s). Note also that, like equations, all such methods must have formal mathematical representations, since they must be expressible as computational instructions in the simulation program.

If one insists on using the distinction, then we think the cultural transmission model developed in this book should be classified as agent-based. We hold this view because the model depicts the behaviors of individuals in an organization who interact to influence each other's enculturation and turnover behavior.[8] At the same time, we specify equations for how agents change over time. In the basic model described in chapter 4, individual enculturation is influenced by the mean enculturation of peers, and the individual also influences others as a factor in the peer influence on them. In this specification, the influence of each peer has equal weight. In chapter 8, we relax this constraint and permit person-to-person influence to vary as a weighted function of cultural similarity.

Comparisons of these forms of simulation models also entail a level-of-analysis issue. When the research interest resides at the system level—aggregates of individuals and relations among their properties—it is usually easier and more efficient to represent this in a model based on these properties and relations directly rather than starting with the individuals and then aggregating up to get to the level of interest. (Of course, one needs a theory of the system-level process to do so adequately.) While some social scientists always prefer a micro model over a macro one, the issue is general and really has little or nothing to do with classes

---

[8]There is, of course, a question of the degree of agent interactivity inherent in a model. We recognize that some agent-based models depict interactions on a more agent-specific basis than in the basic model developed here, and we adapt the model to include person-by-person influence patterns in chapters 8 and 9.

of simulation. Implicit in much discussion of agent-based modeling, however, is the notion that micro (agent) behaviors combine to produce macro (aggregate or system) behaviors through complex, nontransparent interactions, in which case it may not be feasible to model relationships among system variables directly.

2.6 CHALLENGES OF SIMULATION

Because it is a comparatively new third form of science, simulation presents some special challenges to social science. Several issues about modeling and the research process that arise as the book unfolds deserve some attention here, including explanations of how we deal with them.

Model Specification

The theoretical rigor introduced by formal modeling is one of the strengths of (some kinds of) simulation work. A process may appear to be well understood, but attempting to specify an equation for the operation of the process over time often exposes gaps in this understanding. Organizational culture researchers, for example, address cultural change but usually do not develop formal models. Perhaps the empirical work from which the operation of a process was inferred was based on cross-sectional data, leaving the dynamic specification unclear. Formalizing processes imposes a discipline on theorizing, forcing researchers to come to grips with thorny issues that have previously been dealt with by hand waving or were not even recognized. Simulation often makes even greater demands, since the computer program must be complete in the sense that the processes for change in all relevant system variables must be addressed. Whether or not the formalization is correct in some sense, at least it promotes scientific advancement by forcing cloudy areas to be addressed, resulting in a clear specification that can be subjected to analysis, testing, and subsequent refinement.

Model specification also requires parameter values to be set. Sometimes empirical work can provide information on parameter values—for example, extensive empirical work in organizational ecology has resulted in estimates of the parameters of founding and mortality functions for a variety of organizational populations (and also refinement of the functional forms); see Carroll and Hannan (2000). In many cases, however, there is no reliable empirical guidance, so the simulator must enter uncharted territory in determining parameter settings. Various techniques are available to examine how reasonable the settings are for the behavior of the model, and sensitivity analysis can assess their robustness.

In the case of the models presented here, we take a fairly pragmatic approach to model specification and parameter setting. For many processes of interest, received social science theory and research give a general description of the expected relationship between variables. Often this relationship is stated in terms of simple covariation, a static notion. Sometimes the relationship is described in dynamic terms—for example, how the direction of change in one variable (and perhaps even the magnitude of change) depends on another variable—although the description is usually not quantified. So, most of the time we do not find precise mathematical specifications of the change process implied by the theory and empirical evidence. Because there are many possible specifications and parameter settings implied by the general verbal statements found in the theories, we are often forced to make some choices. We call our approach pragmatic because we do not usually belabor the modeling effort in these situations, attempting to develop a novel and elegant specification with new theoretical insight (however desirable and admirable that task might be). Instead, we draw upon our knowledge of basic functions and distributions to specify a workable model that yields a relationship or pattern consistent with that expected by received theory. And, where possible, we calibrate parameter settings to correspond to realistic behavior, as we discuss in later chapters.

Such pragmatic models may capture accurately the global behavior in a relationship or process, but they may not always reflect the details of the underlying mechanisms responsible for the relationship. As a result, to some the specifications may appear overly simple or even arbitrary in places, an issue discussed in the next section. This issue is not unique to simulation or even to formal theory, as all theory assumes some primitives and treats the insides of some processes as black boxes.

A final specification issue concerns the translation of the formal model into computer code. Even with a clearly specified formal model, there will be choices entailed in writing the code. Take as an illustration the cultural transmission model we develop here, which involves three interdependent processes. Since the computer executes instructions sequentially, the order in which these three processes are carried out in a given time period could possibly make a difference in the results. Based on our experience in running many versions of the cultural transmission models for more than a decade (including many versions of the specific model forms for each chapter as the models were developed), we do not think this is the case. We believe that the findings are robust with respect to translation issues. But suppose that we had discovered that operationalizing one of the models differently produces different findings. We would have interpreted this situation as an opportunity to extend or refine the theory and sought to identify additional conditions upon which the results depend.

Model Development

Construction of the model to be simulated involves a tension between simplicity and elaboration. When we give talks on our simulations, a frequent question (perhaps the most frequent) from the audience is, "Why don't you add variable X to the model?" Undoubtedly, a model can be made more realistic by adding more variables or processes. At the same time, the more complex the model becomes, the more difficult it is to understand what is really driving the results. Accordingly, our objective entails a balance—to develop a model based on a simplified abstraction of a system that retains what are believed to be the key elements of the relevant processes without unduly complicating the model. As Nelson and Winter (1982: 402) advocate about models in economics, "Willingness to recognize complexity is not an unmitigated virtue. Models . . . must be greatly simplified abstractions of the situation they are intended to illuminate; they must be understandable and they must have a certain transparency. Artful simplification is the hallmark of skillful modeling."

Axelrod suggests the KISS principle—Keep It Simple, Stupid. The simpler the model, the easier it is to gain insight into the causal processes at work. This is sound general advice, but it is more appropriate for some simulation uses than for others. The downside of this approach is that important elements may be inadvertently excluded from the model, limiting the usefulness of the insights for understanding the system's behavior. One strategy for addressing this dilemma is to start with a very simple model and then add components and observe changes in the system's behavior. If the new component makes a significant difference, then its role may be important; otherwise perhaps it can be excluded. Because system components may interact in a complex manner, however, it is often difficult to be sure that a component is not important or may not produce significant interactions with still other possible components—and if you keep adding things, at some point the simulated system becomes too complex to infer causality. So a variety of model structures can be tested, but eventually choices must be made.

To avoid excessive complexity in computer simulation, we often develop simplified models of the phenomenon under investigation, ignoring many plausible influences to concentrate on the processes deemed to be the most crucial or of greatest interest. This strategy permits us to examine the consequences of the focal processes unencumbered by complicating influences (without denying their existence—and additional processes can always be incorporated in the model in subsequent studies). The simulation findings help in understanding the phenomenon studied to the extent that the focal processes play an important role in influencing it.

For example, in a simulation reported in chapter 8, we examine the relationship of tenure distributions and cultural similarity to organizational influence networks. Influence networks may be affected by many social and psychological mechanisms, such as political processes, similarity-attraction processes, and social identification processes; but, by confining our attention to the effects of tenure distributions and cultural similarity, we are able to isolate the relationships of interest for the purpose of the analysis. In a sense, this strategy is analogous to that of controlled laboratory experiments. Simulations obviously have some disadvantages relative to laboratory experiments, since the actors are artificial agents rather than human subjects (although many laboratory experiments are conducted in artificial settings). But they also have a number of advantages, including perfect control (unobserved heterogeneity and unwanted influences are eliminated), less restriction on sample size, the ability to manage greater complexity in experimental design, and the ability to track precisely the behavioral steps leading to the outcomes of interest (the computer's memory is not subject to the biases of subjects' recollections and other problems of reconstructing causes for human and organizational behavior).

Program Development

At this point, it might seem that a simulation-driven theoretical research program would naturally proceed by constructing an increasingly elaborate model around an initial scaffolding. Because a simulation can expand without limit, however, the edifice created would eventually run counter to the goal of creating elegant and parsimonious theory. So, it is useful to contemplate alternative conceptions of successful programmatic development.

Two different stylized program types come to mind for us. In the first, an initially useful simulation model tightens or condenses over time as a series of studies shows certain parts of the model to be unnecessary, irrelevant, or simply subsumable within other parts of the model. In other words, in this type of program, parts of the model get eliminated (while other parts may recede into the background as abstractions), yielding a simpler but more powerful structure overall. Although they are attractive in principle, we unfortunately know of few such simulation models in the social sciences. Rather, it seems that there is strong general tendency in the other direction, for the simulation model to grow in complexity over a set of related studies.

The second type of program uses what we called disciplined flexibility in the preface. It comes to us from observing research in biology, specifically in evolutionary ecology. For a number of fundamental research questions in this field, there are one or two basic general models of the relevant process along with a series of increasingly detailed models where analysts have built in layers of complexity for certain specified contexts (MacArthur, 1972). That is, the basic model is adaptable and is regularly reengineered so as to bring into greater relief the current issue of primary concern. Such a series of related and partially nested models develop when field investigators uncover empirical regularities of ever-increasing detail while theorists devised ways to incorporate these systematic patterns into models of the underlying basic process. This type of theoretically driven, cumulative research program also characterizes much demography (Keyfitz, 1977).

A notable aspect of the models underlying this type of program is their generality but lack of universality. In bioecology, models contain features that apply to more than one species or habitat (and often to many) but not to all. Although much bioecological work relies at its start on one of several basic models of population dynamics, these are usually modified for the specific context. For any given process, a series of models graded by level of detail can be found (Roughgarden, 1979). The detailed models are not necessarily extensions from the same branch of the underlying tree but rather amplifications of certain issues of interest. So the overall research program proceeds by developing models that may not be identical across contexts, but that may build upon a basic model in nested fashion within a given context.

A similar strategy underlies our simulation-based research program on organizational culture. In the next chapter, we describe and analyze a general representation scheme for culture that we use in our theories and models in the book. In chapter 4, we describe a basic model of cultural transmission in organizations with demographic activity. This model constitutes the cornerstone of our research program. In subsequent chapters, we adapt and extend this model in a variety of directions, depending on the topic of interest and the theoretical goals. These extensions are designed to examine demographic heterogeneity, influence networks, terrorist organizations, mergers, and organizational mortality. In these explorations, the basic model is usually modified by adding some new elements that address the issue of interest, and exact comparisons to the model's earlier behavior are appropriate. At times, however, some aspect of the basic model may be modified as well to make the application more meaningful. On many occasions, the types of simulation experiments are also changed. Finally, we sometimes derive implications of the basic model and use these in fashioning a model more appropriate to the topic.

We regard the research reported here as a unified and cumulative research program, mainly because it attends to the same demographic concerns and flows primarily from the same basic formal model described

PART II

Model of Cultural Transmission

The four chapters in this part of the book describe the basic model of cultural transmission. Chapter 3 describes enculturation—the way organizational culture is represented in the model—and compares it to other commonly used representations. This chapter also explores the implicit relationship between the enculturation representation used here and others based on direct measurement of multiple dimensions of cultural content. Chapter 4 presents the model in formal detail while motivating the specifications. It describes the three major components of the model: functions having to do with hiring, socialization, and turnover. Chapter 5 examines the model's behavior in simulation. For conceptual convenience, this chapter groups findings by organizational type—commonly observed constellations of demographic and policy features. Chapter 6 continues the examination of model behavior by looking directly at conditions of growth and decline. This chapter also unpacks the organizational types, investigating cultural outcomes as consequences of model functions and parameters.

CHAPTER 3

Representing Culture

3.1 INTRODUCTION

As mentioned in chapter 1, social scientists often conceptualize organizational culture as a multidimensional construct. This conceptualization carries through to the measurement of culture in empirical work, where the contents of the actual dimensions used to represent culture vary considerably. For example, Hofstede et al. (1990) found six different dimensions in the cultures of a sample of Dutch and Danish organizations: process versus results orientation; employee versus job orientation; parochial versus professional; open versus closed system; loose versus tight control; and normative versus pragmatic. By contrast, in examining a medium-sized conglomerate, Sackmann (1992) analyzed four types of cultural knowledge: dictionary knowledge, directory knowledge, recipe knowledge, and axiomatic knowledge.[1]

Our interest in this book lies with examining the demographic-based processes of cultural transmission over time in organizations, and with exploring some of the consequences of these processes. As discussed in chapter 1, investigating the demography of cultural transmission is not antithetical to studying cultural content but complementary to it; the two issues can be seen as related but distinct avenues for research on organizational culture.[2] Indeed, the synthetic model used in this book allows us to separate cultural content and distribution analytically but to retain aspects of both. The approach allows progress to be made in one area without encountering the obstacles that might be troubling the other. For instance, cultural transmission can be modeled and understood without taking a position in the ongoing controversy over the empirical measurement of organizational cultural content (see Rousseau,

---

[1]We imagine that the content dimensions used in any particular study depend on such factors as the theoretical orientation, the interests of the researcher, the types of cultures studied, and, for empirical work, the methodologies employed (e.g., content dimensions uncovered by ethnographers versus those extracted through the use of established questionnaire instruments).

[2]Exceptions to this division are sometimes found in rational action theories about norms, which on occasion develop content-based explanations that do not require an additional explanation for cultural persistence (e.g., Coleman, 1990: 247).

1990); the models we develop are potentially applicable even if organizational culture requires intense ethnographic effort to measure.

Throughout the book, we assume that from the perspective of the organization's management, an individual's cultural fitness for an organization can be represented by a single number, which we call the individual's *enculturation level*. This is an unusual and perhaps even unique way to represent organizational culture. In this chapter, we describe our rationale for representing organizational culture in this way and compare it with other common modeling approaches. We describe how this single scale for individuals can be aggregated to obtain properties of an organization's culture. Given the research tradition on cultural content, an obvious question concerns the relationship of our representation to any underlying dimensions of content: Does heterogeneity in enculturation imply heterogeneity in the culture's content? So, we also undertake and report technical analyses designed to understand the relationship of our approach to possible underlying content dimensions of culture. Specifically, we investigate the relationship between heterogeneity in enculturation scores and heterogeneity in underlying content dimensions, using different specifications of content. The findings show that, under reasonable conditions, the modeling framework we use is very amenable to interpretations about content, and specifically to inferences concerning cultural heterogeneity.

3.2 ENCULTURATION

Many attempts to model culture and related phenomena (such as beliefs, tastes, or knowledge) start with an objective representation of each individual on a set of specified attributes.[3] Economists often use a simple scheme, whereby a person is seen at any time as embracing one (and often only one) of several possible alternative beliefs, norms, facts, languages, preferences, behavioral rules, or discrete combinations of these cultural factors constituting competing regimes of a sort (see Kreps, 1990a; Cremer, 1993; Lazear, 1995; Harrington, 1998, 1999). For instance, Kreps (1990a) sees culture as the norm or convention one uses to guide behavior in repeated games with multiple equilibriums. Lazear (1995) uses sets of alternative preferences to define cultural differences. Harrington (1998, 1999) uses a binary distinction among flexible and rigid agents to represent their behavioral rules in environments with hierarchical selection. And Van den Steen (2003) analyzes culture by looking at the organizational action each person in the organization expects will yield the highest payoff.

[3]Parts of this section are adapted from Harrison and Carroll (1991).

Among simulation modelers, culture is usually derived from a finite and unordered set of attributes represented as binary (or restricted to a highly limited set of integer values). For instance, March (1991) uses thirty variables that can each take on three values (-1, 0, 1) to represent the dimensions of beliefs in a model of organizational knowledge. Carley (1991) uses up to forty binary variables to represent the facts known by individuals in a group's culture. Axelrod (1997) sets attributes as a set of finite nominal-scaled variables. Epstein and Axtell (1996) use a string of eleven binary variables to represent the cultural attributes of individuals.

From these objective representations, the cultural attachment of individuals is then ordinarily assessed via criteria imposed by the researcher—in the simple schemes, those with identical scores are culturally similar; in more complex schemes, similarity may be assessed by degree of similarity or distance. Carrying this representation through to the organizational level, cultural intensity, strength and homogeneity are evaluated through some kind of aggregation. Obviously, within this framework an organization where many individuals have similar scores on all or most of the dimensions possesses a more homogeneous culture (an important dimension of so-called strong culture, as discussed in chapter 1) than one where the individual scores show high variability.[4]

The models we use here employ a very different type of representation scheme for organizational culture. We assume that an individual's propensity to embrace the values and norms of a particular organizational culture can be meaningfully represented by a single measure indicating the degree to which an employee fits management's cultural ideal. This measure of cultural fitness, the enculturation level, represents a very specific conception of organizational culture, a certain fitness measure of an individual to the culture. Although management teams will differ in types of factors they use to assess the level of enculturation, it includes knowledge, qualification, and willingness to embrace and comply with the culture and may reflect such factors as work experience and education. Enculturation can occur before an individual joins an organization (e.g., in a professional school), and employees can be further enculturated through socialization within the organization.

Formally, we designate an employee's enculturation level, or fitness score, as C_i and measure this on the unit interval;[5] that is, if C_i is the

[4]It is a curious aspect of this framework that variables representing cultural attributes typically are nominal and unordered. Management also seems to play no special role in defining and supporting appropriate cultural attributes. By themselves, such schemes fail to reflect the goal-directed nature of organizations and the authority usually held by management.

[5]In subsequent chapters, we specify the enculturation score to be a function of time and introduce processes that govern its change over time.

fitness score for employee i, then $C_i \in [0, 1]$, where the ideal employee would have a fitness score of 1.

Because we are primarily interested in organizational culture, we aggregate these scores for all those individuals in an organization and calculate distributional measures. Specifically, in most of our analyses that follow, we examine two summary statistics about the enculturation scores of an organization, the mean level of enculturation among the members of the organization and the standard deviation of enculturation. These statistics allow us to pursue our main interest, understanding how organizational demography affects the extent to which an organization embodies and sustains management's cultural ideals.[6]

Representing culture by a single variable does not imply that it is inherently unidimensional but, rather, that in a specific organizational context some overall managerial assessment about one's cultural predisposition and acceptance is possible. That is, we assume that all relevant cultural characteristics of an employee can be combined to produce a single score measuring the extent to which the employee conforms to the ideal employee from the perspective of management. This is analogous to the way in which economists use the concept of utility to measure the desirability of multidimensional decision alternatives; for example, a consumer might combine multiple characteristics of a product to assign a single utility score indicating the product's value to the consumer.

Of course, it would be incorrect to regard this representation as a model of organizational culture, just as it would be incorrect to regard a utility score as a model of choice. In fact, at this level of abstraction, such representation could potentially apply to many phenomena. What is essential for current purposes is that it apply plausibly to organizational culture. What is critical for developing it into a model of cultural transmission are the specific culturally based processes (e.g., hiring, socialization by management, socialization by peers, turnover, alienation) that we embed it within in chapter 4.

Technically, the validity of measuring cultural fitness (from management's perspective) on a single scale—C_i for person i—rests on two simple assumptions. First, individuals must be rankable in terms of their cultural desirability to management; that is, it is meaningful to say that person i actually is preferred to person j. Implicit here is the assumption

---

[6]A question might arise as to the inferential interpretation of tests of difference (from zero say) using such statistics, given the data are simulated rather than drawn in a sample from a population. Our view is that such tests are still useful and meaningful; we think that the appropriate analogue to the population in this context is the set of all possible realizations that the model and its parameters might generate, of which the observed simulation data are a subset.

that management as a group has consistent preference orderings for the cultural desirability of employees. This is justified either if a superordinate cultural ideal is imposed on management—for example, by the CEO or the board of directors—or if the variation in managerial preferences is trivial compared with the cultural variation among employees (March, 1962), which is a sensible view, given the filtering process that tends to select individuals with similar preferences for managerial positions (March and March, 1977).

Second, the preference ordering needs to be transitive. That is, if i is preferred to j and j is preferred to k, then i is preferred to k. These two assumptions are sufficient to prove $C_i > C_j$ if and only if i is culturally preferred to j (Coombs, Dawes, and Tversky, 1970). This representation theorem justifies the use of a single scale (C_i) to measure cultural desirability, even though an individual's cultural characteristics are multidimensional.

A major attraction of the enculturation measure is that it allows us to be analytical without abstracting too far away from the phenomenon. We thus retain a degree of naturalism about culture, as advocated by Barth (1993). A member of an organization would likely not know what to think about a factor analysis reporting multidimensional scores describing the cultural content of his or her organization. But that same person could clearly relate to a measure of how well he or she fits in, as could his or her peers and boss. Endlich (1999: 20), for instance, observes that at the investment bank Goldman Sachs even job candidates often discovered that they were a poor fit, because they preferred "more eclectic cultures where individual performance was applauded," whereas at Goldman Sachs "rugged individualism has no place." In other words, the fitness-based enculturation variable we use is very meaningful socially.

Cypress Semiconductor, discussed briefly in chapter 1, formalizes assessments of overall cultural fit during the employee interview and evaluation process, using a single scale. CEO T. J. Rodgers (1990: 88) describes the techniques the company uses as the last step in a rigorous interview process:

> *Check for cultural fit.* Most companies claim to do this, but few are systematic. We probe work attitudes and career goals through a questionnaire that requires brief but direct answers to open-ended questions. The questionnaire forces candidates to be as specific as possible about hard-to-quantify issues that are addressed only obliquely, if at all, in most evaluation processes. Among the questions are: How is the morale in your company or department? Why? What do you expect Cypress to offer you in the way of a work environment that your employer doesn't offer? What would your boss say is your best

attribute? What would the "needs improvement" section of your performance review address? Can you describe your personal experience with a difficult boss, peer or subordinate? (Rodgers, 1990: 88)

Organizations typically are not so formal in their cultural assessments; in fact, they may not even be able to articulate fully the evaluation criteria in use (instead simply letting cultural selection express itself in subjective employee preferences for individuals after exposure and interaction). Neither issue presents a problem for the representation of culture, so long as the conditions of rankability and transitivity in preferences hold. We think that this is usually the case, as cultural and social criteria manifest themselves systematically in interactions, interviews, and evaluations driven explicitly by organizational routines and implicitly by homophily.

Although our focus here is on theory, it is worth noting that the concept of individual fitness or enculturation in organizational cultures is readily amenable to empirical research. An obvious empirical research strategy would be to obtain regularly collected measures from a company such as Cypress, where the enculturation scores likely exist in individual personnel files. Perhaps the most popular analytical method for measuring enculturation empirically comes from O'Reilly, Chatman, and Caldwell (1991), who use Q-sort techniques to identify descriptors of an organization's culture and its compatibility with an individual's beliefs, values, and norms (see also Chatman, 1991). Another strategy for measuring enculturation is found by Chatman et al. (2004), who use survey data from a large public financial services corporation to develop an enculturation measure in four steps involving (1) assessing business unit culture from Likert-type ratings of survey items (e.g., innovative, cooperative, detail oriented); (2) factor analyzing the culture assessment using principal component analysis; (3) creating factor scales; and (4) constructing a peer fit measure by comparing an individual's description of his or her business unit's culture to the business unit peers' aggregated descriptions, that is, as the distance between an individual's level of enculturation and the aggregate peer level of enculturation.[7]

One natural complication to our approach arises from cultural variation across organizational subunits. Management teams of different subunits may differ in the values and behaviors they deem important. A classic example is an organization with a research and development

---

[7]Chatman et al. (2004) also computed management fit by comparing an individual's description of his or her business unit's culture to the business unit head's description, that is, as the distance between an individual's level of enculturation and the manager's level of enculturation.

subunit, whose cultural ideal may include open-minded exploration, and a production subunit, where the cultural ideal may embrace the efficient exploitation of resources. But if the concept of an organizational culture is meaningful—and the research we reviewed earlier certainly suggests that it is—this complication is not necessarily problematic. An organization can have both an overarching cultural ideal shared by management composed of the core dimensions of the organization's culture, as illustrated in chapter 1 with the examples of Dreyer's and Cypress Semiconductor, and additional cultural dimensions added to this ideal that suit the unique purposes of the managers of different subunits. These additional cultural dimensions could be viewed as constituting subunit-specific cultures—an extra layer of culture—that supplement the core culture of the organization for these subunits. Our approach of using a single measure to represent culture can still be applied to the culture of the organization as a whole; it can also be applied separately within specific subunits to represent the expanded sets of cultural dimensions relevant for those subunits. When members of some subunits do not buy in to the core cultural ideal of the organization, this is a case where the overarching culture of the organization is characterized by high cultural heterogeneity.

A complex issue concerns whether it is possible to detect subcultures using our representation of culture. In the usual way of identifying subcultures, content dimensions of culture are examined directly to see if there are any distinct clusters of individuals. Of course, the content dimensions might combine in many ways to generate an enculturation score, and the exact transformation rules involved are likely critical to determining whether and how subcultures might be detectable from the enculturation scores. The issue clearly requires deep study. But our current speculation is that gaps or separations in the distribution of enculturation scores within an organization may signify certain types of subcultural clustering in content.[8]

It is important to recognize that the assumption of a stable preference ordering for cultural fitness may not always hold. Management's cultural preferences may change over time, or there may be inconsistency in the ways various cultural dimensions are combined to determine overall cultural desirability. Nonetheless, we think that managerial assessments and preferences on cultural grounds are fairly stable over time, certainly

---

[8]The issue could be investigated with simulation techniques, to identify the possible assumptions and conditions where the conjecture advanced here is true, if they exist. Of course, there may always be subcultures evident in the content dimensions that are not discernible in the enculturation scores; obviously, these are best studied with an alternative approach.

more stable than individual consumer preferences are for, say, automobiles. We believe that day-to-day behavior is often ignored or excused when it does not agree with the overall cultural assessment made of an individual (see Goffman, 1959); in our view, it usually takes a long pattern of inconsistent behavior or an egregious action to cause reassessment of one's cultural fit. In any case, a stable preference ordering seems to be a reasonable assumption for a model of cultural transmission designed to examine demographics.

Now we turn to the primary issue of analysis in the chapter. Although our approach represents cultural fitness on a single scale, there can obviously be several, and perhaps many, underlying cultural content dimensions relevant to management for determining individual scores on the scale. So the question naturally arises, What is the relationship between enculturation (the cultural fitness score) and the underlying (multiple) content dimensions of culture? This question seems especially important to show the connection between our models and findings and the larger literature on organizational culture, which tends to view culture as multidimensional. Accordingly, the rest of the chapter is devoted to exploring this question. Of particular interest is examining the relationship between heterogeneity in enculturation scores and heterogeneity in the configurations on the underlying content dimensions.

3.3 CONTENT DIMENSIONS OF CULTURE

We start the analysis by assuming that several content dimensions of culture are of interest to management. Each can be thought of as falling somewhere on a measurement scale. Without loss of generality, we can view this scale as running from 0 to 1; if the dimension is measured empirically on, say, a scale of 1 to 7, a simple linear transformation will convert it to a [0–1] scale. Formally, if there are k dimensions of interest, and c_{ij} is individual i's value on dimension $j \leq k$, then $c_{ij} \in [0, 1]$.

Matching Dimensional Scales to Management Preferences

In developing our approach, we wish to work with 0–1 dimensional scales for culture for which 1 is the ideal score from management's perspective, and 0 is the least preferred. An arbitrary scale for a cultural dimension—say, constructed from a questionnaire instrument—may or may not capture management values in this fashion. For example, if a service firm prefers employees who are politically moderate, this might indicate a preference for people who score .5 on a 0–1 scale ranging from far left to far right. Preferences of this kind can be handled with a simple transformation; in the example, the scale can be converted to one of degree of moderateness: if v_{ij} is the original 0–1 scale value, then the transformation

$$c_{ij} = 1 - 2 \, |.5 - v_{ij}| \qquad (3.1)$$

will produce a scale with the desired characteristics—an original score of .5 becomes 1 (completely moderate), and an original score of 1 or 0 will be 0 (maximally extreme).

In general, if m_j is management's ideal score on dimension j, and individual i has score v_{ij}, then

$$c_{ij} = 1 - \frac{|m_j - v_{ij}|}{\max[(1 - m_j), \, m_j]} \qquad (3.2)$$

gives the cultural dimension score that we will work with. Notice that if $m_j = 1$ then $c_{ij} = v_{ij}$, and if $m_j = 0$ then $c_{ij} = 1 - v_{ij}$ (i.e., the scale is simply reversed).

The basic point here is that we can treat any underlying cultural dimension as a 0–1 scale, with 1 being the most preferred and 0 the least preferred, from management's perspective.

Combining Dimensions to Find Enculturation

The enculturation score of an individual will obviously be some function of the underlying cultural dimensions of interest to management. For simplicity, we assume that management's cultural fitness function for individual i, C_i, is a linear function of the k cultural dimensions:

$$C_i = \frac{\sum_{j=1}^{k} \beta_j c_{ij}}{\sum_{j=1}^{k} \beta_j} \qquad (3.3)$$

where $\beta_j > 0$ is the weighting assigned to dimension j and the c_{ij}, if necessary, have been transformed as just discussed so that a value of 1 is most preferred by management. Since $c_{ij} \in [0, 1]$, then also $C_i \in [0, 1]$.

The linear function for assessing cultural fitness seems to us a reasonable approach. Note that it includes cases where management may prefer a particular combination of underlying cultural characteristics. In such situations, the weightings for the desired dimensions would be high, and the scores on these dimensions for individuals in the organization would likely be correlated. We will specifically examine the case of correlated dimensions in the following.

3.4 ENCULTURATION AND CULTURAL DIMENSIONS

It is clear from the earlier equation for C_i that higher enculturation scores correspond to higher (weighted) average scores on the cultural dimensions of interest to management. The highest enculturation score of 1 corresponds to an ideal rating of 1 on each dimension, while the lowest score of 0 corresponds to the poorest rating of 0 on each dimension.

If a management team actually used a rating system for enculturation based on cultural dimensions, it would be highly unlikely for anyone to get an extreme fitness score. Any rating system is inherently noisy, and regression would drive the weighted averages toward the group mean. In an organization, a fitness scoring system is probably more useful if it exhibits greater variation, and hence better differentiation among employees in terms of enculturation. So as a practical matter, it may be useful to rescale the enculturation score so that it is spread over a broader range of the [0, 1] interval. The simplest approach would be to expand the score's variance around the mean until the most extreme end point reaches either 0 or 1. In other words, rescaling would increase the variance of the scores.

For analytic purposes, it does not matter whether the enculturation scores are rescaled. The relative location of each individual in the score distribution is the same in either case. And the meaning of our enculturation measure in terms of underlying cultural dimensions does not change: an employee with a higher fitness measure has a higher weighted average score on appropriately scaled underlying cultural dimensions; both the appropriate underlying dimensions and the weighting for the dimensions are functions of management's cultural preferences.

Cultural Homogeneity/Heterogeneity

In many later chapters, an outcome of great interest is the level of cultural homogeneity/heterogeneity in an organization. We speak of cultural homogeneity only in the sense of similarity in terms of work-related cultural dimensions, and specifically those considered relevant to management. Of course, individuals may have (dis)similarities on many other cultural dimensions that are not addressed by our focus on organizationally related cultural homogeneity.

Since we make inferences about cultural homogeneity based on the variance (or standard deviation) of the enculturation measure, it is important to establish the relationship between variation in the enculturation score and variation on the underlying cultural dimensions. Obviously there is no variation in the two extreme cases: a fitness score of 0 means 0 on every dimension, and fitness 1 means 1 on every dimension.

Intuitively, however, one may think that the correspondence between variation and fitness becomes more problematic for intermediate fitness values, since there are many combinations of underlying dimensions that could produce a fitness score of, say, .5. But how can one be sure? What is needed is a systematic way to assess this issue.

It makes sense to us to do so by investigating the relationship between the standard deviation of the enculturation measure and the average Euclidean distance for the underlying dimensions. The standard deviation of enculturation scores is given by

$$\sigma_c = \frac{1}{(n-1)} \left[\sum_{i=1}^{n} (C_i - \overline{C})^2 \right]^{1/2},\qquad (3.4)$$

where $\overline{C}$ is the mean enculturation or fitness score. The Euclidean distance between any two individuals i and j in an organization on their k underlying cultural dimensions is given by

$$d_{ij} = \left[\sum_{m=1}^{k} (c_{im} - c_{jm})^2 \right]^{1/2}.\qquad (3.5)$$

Then the average Euclidean distance between n individuals can be calculated as

$$\overline{d}_n = \frac{\sum_{i>j} d_{ij}}{n(n-1)/2}.\qquad (3.6)$$

With these formulations in hand, we now narrow the research question and ask whether a lower standard deviation of the enculturation scores corresponds to a lower average distance between underlying cultural dimensions. We use simulations to help us provide answers.

Design of Experiments

Our objective is to compare the average distance among individuals on their underlying cultural dimensions to the standard deviation of their enculturation scores—that is, to compare $\overline{d}_n$ and σ_c. We started this task by using the computer to generate the underlying dimension values for n individuals on k dimensions. We then drew individual dimension scores c_{ij} from a beta distribution, as described later. We next used the c_{ij} to calculate $\overline{d}_n$ and σ_c with equations (3.3–3.6), and then their ratio $\overline{d}_n/\sigma_c$. The relationship between underlying cultural distance and standard deviation in enculturation can be assessed by comparing this ratio across a range of values for σ_c; in particular, if the two measures are perfectly correlated, then the ratio will be constant.

As discussed earlier, the c_{ij} are in the [0, 1] interval (with 1 representing the management ideal on dimension j). Accordingly, we drew the c_{ij} scores from a beta distribution with parameters $a_1 > 1$ and $a_2 > 1$. Because such a distribution is unimodal and bounded by 0 and 1, random numbers generated from it have the characteristics desired for the c_{ij}.

We designed variations to examine the ratio $\bar{d}_n / \sigma_c$ over a range of values for σ_c. Since it is possible that the ratio value depends on the mean of $\bar{C}$ as well as its standard deviation, we also varied the value of $\bar{C}$. Specifically, we designed the simulation to generate values for c_{ij} that would create a grid of $\bar{C}$ and σ_c combinations, with means running from .05 to .95 in intervals of .05, and with standard deviations running from .02 to .18 in intervals of .04. For each of the ninety-five resulting mean/standard deviation pairs, we calculated the a_1 and a_2 parameters for the beta distribution used to generate the underlying dimensions c_{ij} that would produce the desired mean and standard deviation for C_i, and used those values in the simulation. In all cases, we set the organizational size to 1,000 ($n = 1,000$). Initially, we treated all dimensions c_{ij} as equally weighted in determining C_i—that is, in equation (3.3), $\beta_j = 1$ for $j = 1, \ldots, k$.

The simulation then proceeded in the following manner:

1. For one of the ninety-five paired parameter settings of a_1 and a_2, draw independently the underlying dimension values c_{ij} for 1,000 individuals from the corresponding beta distribution with the number of underlying dimensions k set to 2.
2. Using these c_{ij} values, calculate $\bar{d}_n / \sigma_c$ for the organization.
3. Repeat this process 100 times and calculate the average value of $\bar{d}_n / \sigma_c$ for the 100 iterations. The result is one point plotted on the graphs shown in figures 3.1 through 3.4.

Repeating this procedure for all ninety-five paired parameter settings of a_1 and a_2 results in ninety-five points for the $\bar{d}_n / \sigma_c$ average: nineteen points each, across a range of $\bar{C}$ values, for each of five values of σ_c. The entire procedure was then repeated for two additional values of the number of underlying dimensions k, 3 and 7.

Findings

Figure 3.1 presents the results of the simulations investigating the relationship between enculturation and uncorrelated content dimensions of culture. The top graph is for the case of two underlying cultural dimensions ($k = 2$), and the next two are for $k = 3$ and $k = 7$, respectively. In each graph, the x-axis is the mean value of enculturation C_i, and the y-axis gives the value of the ratio of Euclidean distance on the content

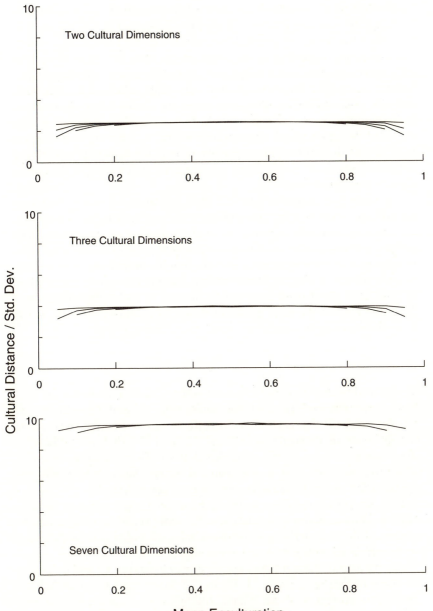

FIGURE 3.1 Ratio of cultural distance to standard deviation of enculturation $(\bar{d}_n/\sigma_c)$ for uncorrelated dimensions

dimensions to the standard deviation of enculturation, $\bar{d}_n/\sigma_c$. The lines in each graph connect points with the same values for σ_c.

Consider first the top graph. It is obvious that the ratio $\bar{d}_n/\sigma_c$ is essentially constant, regardless of the mean or standard deviation of C_i. The only exception is for mean values of C_i at the extremes—the ratio begins to vary somewhat for very low and very high values of C_i. But such extreme values of the enculturation mean are almost never encountered in the findings presented in this book. For practical purposes, then, the standard deviation of the enculturation mean, σ_c, appears to be a good indicator of the cultural heterogeneity of individuals on the underlying cultural dimensions of interest to management (at least under the conditions of the simulation).

The other two graphs in figure 3.1 yield the same conclusion. Although the average values of $\bar{d}_n/\sigma_c$ vary with the number of underlying dimensions, the value is essentially constant for a given number of dimensions. The variation across number of dimensions does not concern us, since the ratio of $\bar{d}_n/\sigma_c$ to σ_c is constant regardless of the number of dimensions of interest to management. Rather, by demonstrating that an essentially constant value of $\bar{d}_n/\sigma_c$ does not depend on a specific number of underlying dimensions, the pattern across the three graphs in figure 3.1 gives us confidence in the generalizability of the conclusion drawn from the top graph.

Extensions

The preceding findings are based on some specific conditions. In particular, we assumed (1) that the underlying cultural dimensions are uncorrelated, (2) that each underlying dimension is equally weighted by management in determining cultural fit, and (3) that all underlying dimensions conform to the same distribution. To strengthen our claim about the usefulness of σ_c as a measure of cultural heterogeneity, we conducted additional simulations to examine its generalizability.

First, we considered cases in which the underlying dimensions are correlated. The simulation procedure was the same as earlier, except that we generated the k underlying dimensions for each individual so that they were correlated with $\rho = .4$ and again with $\rho = .8$.

The findings of these simulations are shown in figures 3.2 and 3.3, using the same format as in figure 3.1. Figure 3.2 shows the case for underlying dimensions correlated at the .4 level, and figure 3.3 for a correlation level of .8. The overall pattern is similar to the findings for uncorrelated dimensions: while the value of $\bar{d}_n/\sigma_c$ varies by condition, within any given context this ratio is essentially constant except for extreme values of the mean enculturation level. So conclusions concerning the usefulness of σ_c appear to generalize to the case of correlated underlying dimensions.

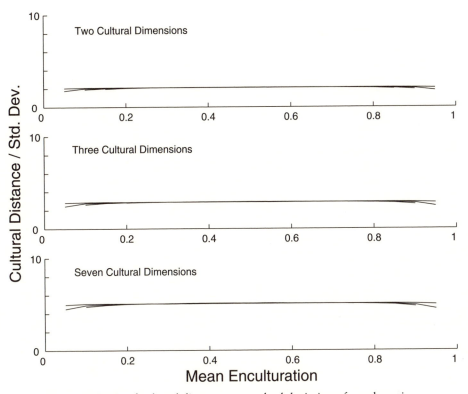

FIGURE 3.2 Ratio of cultural distance to standard deviation of enculturation ($\bar{d}_n/\sigma_c$) for dimensions with .4 correlation

In the simulations for figures 3.2 and 3.3, we assumed that all underlying dimensions were correlated at the same level within a given condition. To examine further the robustness of our conclusions for σ_c, we conducted two additional simulations. For the first simulation, we addressed the case of three underlying dimensions where (1) two of the dimensions are correlated at the .8 level, but the third dimension is uncorrelated with the other two, and (2) the dimensions are not equally weighted by management in determining cultural fitness (we chose $\beta_1 = 1$, $\beta_2 = .2$, and $\beta_3 = .7$ in equation 3.3). We also used the dimension weights in calculating the Euclidean distance between individuals, d_{ij}, to reflect the differential importance to management of different dimensions.

Figure 3.4 shows the result of the first additional simulation. As before, we see that the ratio $\bar{d}_n/\sigma_c$ is essentially constant except for very extreme values of the mean enculturation level.

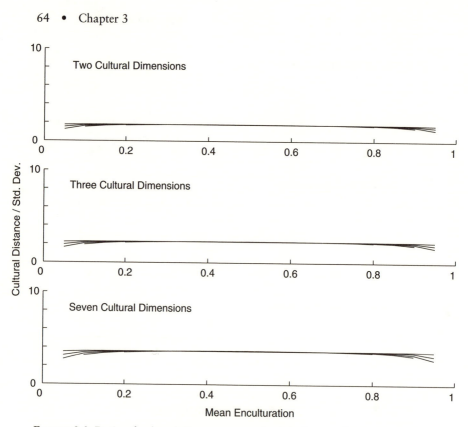

FIGURE 3.3 Ratio of cultural distance to standard deviation of enculturation $(\bar{d}_n/\sigma_c)$ for dimensions with .8 correlation

For the second additional simulation, we also used three underlying dimensions. But rather than determining the values of the mean and standard deviations for the beta distributions using the experimental design described earlier, for each point we drew the mean from a uniform distribution on [.05, .95] and the standard deviation from a uniform distribution on [.01, .15] and then proceeded as before to produce 500 points representing averages of 100 iterations each for 1,000-person organizations. The outcome of this simulation is presented in figure 3.5. Again, the ratio $\bar{d}_n/\sigma_c$ is essentially constant except for very extreme values of the mean enculturation level.

The final issue involves the distributions of the underlying dimensions. In the simulations presented so far, we assumed that each underlying dimension had the same distribution. This assumption is not too heroic, since the values of individuals on these dimensions contribute to the enculturation scores that form the basis for selection of new entrants and

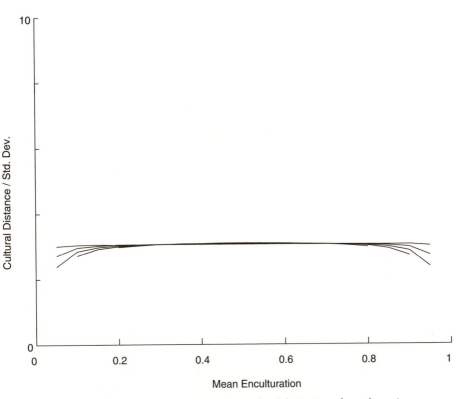

FIGURE 3.4 Ratio of cultural distance to standard deviation of enculturation $(\bar{d}_n/\sigma_c)$ for three dimensions with various correlations and weightings

are subject to further socialization within the organization, and also play a role in the turnover process. In fact, socialization processes, at a fine-grained level, operate on the dimension values rather than on the enculturation score itself. Still, because these underlying distributions may vary across cultural dimensions, we examined the case in which the distributions of the underlying dimensions are allowed to differ.

Simulating different distributions for the underlying dimensions is straightforward when the dimensions are uncorrelated. However, for cases when the underlying dimension values are correlated, technical constraints intervene. Generating correlated random variates from joint (or multivariate) distributions can be problematic, and techniques are in general not well developed. According to Law and Kelton (1991: 505), the practical utility of this approach "is probably quite limited. Not only is specification of the entire joint distribution required, but also derivation of all the required marginal and conditional distributions must be

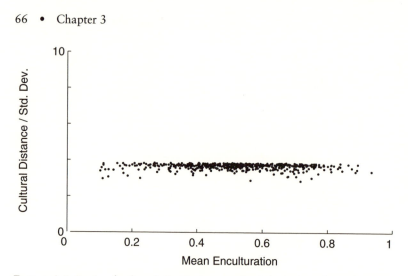

FIGURE 3.5 Ratio of cultural distance to standard deviation of enculturation $(\bar{d}_n/\sigma_c)$ for three randomly selected dimensions with randomly selected means and standard deviations

carried out. Such a level of detail is probably rarely obtainable in a complicated simulation." The solution to this problem is known for special cases, such as for the normal and gamma distributions, but we could find no solution for the beta distribution we use in this chapter.

We were able to derive a method for generating correlated random variates for the special case of beta distributions with identical parameters, which we used in producing figures 3.2 through 3.4 but we were unable to generalize it to the case of multivariate beta distributions with differing shape parameters. So we present simulation findings only for the case of different distributions for the underlying cultural dimensions when they are uncorrelated.

Figure 3.6 shows the findings for uncorrelated dimensions where the means and standard deviations of each dimension (and also the weightings for the dimensions) vary according to random assignment. Since the relationship between $\bar{d}_n$ and σ_c is no longer constant, we show plots of this relationship for two, three, and seven underlying dimensions. There is still a strong correlation between these measures ($\rho = .69$ regardless of the number of dimensions), but the relationship becomes weaker as their values increase. Note that the highest values for $\bar{d}_n$ and σ_c occur at the center of the enculturation scale ($C_i = .5$), since both must go to zero at the end points (C_i of 0 or 1). Note also that, in a sense, figure 3.6 shows a worst-case scenario, because the means for each dimension are drawn from a uniform distribution on [.05, .95]. In practice, the means for the

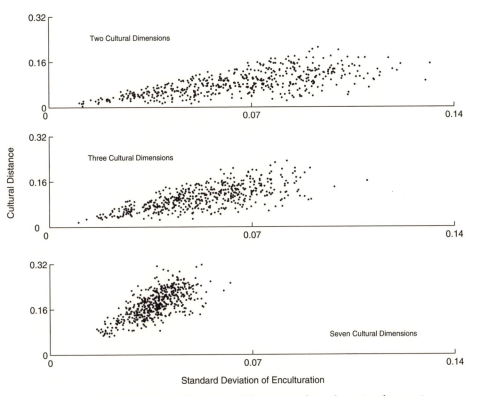

FIGURE 3.6 Cultural distance by standard deviation of enculturation for varying numbers of dimensions

dimensions are likely to be less dispersed, perhaps following a normal distribution, so the relationship addressed in figure 3.6 is likely to be stronger at high values than that shown in the figure.[9]

We conclude that heterogeneity in enculturation is still a good indicator of heterogeneity in the underlying cultural dimensions when the underlying dimensions follow different distributions and are uncorrelated, but not as robust an indicator as in the case of identical distributions, particularly when heterogeneity is high. And for the technical

[9]In figure 3.6, we use cultural distance and the standard deviation in enculturation as axes, rather than plotting the ratio of the two, to show the dispersion of points. If we had used the same method with the earlier figures (where the underlying dimensions in any condition have the same distribution), the plots would essentially be straight lines with slopes equal to the ratios in those figures, so the slopes would increase with the number of dimensions. The primary advantage of our strategy for the earlier figures is to demonstrate that the ratios do not depend on the means of the distributions.

constraints cited earlier, we cannot quantify the case for which the dimensions have different distributions and are correlated, although the findings presented here suggest that correlated underlying dimensions will not affect this conclusion in a qualitative sense.

Taken together, the set of findings presented in this section strongly suggests that the standard deviation of the enculturation level, σ_c, is a good measure of heterogeneity in the underlying cultural dimensions of interest to management, regardless of the number of relevant dimensions, the correlations among the dimensions, or the relative weightings assigned to the dimensions by management.

3.5 SUMMARY

In this chapter, we described our approach to representing organizational culture with a single scale indicating individuals' enculturation levels from the perspective of management. We also examined the relationship of our representation to the set of underlying cultural dimensions relevant to management for assessing the cultural fitness of workers. The findings show that for a very broad range of enculturation values—in fact, for all values except those approaching the end points of the scale—there is a strong relationship between the standard deviation of the enculturation measure and the average Euclidean distance for the underlying dimensions. Further, this relationship appears to hold regardless of the level of correlation between scores on the underlying dimensions.

Obviously, an individual with higher values on the underlying cultural dimensions of relevance to management will have a higher enculturation level, and a higher mean enculturation level for the organization directly implies higher average values for individuals on the underlying cultural dimensions. Perhaps more important for our purposes, we have shown that the standard deviation in the organization's enculturation level is a good measure of heterogeneity among individuals in the organization on the underlying cultural dimensions of relevance to management; as a consequence, we conclude with confidence in the work in the following chapters that organizations with smaller standard deviations in their enculturation levels are more culturally homogeneous from a managerial perspective. We think that this establishes the validity of our measure of cultural fitness and its interpretability from a multidimensional cultural perspective.

CHAPTER 4

Cultural Transmission

4.1 INTRODUCTION

As reviewed in chapter 1, cultural analyses of organizations tend to focus on the substantive content of culture and its effects on behavior. Because cultural content cannot have strong behavioral effects without a certain minimal inertia, any content-based analysis implies that culture is somewhat persistent across time. Yet, in contrast to societies and ethnic groups, the participants in formal organizations come and go more quickly, in larger relative numbers, and with less overlap in their periods of membership. They also must be enculturated to the organization through a process of secondary rather than primary socialization (Berger and Luckmann, 1967). These factors mean that cultural persistence in formal organizations is potentially problematic, at least more so than in other cultural systems, and worthy of study in its own right.

Cultural persistence is essentially a question of transmission (Cavalli-Sforza and Feldman, 1981). If new members of the culture enter and leave the system slowly, then the mechanisms of transmission can be slow and diffuse. If new members join and exit rapidly, or in large numbers relative to those who stay, then culture must be transmitted quickly and intensively if it is to be maintained. The former situation is characteristic of a society, the latter of an organization. Obviously, culture can be maintained more easily in the first than in the second. This does not, however, necessarily mean that organizational culture will be weaker or that it is predisposed to collapse. Rather, the conditions under which organizational culture can be maintained are narrower and more restrictive. In the scenario presented earlier, maintenance is a matter of socialization intensity relative to demographic flow. If that intensity is great enough, then even a strong or homogeneous culture can be maintained in the face of high turnover and high growth. College fraternities and sororities, whose socialization mechanisms include severe hazing activities, provide a good example: despite heavy and lumpy turnover in membership, the cultural character of local chapters often persists.[1]

---

[1]Stinchcombe (1965) links the cultural content in fraternities and sororities to the social conditions surrounding the founding period of their national unit.

Current understanding of these issues often succeeds in identifying plausible trade-offs. For instance, management textbooks contain much advice about how homogeneity among new members to a firm reduces socialization requirements (Ott, 1989). Likewise, long-term employment is widely believed to enhance cultural persistence. Yet the value of these important arguments is limited because they lack analytical precision. For instance, we do not understand the extent to which selective recruitment diminishes the need for intensive socialization. Nor do we know how long-term employment obviates either process. In other words, the demographic constraints on homogeneous organizational cultures are not well understood.

How is culture within an organization transmitted? How do organizational demographics affect the transmission process? What roles do peers and management play in the transmission process? Our efforts in this and later chapters represent an attempt to refine thinking on these matters. In this chapter, we address fundamental issues involved in cultural transmission in organizations.[2] In particular, we motivate and explain the basic model of cultural transmission used in the book. We build on the representation scheme described in chapter 3 and then rely on accepted social science theory and research to specify the model. What is perhaps unique about our analyses is the ability to put these processes together in a unified model and to understand its long-run dynamic behavior. This chapter and the next two explore the model's general behavior. Later chapters build on and adapt this model as dictated by different research questions.

4.2 Modeling framework

As explained in chapter 2, we use a formal modeling approach in studying culture. We do so because of its analytical rigor and because the transmission problem is suited to this approach: its constituent parts are understood reasonably well and are time dependent. This means that we can write simple but defensible equations of each component of the process but concentrate our analysis on the joint outcomes.

The model we develop contains three basic functions, one each for hiring practices, socialization processes, and employee departures in a given time interval. In specifying each function, we aim to represent the essential mechanisms by which organizational culture gets transmitted over time. We evaluate the simulated transmission processes by examining the

---

[2]Parts of the chapter are adapted from Harrison and Carroll (1991).

mean and standard deviation of enculturation obtained within each organization, as well as the length of time required to reach equilibrium.

The basic model of cultural transmission in organizations we develop and work with is a multilevel model. It represents processes of change in both individuals and organizations and can be used to make comparisons in structural characteristics across organizations. In subsequent chapters, we extend the basic model described here to examine both microscopic issues such as influence networks (chapter 8) and macroscopic ones such as organizational mortality (chapter 11).

4.3 MODEL SPECIFICATION

The cultural transmission model consists of three mathematical functions and a set of embedded parameters. The functions give (1) the number of persons hired in a period of time, (2) the process of change in the enculturation level of each person within the organization, and (3) the number of persons departing from the organization in a period of time. Each function contains both systematic parts, which describe the relations among variables and processes, and stochastic parts, which depict the random aspects of the processes. The parameters of the model control the growth rate of the organization, the recruitment rate to vacancies, the selectiveness of the recruitment process with respect to cultural criteria, the sources and intensity of socialization, the natural decay rate of socialization, and the components of the turnover rate. We discuss each function in turn, using the relevant parameters as necessary.

We introduce the model parameters along with their associated functions. In later chapters, parameter values are varied as a part of the experimental design. What substantive meaning do specific parameter values have? For the hiring and turnover processes, the parameters make sense only in the context of a time frame and are therefore calibrated to the time intervals in the experimental designs. These designs will be presented in detail in later chapters, but for present purposes, it is important to note that we treat each simulation time period as one month. This allows us to interpret parameter values in terms of what effects they have on a monthly basis. As we describe the functions, we also provide a sense of the magnitudes of effects for the range of parameter variations used in later experiments.

We begin by defining organizational size, N, in terms of the number of persons within the organization. We next note the definitional relation between organizational size N and demographic flows over time t. Let N_t denote organizational size at t, $N_{B,t}$ be the number entering (hired by) the organization between t and $t + 1$, and $N_{D,t}$ be the number of individuals departing from the organization in the same interval. Then it is the case for any interval that

$$N_{t+1} = N_t + N_{B,t} - N_{D,t}. \tag{4.1}$$

The organizations we simulate grow through the creation of new positions, which are then filled with persons as they are hired. The potential size of the organization is controlled by the number of positions N_t. This number changes over time as a function of the stochastic growth rate r_g. That is, the growth rate r_g operates on current size N_t, making growth proportional to size, and new persons enter the organization as vacancies to be filled through recruitment. To see this clearly, let the number of vacancies at t be indicated by V_t. Then the relation between size and vacancies over time is defined by the relation

$$V_t = (V_{t-1} - N_{B,t} + N_{D,t}) + r_g(N_t). \tag{4.2}$$

In our experiments, we consider growth rates varying from 0 to .08 (we also consider decline, the removal of positions, in chapter 6). The .08 value represents very high growth, averaging 8 percent a month, a doubling in size for the organization in about 9 months on average. More common values used in the experiments are .04, doubling in size on average about every 18 months, and .0035, doubling in around 16.5 years.

As explained in chapter 3, for a given individual i, we denote his or her enculturation level at time t by the variable $C_{i,t}$, which is defined to vary between 0 and 1 inclusive. Distributional measures of these $C_{i,t}$ scores characterize the organizational culture at any particular point in time. In particular, the mean level of enculturation $\bar{C}_t$ represents the degree to which the culture conforms to the management ideal, and a measure of dispersion, such as the standard deviation of enculturation across all individuals, $\sigma_{c,t}$, indicates cultural heterogeneity.

Hiring Function

Organizations hire employees to fill vacancies created by departures and to staff new positions generated by growth. Recruitment is not, however, usually matched perfectly to positions available, since search processes take time and effort. Realizing this, firms can project labor needs and over-recruit to the immediate situation, or they can attempt to fill openings as they occur, accepting that there will always be a gap between labor needs and staffing. We follow the latter approach in developing the basic model.

Think about hiring within an organization. Organizations vary in the speed with which they fill positions, in part because hiring selectively takes more time and effort: searches must seek out rarer types of individuals, and many desired characteristics are not easily discerned. Consider, for instance, the following account of selection at Goldman Sachs, an investment bank where culture is taken very seriously:

> It begins in the recruitment process, long before a formal offer is extended. Brains are not enough. The first couple of interviews determine whether a candidate meets the firm's intellectual standards; the remainder, where far more candidates stumble, are used to determine "fit." It is a grueling process that tests endurance as well as aptitude. Those candidates who do not evince a scorching ambition, total commitment, and an inclination for teamwork are quickly weeded out. (Endlich, 1999: 20)

To enable the model to reflect such processes, we specify a stochastic recruitment rate r_r at which vacancies are filled. We use lower rates to represent more selective hiring processes and higher rates for less selective ones. The probability of filling a vacancy within one month is $[1 - \exp(-r_r)]$. In our experiments, we vary the recruitment rate from 1.9 for hiring with very low selectivity to .4 for very high selectivity (we also vary the enculturation means of the hiring pools across these conditions, for reasons explained later). The low-selectivity setting results in an 85 percent probability of filling a vacancy in a month, whereas the probability is only 33 percent with the high-selectivity setting.

We can now specify the hiring function. Recall that $N_{B,t}$ gives the number of persons hired in period t, and $N_{D,t}$ gives the number departing. Then organizational hiring is given by

$$N_{B,t} = \sum_{i=1}^{V_{t-1}} H_{i,t}, \tag{4.3}$$

where

$$H_{i,t} = \begin{cases} 1 & \text{if position } i \text{ is filled in period } t, \\ 0 & \text{otherwise.} \end{cases}$$

where the stochastic rate of recruitment to vacant positions (r_r) is used to find values of $H_{i,t}$.

Where do the new individuals come from? What do they look like? For the simulation model, organizational hiring can be conceived as drawing individuals from a pool of candidates. The hiring pool has a distribution of values on the desired cultural characteristics and the distribution is set for the pool, but the choice of any particular individual is somewhat random. In fact, the distributional characteristics of the hiring pool are determined by the selectiveness of the hiring policies of the organization. As mentioned earlier, hiring can be selective, in that a particular type of person can be defined as needed and then sought after, or it can be more opportunistic, in the sense of using a wider segment of the population for the recruitment pool. Selectivity usually requires more time and resources than opportunism. But this presumably is balanced to some extent by the reduced socialization requirements and lower turnover associated with selectivity. In either case—or, more precisely, over the range of cases from very low to very high selectivity—hiring decisions will be imperfect because some relevant information about potential employees may not be observable or accurate. Thus even under high selectivity, some individuals will require substantial efforts in socialization (or removal from the organization) if a preferred and homogeneous culture is to be maintained. To reflect this reality, the candidate hiring pool can be more or less centered on the desired characteristics (set by the mean of the distribution), and more or less noise can be tolerated in the information (variance of the distribution).

To keep things simple, imagine that there is only a single cultural measure of interest and that it can be represented on a continuous scale from 0 to 1. As explained in chapter 3, in our modeling efforts we assume that an individual's propensity to embrace the values and norms of a particular organizational culture can be meaningfully represented by such a single measure—the enculturation level—indicating the degree to which an employee fits management's ideal.

The hiring pool of candidates can then be defined by its mean and variance on this variable. The case of high selectivity would imply a relatively high mean, say, .8. By contrast, an opportunistic hiring policy implies a much lower mean for the candidate pool.

We simulate hiring on the basis of cultural criteria by randomly drawing values of $C_{i,t}$ from normal distributions parameterized to yield a mean of $\bar{C}_h$ and a standard deviation of σ_{ch}. The parameters of the distribution are defined by the hiring policies simulated. The average number of persons hired is driven by equation (4.3), given earlier. At each time period, therefore, a number of persons with a variety of dispositions toward the culture of the organization are hired.

On average, more selective hiring involves a slower process. The higher the mean $\bar{C}_h$ of the organization's recruitment pool, the lower the stochastic recruitment rate (r_r), and the lower the percentage of vacancies filled per time period.

Socialization Function

Once an individual is hired, he or she is subject to a variety of influences with respect to the culture of the organization. Management may attempt to inculcate the new employee fully in the aims, ways, and whims of the organization. This might take the form of explicit orientation programs and activities or reward and punishment systems, or it might be produced through more subtle means. For instance, Lewis (1989: 48) describes the training sessions offered to newly recruited traders at the investment bank Salomon Brothers in the 1980s:

> Over three months leading salesmen, traders, and financiers shared their experiences with the class. They trafficked in unrefined street wisdom: how money travels around the world (any way it wants), how a trader feels and behaves (any way he wants), and how to schmooze a customer. After three months in the class trainees circulated wearily around the trading floor for two more months. Then they went to work. All the while there was a hidden agenda: to Salomonize the trainee.

Likewise, the now famous Hamburger University of McDonald's was launched to impart uniform operational and behavioral guidelines through the franchisee system. While much of this is accomplished through formal rules, a leading executive at the time explained that "We [McDonald's] had to have a classroom atmosphere to teach some of these guys the operating philosophy and theory of the McDonald's operation" (quoted in Love 1995: 147).

Whatever the actual form of management influence efforts, in these cases it is clear that management has a conception of the ideal employee on the cultural dimensions it considers relevant, and the objective from its point of view is to produce a person socialized to within some acceptable distance of this ideal. Obviously, management's clarity of thought about what constitutes an ideal employee may be more or less specific, it may invest more or less in attempting to influence culture, and its efforts to produce such a person may be more or less successful.

Another important source of cultural socialization arises from existing employees or peers. Group and peer pressure toward conformity are some of the best-documented phenomena in the social science world (e.g., Sherif, 1935; Asch, 1951; Kiesler and Kiesler, 1969; O'Reilly and Caldwell, 1979). Peer effects can operate through direct and personal advice by one's peers, as when a senior manager tells a new employee at Goldman Sachs, "We say 'we,' we never say 'I'" (Endlich 1999: 21). Or they can operate in a less obvious manner, through identification and imitation or tacit collusion.

Regardless of the mechanism, if an individual enters an organization filled with persons more highly socialized to the norms of the culture, then it is reasonable to expect that, in the normal course of interaction and work with these persons, the individual will become more enculturated. Likewise, if an individual enters an organization where the existing employees are only weakly socialized to the cultural norms, then he or she will tend to become weakly enculturated even if he or she entered in a state more accepting of the norms encouraged by management. In other words, in a simple model neglecting social distances and innate individual differences, individuals get pulled toward the mean level of enculturation among others.

There is also apparently a natural source of desocialization. Laboratory studies have shown that socialization decays over time in the absence of other stimuli (Jacobs and Campbell, 1961). So in addition to the other two pulls—toward the group mean and toward the management ideal—there is also a pull toward no or zero enculturation.

Any individual's change over time with respect to socialization is a combination of the pulls from the three sources of management, peers, and decay. The three forces likely vary in their relative strengths. The expected change in socialization is modeled as a function of the individual's current distance from a target for each source (1.0, the maximum value of C, for management; $\bar{C}$, the group enculturation mean, for peers; and 0, the minimum of C, for decay), multiplied by weighting parameters. The use of the mean socialization level of peers in the specification assumes that all peers are in communication with each other and are equally influential (French, 1956). We use this assumption here in developing the basic model, recognizing that it may be implausible in many organizational settings. In chapter 8, we extend and refine this aspect of the model, letting influence be dynamic and unequal across an individual's social network. The model also introduces an error term to allow for noise in the cultural transmission process.

Putting together these formulations, we posit socialization-change intensity as

$$A_{i,t} = \frac{\alpha_{mgt}(1 - C_{i,t-1}) + \alpha_{peer}(\bar{C}_{t-1} - C_{i,t-1}) + \alpha_{decay}(0 - C_{i,t-1})}{\alpha_{mgt} + \alpha_{peer} + \alpha_{decay}} + e, \qquad (4.4)$$

where e is an error term and α_{mgt}, α_{peer}, α_{decay} are parameters representing the pulls toward ideal socialization (from management), mean socialization level (from peer pressure), and zero socialization (from decay), respectively. In effect, the denominator normalizes the function $A_{i,t}$ to ensure that an individual's $C_{i,t}$ score remains between 0 and 1 inclusive or, equivalently, that the sum of the parameters α_{mgt}, α_{peer}, α_{decay} is constructed to be unity. The error e is defined to be normally distributed with mean zero and adjustable variance.

Figure 4.1 shows the value of the socialization-change intensity function when mean enculturation is at a low level (.2, the figure on the left) and a high level (.8, the figure on the right). In both figures, the vertical axis shows socialization change intensity, $A_{i,t}$, the leftmost horizontal axis gives the management socialization parameter, α_{mgt}, and the rightmost

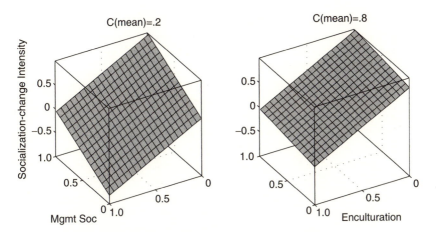

FIGURE 4.1 Socialization-change intensity

axis depicts an individual's enculturation level, $C_{i,t}$. An important insight of both figures is that the lower a person's enculturation, $C_{i,t}$, the greater his or her socialization-change intensity for any given level of management socialization, α_{mgt}; that is, less enculturated individuals get pulled up more for a given effort from management. Moreover, this effect is stronger when the overall enculturation mean is higher, as comparing the slopes of the shaded surfaces of the two figures indicates.

Individuals can be more or less susceptible to socialization, whatever its source. Susceptibility is greatest at the time of entry into the organization and then declines with tenure (Louis, 1980). We simulate susceptibility to socialization forces with the following equation:

$$B_{i,t} = \beta_0 + \exp[-\beta_1 - \beta_2 u_{i,t-1}], \qquad (4.5)$$

where $u_{i,t-1}$ is individual i's tenure with the organization at $t-1$. With the parameter values used here ($\beta_0 = .02$; $\beta_1 = .60$; $\beta_2 = .30$), susceptibility begins with a value less than unity and declines exponentially with tenure toward a nonzero asymptote. (See figure 4.2 for a visual representation of susceptibility, $B_{i,t}$.) It is important for the value of the function to remain between 0 and 1 because it will be used below as a multiplier. In this specification, β_0 is associated with the asymptotic level of susceptibility, β_1 with the level of susceptibility at entry (tenure equals zero), and β_2 with the speed of the decline in susceptibility with increasing tenure from the entry level to the asymptotic level.

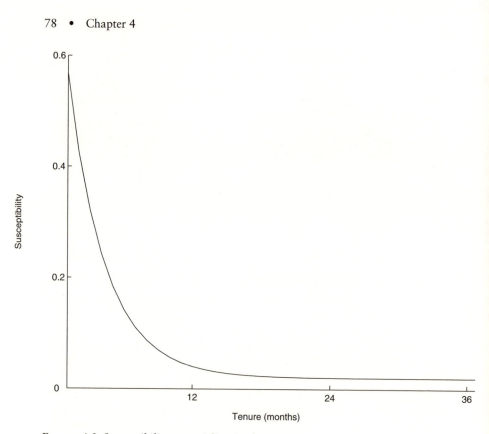

FIGURE 4.2 Susceptibility to socialization by tenure

The socialization function is completed by taking an individual's prior enculturation level $C_{i,t-1}$ and adding to it the effect of socialization-change intensity $A_{i,t}$ multiplied by susceptibility $B_{i,t}$. That is,

$$C_{i,t} = C_{i,t-1} + A_{i,t}B_{i,t}. \tag{4.6}$$

The net effect of the cultural change process is that when peer socialization is strong (i.e., α_{peer} is high relative to α_{mgt}), individual enculturation tends to move toward the enculturation mean, and when management socialization is strong (i.e., α_{mgt} is high relative to α_{peer}), individual enculturation tends to move toward 1.0. But the extent of change in individual enculturation in a time period is attenuated with increasing tenure, dropping to a very low level as tenure increases beyond twelve time periods (one simulation year).

Figure 4.3 shows examples of the amount of cultural change in one time period for cases of peer socialization only and management

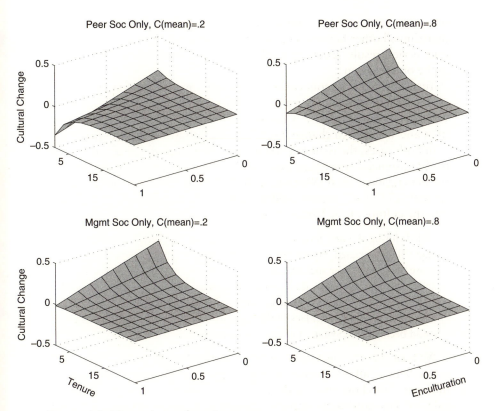

FIGURE 4.3 Change in enculturation

socialization only when the enculturation mean is alternatively low ($\bar{C}$ = .2) and high ($\bar{C}$ = .8). With only peer socialization—the top row of the figure—enculturation increases for individuals with very low encul-turation levels (C_i near zero) and decreases for those with very high enculturation levels (C_i near one), but on average it tends to decrease when $\bar{C}$ is low and to increase when $\bar{C}$ is high. With only management socialization—the bottom row—enculturation tends to increase more for less enculturated individuals (and obviously does not change for the culturally "ideal" individual). In all cases, the amount of cultural change is greatest for new employees and declines with tenure.

Turnover Function

Individuals leave organizations for a wide variety of reasons, including better jobs, dissatisfaction, and family concerns. For present purposes, it makes sense to divide the causes of turnover into two separate factors, one associated with the culture of the organization and the other summarizing all other factors. The number of persons departing in any given time period results from the application of these factors to each person in the organization.

Turnover might be connected to organizational culture for at least two reasons. First, individuals who do not accept the culture might be motivated to leave voluntarily (Chatman, 1991). Second, those who do not fit in and who fail to change might be forced to leave involuntarily.

In both cases, the issue may be thought of as one of alienation, related to the distance between an individual's embodiment of the culture and the management ideal (Wanous, 1980). For instance, consider the anger Gerstel (1982: 167) experienced when he recognized he no longer fit well into the culture of the Synanon cult:

> I tried during the first months that I was back at the Ranch, to suffocate my anger. I excoriated myself for the pathological rebelliousness that would cause me to rage over such trivial matters as ninety minutes of exercise a week and a few new words in the community language. But my efforts failed. My anger ate at me. I began to conclude that I would never be content in the community, that, somehow, I lacked the capacity for trust possessed by those who could become true Synanon people. I had to leave.

We formalize the alienation process with the term $\gamma_1(1 - C_{i,t})^3$, where γ_1 is a parameter allowing more or less sensitivity to alienation as a cause of turnover.[3] We chose to raise the difference to the third power so that the value of this expression increases rapidly as $C_{i,t}$ approaches zero, but in general the effect of alienation on turnover in the model is much smaller than the effect of other (noncultural) factors over most of the range of $C_{i,t}$.

Allowing all other reasons for leaving an organization (Chatman and Jehn, 1994) to be captured in an adjustable stochastic base-turnover rate (associated with the parameter γ_0), the number of persons departing the organization in time period t is then given by

$$N_{D,t} = \sum_{i=1}^{N_t-1} E_{i,t}, \tag{4.7}$$

where

$$E_{i,t} = \begin{cases} 1 & \text{if individual } i \text{ leaves the organization in period } t, \\ 0 & \text{otherwise.} \end{cases}$$

---

[3]In model extensions described in chapters 8, 9, and 11, we respecify the alienation process as $\gamma_1(\bar{C}_t - C_{i,t})^3$. In these model contexts, we see the distance from one's peer base as more critical than distance from the management ideal in producing alienation.

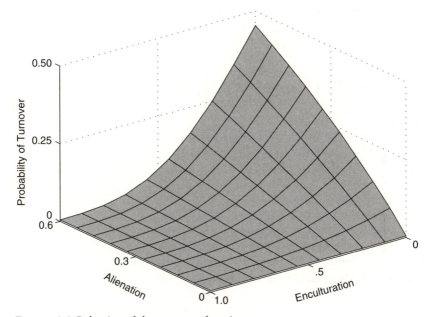

FIGURE 4.4 Behavior of the turnover function

The stochastic rate of departure for individual i, used to find $N_{D,t}$, is

$$r_{i,t} = \gamma_0 + \gamma_1[1 - C_{i,t-1}]^3, \tag{4.8}$$

where both γ_0 and γ_1 are parameters of the rate associated with, respectively, base turnover and alienation.

Figure 4.4 shows the behavior of the simulated turnover function. The vertical axis gives the probability of turnover, the leftmost horizontal axis the parameter associated with alienation, γ_1, and the rightmost axis an individual's enculturation level, $C_{i,t-1}$. As the shaded surface of the plot shows, turnover rises sharply when enculturation is low and the alienation parameter, γ_1, is high. With the highest alienation parameter setting (γ_1) we use in our experiments, 0.6, the probability of alienation-driven turnover approaches .50 per month for someone with zero enculturation; it drops sharply as enculturation rises or as the alienation parameter is lowered. The base turnover parameter (γ_0) has an additive effect on the probability of turnover but no influence on the shape of the surface. In the settings we use in the experiments, the base turnover rates range from .005 (reflecting a .5 percent monthly probability of turnover—implying an expected waiting time of 16.7 years and 11.5 years to wait until 50 percent of persons turn over) to .03 (reflecting a

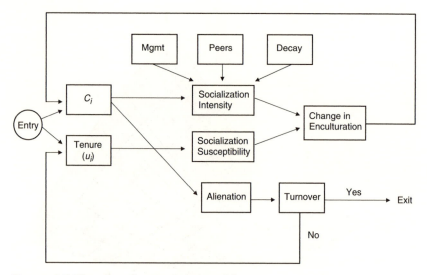

FIGURE 4.5 The cultural transmission model

3 percent monthly turnover probability, with an expected waiting time of 33 months and a wait of 23 months for 50 percent turnover).

4.4 SUMMARY

As a conceptual overview, figure 4.5 shows a visualization of the model. The figure summarizes the elemental processes of the model that operate on an individual during each time period. As mentioned in chapter 2, this model constitutes the cornerstone of our research program. In the next chapter, we examine its behavior with different configurations of parameter settings that correspond to widely observed types of organizations. In chapter 6, we explore the model's behavior under varying levels of growth and decline; these variations essentially modify the rate at which new individuals enter the organization (leftmost component on figure) or leave the organization (lower right). In subsequent chapters, we put the model to a variety of uses, each of which requires us to adapt and extend it in particular ways. Chapter 7 varies parameters of all the model's processes to study the effects of heterogeneity in tenure across individuals on cultural heterogeneity. Chapter 8 elaborates the effects of peers on socialization intensity by specifying exact influence networks among individuals and making these relations dynamic. Chapter 9 continues with the network-based extension of peer influence to explore the resilience of typical terrorist organizations to common governmental intervention strategies. This chapter also sets up a hierarchical influence network that constrains peer-based socialization processes. Chapter 10 investigates the speed with which a merger of two separate organizations converges to a homogeneous culture when influence and demographic processes vary, including how the peers of the acquired organization are influenced by ex-colleagues and by members of the acquiring organization. Chapter 11 links the cultural system to organizational mortality by deriving and studying a macro version of the model.[4]

As with any theory, evaluation of the model should depend on both its plausibility and the ideas it generates. In our effort to build a plausible model of cultural transmission in organizations, we resisted the temptation to be creative and innovative. Instead, we tried to rely on established theories and available evidence to specify a model that most social scientists would find plausible, minor quibbles about theories and evidence aside. Specification of the cultural transmission process in its entirety in mathematical form may be regarded as a contribution in and of itself. But a better test of the model comes in the following chapters, where we examine whether it is capable of generating widely observed differences in organizational behavior.

---

[4]Appendix A provides a guide to the notation in our basic model and to notation specific to individual chapters.

CHAPTER 5

Organizational Types

5.1 INTRODUCTION

Although chapter 4 discussed each component of the cultural transmission process separately, empirical research strongly suggests that organizational features do not vary independently of each other.[1] Indeed, a common observation among organizational analysts holds that certain major organizational features hang together in coherent clusters or constellations. Perhaps the oldest and most famous example is the "bureaucratic organization" of Max Weber (1947), which (among other features) contains a fixed division of labor, hierarchical authority relations, impersonal formal rules, technical skill-based personnel policies, and long-term employment. More recently, after collecting detailed human resource practice data on 170 young high-technology firms in California's Silicon Valley, researchers at the Stanford Project on Emerging Companies (SPEC) identified a range of practices that could generate up to thirty-six possible combinations, but they also found that two-thirds of the firms used only five basic combinations as employment models (Baron, Burton, and Hannan, 1996).

Similarly, the major factors related to cultural transmission, such as recruitment selectivity, socialization intensity, and longevity of employment, are widely thought to cohere in a small number of particular combinations. While for analytical purposes we continue to separate each component of the cultural transmission process, we also think it is worthwhile to consider the model in the context of some commonly used combinations of features. These combinations not only ease the cognitive task of organizing findings, in particular those related to interactions between variables, but also provide an opportunity to check the face validity of the model. We refer to these combinations as *organizational types*.[2]

---

[1]Parts of this chapter adapt sections of text from Harrison and Carroll (1991).

[2]In earlier work, we referred to these configurations as *organizational forms*. The form concept is used in a variety of loose and often-inconsistent ways in the organizations literature. Only recently have efforts been made to introduce theoretical rigor into the form concept (see Romanelli, 1990; Pólos, Hanna, and Carroll, 2002; McKendrick and Carroll, 2001). To avoid confusion, we now use the term *type*, which is mainly an organizing device for presenting findings.

As we describe them here, each organizational type is commonly associated with a certain set of social-demographic features (selectivity, socialization intensity, growth, turnover, tenure), as well as a cultural disposition (consistency with management, heterogeneity). In our analysis, we use these casual observations to define for each type a unique configuration of parameter settings in the three basic components of the model. We then run simulations of the model using these configurations and examine the characteristics of the resulting organizational culture. The first major analytical question we address concerns the model's ability to produce the "known" observed differences in organizational culture across the types. This is a casual test of the basic model's face validity. We next investigate separately for each organizational type the effects of variation in four aspects of the model controllable, at least to some extent, by top management. These arguably controllable aspects are (1) the base employee turnover rate, (2) recruitment selectivity, (3) intensity of management socialization practices, and (4) strength of the alienation effect.

5.2 STYLIZED ORGANIZATIONAL TYPES

Orienting the simulations around stylized versions of organizational types provides some useful guidance as to parameter selection. It also facilitates comparison of outcomes to empirical observations. Consequently, we work with the following seven organizational types around which the initial simulation studies are organized conceptually:

- *Japanese-style type.* The Japanese may be responsible for the strong American interest in organizational culture. Coinciding with the Japanese economy's dominance of international trade in the 1980s is the spread and visibility of the Japanese ways of organizing corporations. While the specific features vary for any individual organization, the essential elements of Japanese organizations are (1) high recruitment selectivity, (2) intensive socialization by management, and (3) long-term employment (Ouchi, 1981). These factors are thought to produce organizations with homogeneous cultures that can persist intact even when growth rates are extraordinarily high. As a result, Japanese-style organizations can adopt strategies aimed at maximizing market share without fear of undermining corporate culture and values (Abegglen and Stalk, 1985).

- *American manufacturing type.* Among many other things, the Industrial Revolution produced the assembly line and its associated traditional manufacturing organization. The essence of this design is standardized work and specialized division of labor. Human factors, including culture, are generally designed out of the type; one person can replace any other with ease in such a system. For this reason, recruitment selectivity is usually low in this type, and management socialization is weak or nonexistent. Fast growth and high turnover run part and parcel with other characteristics.

- *Professional type.* Organizations that are dominated by professionals, such as law firms and universities, have still different cultural and demographic features. Dominant among these, of course, is the high selectivity of recruitment—to be a professional organization means to recruit primarily from a clearly defined and already enculturated pool of professionals. Consequently, there is little socialization done by management within the organization, at least as compared with the professional socialization that has already occurred outside it (e.g., in professional graduate programs). Growth and turnover may vary from low to moderate, but neither is typically high.

- *Governmental-bureaucratic type.* The Weberian ideal of the rational bureaucracy still characterizes many governmental and other organizations. Demographic stability is a primary feature of many of these bureaucratic organizations. Growth in employment, if any, is low if not entirely stable, and turnover is low, the career being conducted mainly within the bureaucracy. Recruitment and socialization practices undoubtedly vary across bureaucratic organizations. However, rarely if ever do they reach the extremes found in the Japanese-style organization. In fact, bureaucracy was originally designed to eliminate particularistic (e.g., cultural) selection, the goal being a purely meritocratic system based on technical criteria. Few would contend this has been achieved often, so it seems best to characterize the bureaucratic organizational type as having low to moderate cultural selectivity in recruitment and low to moderate socialization intensity.

- *Entrepreneurial type.* Less of an ideal type than the others, the predominant characteristic of the entrepreneurial type is high growth. This makes it particularly interesting for the study of cultural transmission: Can culture be maintained in the midst of such rapid change? Because of the many survival pressures experienced by entrepreneurial organizations, little effort is typically devoted to socialization or even selective recruitment. Turnover varies but is usually in the moderate range.

- *Z-type.* Many management theorists recommend that traditional American firms move closer to the Japanese model of organization. The resulting hybrid has been called a "type Z" organization (Ouchi, 1981). Its features include those of the traditional manufacturing type but with intensified socialization by management, greater recruitment selectivity, and reduced turnover. The hypothesized benefits of these efforts hinge on an intensified and more homogeneous organizational culture.

- *Collectivist-democratic type.* Organizations operated on a collective basis and without formal hierarchical authority usually display homogeneous and tightly encapsulated cultures. Such organizations have been described and analyzed by Rothschild-Whitt (1979), who refers to them as collectivist-democratic organizations (not to be confused with cults, which often have a strong but covert hierarchy). The structural and demographic features of the collectivist-democratic organization include extremely high selectivity in recruitment, intensive socialization by coworkers rather than by management, little turnover, and low growth. These are commonly considered ideal, if not extreme, conditions for establishing and maintaining an organization's culture.

Table 5.1 provides a summary of the relative settings of the parameters for each organizational type. As we have noted in our discussion of the various types, there also are known differences among the types in terms of cultural intensity and heterogeneity. In particular, the typical expected ordering of types by ability to achieve high managerial preferredness in culture would include the Japanese-style, professional, and Z-type at the top (generating the most preferred cultures) and the American manufacturing type at the bottom (generating the least preferred culture). In terms of cultural heterogeneity, we would expect it to be lowest for the professional, collectivist-democratic, and governmental types. Although the matter has not been studied directly, it is widely believed that recruitment selectivity, socialization intensity, turnover, and growth can account for many of these differences.

Comparison with SPEC Models

For empirical grounding, we find it useful to compare the stylized types with the employment models of the Stanford Project on Emerging Companies (SPEC; Baron, Burton, and Hannan, 1996). SPEC sampled firms no more than ten years old and with at least ten employees when sampled. As noted earlier, the SPEC researchers identified five basic employment models: (1) a star model that involves challenging work, autonomy and professional control, and selection of elite personnel based on long-term potential; (2) an engineering model that combines a focus on challenging work, peer group control, and selection based on specific task abilities; (3) a commitment model that relies on emotional/familial attachments of employees to the organization, selection based on cultural fit, and peer group control; (4) a bureaucratic model that is based purely on monetary or task motivations, control and coordination through formal organization, and selection of employees to perform

TABLE 5.1
Stylized organizational types

Japanese-style	High recruitment selectivity
	Intensive socialization by management
	Long-term employment
	High growth rate
American manufacturing	Low recruitment selectivity
	Weak socialization by management
	High turnover
	High growth rate
Professional	High recruitment selectivity
	Weak socialization by management
	Moderate turnover
	Low growth rate
Governmental	Moderate recruitment selectivity
	Weak socialization by management
	Low turnover
	Low growth rate
Entrepreneurial	Moderate recruitment selectivity
	Moderate socialization by management
	Moderate turnover
	Very high growth rate
Z-type	Moderate recruitment selectivity
	Moderate socialization by management
	Low turnover
	High growth rate
Collectivistic-democratic	High recruitment selectivity
	Intensive socialization by peers
	Low turnover
	No growth

Source: Harrison and Carroll (1991). Copyright © 1991 by Cornell University. All rights reserved. Used by permission.

prespecified tasks; and (5) an autocratic model based on pecuniary attachment, selection based on current competence, and direct oversight and control by managers.[3]

The SPEC employment models do not map directly to all the stylized organizational types. This is mainly because they focus on the substantive nature of the attachment to the firm (including emotional involvement and homogeneity), whereas the stylized types are based directly on demographics and the strength of the processes (e.g., socialization) generating the attachment. Some models and types do seem roughly equivalent, though. In particular, the commitment model of SPEC displays high similarity to the Japanese-style type in the simulation. Likewise, the bureaucratic model of SPEC aligns with the governmental-bureaucratic type. Finally, the star and autocratic models loosely correspond to the professional and entrepreneurial types.

The SPEC analysis of employee turnover by Baron et al. (2001) is very interesting for present purposes because it shows that the culturally based commitment model has a significant amount of employee turnover. In particular, when stable over time, the commitment model shows an intermediate level of turnover compared with the other models. Thus, by these data at least, some level of demographic activity in the organization does not undermine the ability to set up and maintain a persistent and homogeneous organization culture.

More broadly, the SPEC turnover analysis provides a kind of validity check of the four roughly equivalent stylized types. Looking at stable models and estimating their relationship with turnover, Baron, Hannan, and Burton (2001, table 5) find that the bureaucratic model has lowest turnover, followed by (in order) engineering, commitment, star, and autocratic. The ordering of types by turnover level (not rate) is a function of both the growth rate (r_g) and the base turnover rate (associated with γ_0 in $r_{i,t}$ in equation 4.8).[4] Looking only at the base rate gives an ordering of types into two groups: a first with the lowest rate consisting of governmental-bureaucratic and Japanese-style, and a second with professional and entrepreneurial. Combining growth rate and the baseline turnover rate would yield the following order of turnover level in our view: governmental-bureaucratic, Japanese-style, professional, and entrepreneurial. This ordering corresponds exactly to what we would expect from the empirical SPEC study.

---

[3]A variety of analyses reveals that the responses that do not correspond to one of these basic model types can be combined with the closest basic-type observations without significant loss of information.

[4]The parameter associated with the alienation effect is constant for these four organizational types.

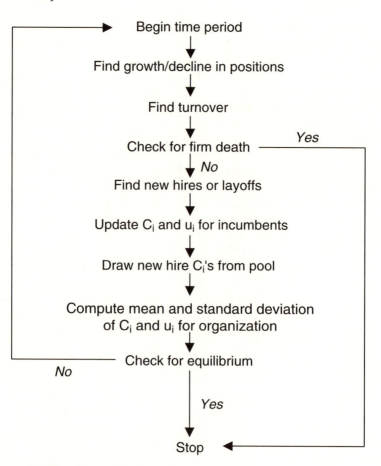

FIGURE 5.1 Flowchart of the simulation

5.3 SIMULATION METHODS

The original simulation program of the model was written in the BASIC language using MicroSoft's QuickBASIC 4.00b. Some later simulation programs were written in PowerBASIC Complier for Windows IDE 7.02 to take advantage of both software and hardware advances that occurred during the course of the research.[5] Figure 5.1 shows a flowchart for the code governing the simulation, depicted at the organizational level. It shows the sequence of operations the program conducts for each time period of the simulation.

[5] Comparisons of output for the simulations coded in both QuickBASIC and Power-BASIC verified that model behavior was not affected by the software change.

A number of the components of the simulation require drawing from probability distributions. The enculturation scores of the initial members, new recruits, and the noise term in the socialization function all use normal distributions. These were simulated with the uniform random deviate generator in the BASIC compiler by constructing random normal deviates using the polar method. Rate parameters in the model were simulated as parameters embedded in stochastic processes. For the recruitment rate r_r and the departure rate $r_{i,t}$, the rate is assumed to be part of the basic framework

$$G(u) = \exp\left[\int_0^u r(s)\,ds\right], \tag{5.1}$$

where $G(u)$ is the stochastic survivor function and $r(u)$ is the rate. In the basic model, r_r and $r_{i,t}$ are set at values typical of calculations made on the basis of monthly data. The rates are used to solve for waiting times, $u = -\log G(u)/r$, which are used directly in the simulation.[6]

As is conventional, the survivor function is simulated as a uniform distribution using a uniform random deviate generator (Tuma and Hannan, 1984). The organizational growth rate r_g is associated with an underlying stochastic process of growth in the number of positions. A size-dependent Poisson growth process is assumed.

The simulation is initiated with an organization size of 100, except for the entrepreneurial type, which is started at a size of 5. Initial enculturation scores are randomly assigned from a normal distribution with mean 0 and standard deviation .10 (with negative draws reset to 0). Initial tenure scores are drawn from a lognormal distribution, with mean 12 and standard deviation 1 for the underlying normal distribution, giving an initial tenure distribution with median 12 and standard deviation 25.9. After each time period (simulation "month"), each individual enculturation score ($C_{i,t}$) is updated and the mean enculturation level ($\overline{C}_t$) and standard deviation ($\sigma_{c,t}$) for the organization are calculated. Enculturation levels are compared over time. When the mean enculturation level for the twelve most recent time periods differs by less than .01 from the means for the two previous sets of twelve time periods, the organization's culture system is assumed to be in equilibrium. The simulation is then stopped and the following outcome variables are examined: mean enculturation level ($\overline{C}$, at equilibrium denoted by $\overline{C}_e$), time elapsed until equilibrium t^*, and dispersion of enculturation scores at equilibrium (σ_{ce}).

---

[6]Empirical analysis of the tenure distributions generated by the specification for $r_{i,t}$ suggests a slight duration dependence (with respect to tenure) in the overall employee departure rate. Although this duration dependence varies by organizational type, the pattern is generally consistent with the findings of Petersen and Spilerman (1990), who analyzed comparable departure data from a large organization with an established internal labor market.

In conducting the simulations, we first examined some of the simulation model's basic properties by experimentally varying the mean level of enculturation of the initial employees for each organizational type. Our primary goal in these experiments was to learn how sensitive the model is to the initial setting of mean enculturation. The experiments showed that the mean level of enculturation in the initial employee base affects the time required to reach equilibrium. In all instances, the further the initial mean is from the equilibrium mean, the longer the time to equilibrium. Thus, starting with a low mean level of enculturation usually implies a longer dynamic process for homogeneous-culture organizations. The variation in time to equilibrium was greatest for the governmental, professional, and collectivist-democratic types. The mean enculturation level of the initial employees affected the equilibrium levels attained for some types, but not all. The Japanese, American manufacturing, entrepreneurial, and Z-type types all reached the same equilibrium levels regardless of the initial mean level of enculturation. Governmental, professional, and collectivist-democratic types each depended slightly on the mean of the initial employee base.

5.4 Findings by type

Figure 5.2 shows the cultural outcomes by organizational type, each identified on the graph by the first letter of its name. The figure plots the equilibrium behavior of the types in terms of time to equilibrium (x-axis) and enculturation level (y-axis), averaged across 1,000 simulation runs for each type. The center point of a rectangle's horizontal border shows the mean time to equilibrium for that type across the runs; the width of a rectangle shows average dispersion in that time as given by one standard deviation above and below the mean. Similarly, the center point of a rectangle's vertical border shows the average mean enculturation level at equilibrium for that type across the runs; the height of a rectangle indicates average dispersion in enculturation as given by one standard deviation above and below the mean. Thus, for instance, for the entrepreneurial type (rectangle labeled E) the mean time to equilibrium is 74.7 and its average dispersion is 12.2, while its average mean enculturation level is .65 with an average standard deviation of .16.

Comparing across types, the patterns give substantial credibility to the simulation model in that the organizational types behave in plausible ways. First, the most managerially preferred cultures, as indicated by the mean level of enculturation (the center point of a rectangle's height), are found in the Japanese (J rectangle), professional (P), and Z-type (Z). The least managerially preferred culture is in the American manufacturing type.

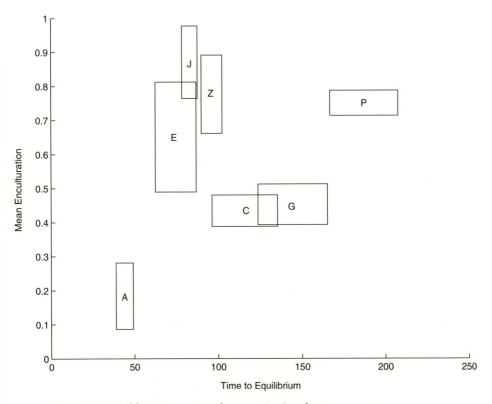

FIGURE 5.2 Equilibrium outcomes by organizational type

Second, cultural heterogeneity, as given by dispersion around the mean enculturation level at equilibrium (the height of a rectangle), is lowest for the professional, collectivist-democratic (C), and governmental (G) organizational types, again conforming to expectations. Third, time to equilibrium is greatest for the professional type, followed by governmental and collectivist-democratic.

Overall, this pattern of findings shows that the model can reproduce the basic "known" or observed differences in cultural preferredness and heterogeneity across organizational types, providing some face validation for the model.[7] We now proceed to investigate, for each type, the

___

[7]Multiple simulations were conducted for each set of parameter values investigated. For ease of communication, we present results in graphic form. However, we did conduct a stability analysis for a variety of models to ensure that the findings are not idiosyncratic. This effort included a sensitivity analysis to determine that the findings reported here do not

effects of variations in: (1) the base employee turnover rate, (2) recruitment selectivity, (3) intensity of management socialization practices, and (4) strength of the alienation effect. In these simulations, each variation is run for 100 iterations, and the average outcomes for each variation are reported.

Base Turnover Rate

The turnover process can be managed to enhance the retention of highly socialized employees and to encourage the departure of those who have not been successfully socialized. Alternatively, if the goal is to foster innovation and creativity, then perhaps some variation is desirable and an optimal number of less socialized employees should be retained. In either case, the available management tools include evaluation procedures and promotion and compensation policies.

Figure 5.3 shows the equilibrium outcomes by organizational type when the parameter associated with the base employee turnover rate (γ_0) is varied. The graphs depict five variations in turnover for each type, ranging from 0 (shown as LO on the plot) to .03 (shown as HI) in increments of .0075. All other parameters are held fixed at the values characterizing the specific type. (We use the same approach for the remainder of figures in this chapter.)

Variations in the base turnover rate affect the equilibrium enculturation levels little. However, turnover does seem to affect the time to equilibrium. In general, higher turnover rates are associated with shorter times to equilibrium—in all cases, the equilibrium points in the figure move to the left as the turnover rate increases. This effect is especially pronounced for the governmental, professional, and collectivist-democratic organizational types. The greater sensitivity of these types to turnover is somewhat surprising, since they are often held to have higher inertia than some of the other types.

These effects can be understood as a combination of the enculturation levels of new entrants and their greater susceptibility to socialization. As the number of new entrants increases due to higher turnover, the cultural equilibrium moves slightly toward the mean enculturation level of entrants; as new entrants constitute a larger proportion of an organization's employees, they have a greater effect on the enculturation mean of

---

depend primarily on the values of single parameters, including those held constant in the results reported here for organizational types (such as the socialization noise term e), and do not vary substantially across changes in many combinations of parameters. In the next chapter, we also report a variance decomposition of the outcome variables for all the simulation data. This analysis allows an overall assessment of the effects of each parameter.

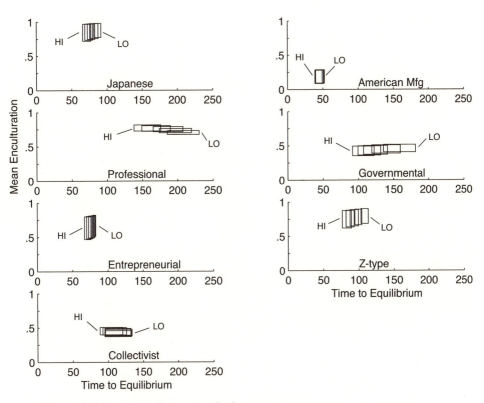

FIGURE 5.3 Equilibrium outcomes by base turnover

the organization. At the same time, new entrants are more susceptible to socialization than the longer-tenured incumbents who leave, so with higher turnover, a larger proportion of employees is more easily socialized, leading to a shorter time to equilibrium.

Recruitment Selectivity

The recruitment process can be managed in terms of how well new employees fit with the organization's current or desired culture. Recruitment factors under management's control include search, selection, and selling procedures. More extensive searches for job applicants, more careful evaluation of candidates, and greater inducements for desirable applicants will generally enable the organization to find new employees who are better matched to management's cultural objectives. So, too, will efforts to promote the organization's image and reputation.

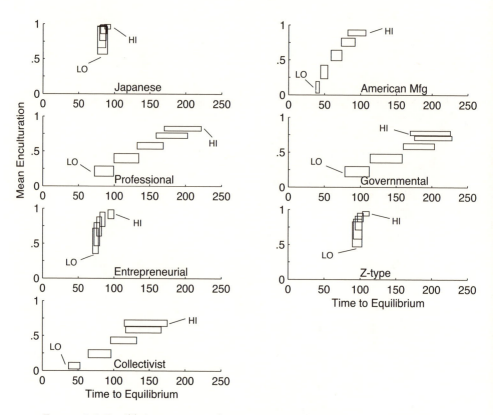

FIGURE 5.4 Equilibrium outcomes by recruitment selectivity

Figure 5.4 shows the results of introducing different degrees of recruitment selectivity into the simulations. We did this by varying the mean enculturation of the recruitment pool ($\overline{C}_b$) from 0 (LO) to 1.0 (HI) in increments of .25. In all cases, greater selectivity is associated with higher mean enculturation in the figure.

Variations in recruitment selectivity produce changes in both the equilibrium means and the times to equilibrium, although these effects are more pronounced in some organizational types than in others. The entrepreneurial, Z-type, and Japanese types show higher enculturation levels corresponding to greater selectivity; equilibrium times are barely affected. By contrast, the other types show longer times to equilibrium in response to enhanced selectivity; they also show higher enculturation means. These results indicate that a given approach to managing organizational culture—selective recruitment in this case—can have substantively different effects for different types.

Obviously, the mean enculturation level will be higher when recruitment selectivity is higher, since new entrants will have higher enculturation scores. But the time to equilibrium depends on the nature of socialization. Intensive management socialization produces faster cultural homogenization, and the three types (E, Z, and J) showing little variation in time to equilibrium across different levels of recruitment selectivity also have the highest levels of management socialization. The other types have low levels of management socialization, relying instead on peer socialization to reduce cultural heterogeneity, and so they are more sensitive to the cultural characteristics on new entrants. Since we start the simulations with $C_i = 0$ for existing employees, low recruitment selectivity leads to fast convergence to a low enculturation mean for the organization. Conversely, when recruitment selectivity is high, it takes longer for the new entrants to pull the organization's enculturation mean up to a high level. In general, when management socialization is high, the time to equilibrium is relatively insensitive to recruitment selectivity, but when an organization relies primarily on peer socialization, time to equilibrium is heavily dependent on the cultural characteristics of new entrants. (If we initialize the simulation with a nonzero mean for existing employees, the time to equilibrium depends on the cultural distance between the initial mean and the mean for new entrants when socialization relies primarily on peers.)

Management Socialization

The socialization process can be managed to intensify the enculturation of employees (Schein, 1968, 1985; Ott, 1989; O'Reilly, 1989). Management can provide intensive orientations for new employees and models for exemplary behavior. Other techniques include systems of employee participation that rely on processes of incremental commitment, reliance on peer groups for control of members, and comprehensive reward systems that use recognition and approval (O'Reilly, 1989). Management can also interpret organizational events for employees and send signals to reinforce cultural values; one technique involves the use of symbols such as language, logos, and organizational rituals and ceremonies (Peters, 1978; Pfeffer, 1981).

Figure 5.5 presents plots of the equilibrium outcomes when the intensity of management socialization practices (parameter α_{mgt} relative to α_{peer}) is varied from 0 (LO) to .98 (HI) in increments of .245, with $\alpha_{peer} = .98 - \alpha_{mgt}$ and α_{decay} held constant at .02. For each organizational type, the enculturation mean rises substantially as a result of more intensive management efforts—in the figure, in all cases as management socialization increases, so does enculturation, while time to equilibrium

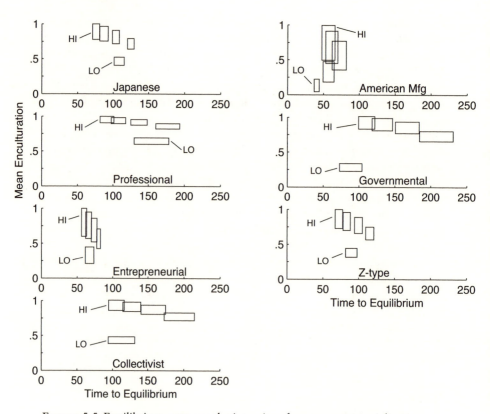

FIGURE 5.5 Equilibrium outcomes by intensity of management socialization

increases and then decreases. The largest gains occur for the governmental and American manufacturing types, although heterogeneity increases as well at intermediate levels of management socialization. The increased cultural heterogeneity likely results from the combination of low selectivity (which continually brings in ample numbers of relatively unenculturated individuals) and an internal mechanism exerting a strong positive effect on enculturation levels (in this instance, management socialization).

Perhaps the most interesting pattern in figure 5.5 is that the greatest returns to increased management socialization apparently come at the variable's lower levels. That is, for each organizational type the effects of intensified management socialization on C_i are especially pronounced when prior management socialization efforts were minimal. When management socialization is already strong, additional efforts still do show some effects. But they are small compared with the returns associated with the same increased effort in a prior situation of weak management socialization. The reason for this is that management socialization produces a change in enculturation per time period proportional to an individual's distance from the ideal enculturation level of 1.0 (see equation 4.4). When management socialization is weak, C_i tends to be lower and the distance from the ideal higher, so an increase in management socialization has a larger proportional effect. When management socialization is already strong, C_i tends to be higher, so the distance from the ideal is lower and the proportional effect on an increase in management socialization is lower.

Time to equilibrium in figure 5.5 is low for no management socialization. As management socialization increases, time to equilibrium first increases and then decreases as management socialization becomes strong. With no management socialization, socialization is carried out by peers and quickly converges at a level close to that of new entrants, who make up a larger proportion of employees over time due to entry and exit processes. High levels of management socialization also show quick convergence driven by strong management influence with little or no peer influence. At intermediate levels of management socialization, the competing influences of management and peers on new entrants create a longer time to equilibrium.

Alienation Effect

Alienation, as we have defined it here, refers to the propensity of those far from the cultural ideal to leave the organization in greater numbers. Some of this behavior is motivated naturally by self-reflection and a desire to fit into a setting where one spends so much time. But the salience of not fitting in and the punitive pressures applied to individuals in such situations are both elements of the process controllable by management. Organizations differ dramatically in how much direct and indirect pressure they exert in making less enculturated individuals feel uncomfortable.

Figure 5.6 shows the equilibrium outcomes by type when the strength of the alienation parameter, γ_1, varies from 0 (LO) to .60 (HI) in increments of .15. In all cases, the main impact of a stronger alienation effect (larger coefficient) is to reduce the time required to reach equilibrium. Equilibrium levels and means in enculturation remain relatively stable except for the collectivist-democratic type, where equilibrium levels rise as the alienation effect becomes stronger, particularly when the alienation factor rises above zero.

Higher alienation produces shorter equilibrium times because it reduces cultural heterogeneity through removing less enculturated individuals

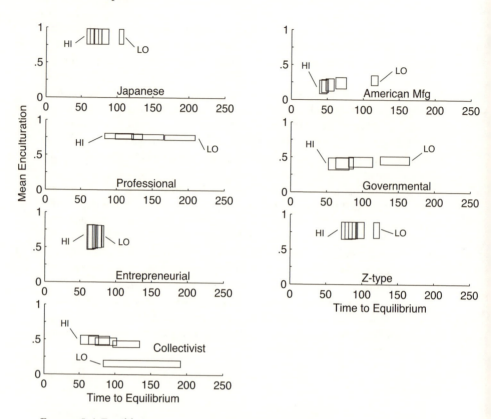

FIGURE 5.6 Equilibrium outcomes by strength of alienation

more quickly. But the effects of alienation on enculturation levels are more complex, depending on the relative enculturation scores of those who leave (and have already been partially socialized, more so when management socialization is high) and those who enter, as well as the numbers in each category. The mean enculturation level of the American manufacturing type actually drops with increasing alienation; the mean enculturation level of new entrants (.1) is actually lower than that of the (at least) partially socialized workers who exit. The governmental type shows a similar but less pronounced pattern. In contrast, the mean enculturation level for the collectivist-democratic type rises with increasing alienation; for this type, the mean enculturation level of new entrants (.5) is significantly higher than that of those who leave. For the other types, the enculturation levels do not change much across alienation conditions, since the less enculturated individuals who leave are culturally similar to those who enter; in these cases, incumbent members already have higher enculturation levels due to either higher recruitment selectivity or stronger management socialization.

The findings presented in this section illustrate the value of using a simulation approach. For example, it is clear analytically that the mean enculturation level changes partially as a function of management socialization intensity and partially as a function of cultural characteristics of entrants relative to those who exit. Further, the relative numbers in each category (entries and departures) also matter. But these numbers of entrants depend on both growth and turnover, and the numbers of exits depend on socialization and alienation, as well as on the base turnover rate. The complexity of the interactions of the entry, socialization, exit, and growth processes makes it impossible to determine outcomes of the model analytically, but it is straightforward to produce outcomes using computational methods.

5.5 CONCLUSION

Because they are based on a simulation model, the findings reviewed in this chapter are comparable to theoretical derivations. Here the model shows high face validity in that it is capable of reproducing observed levels of cultural preferredness and homogeneity in known organizational types based on the demographic, recruitment, and socialization characteristics of these types. Thus, we feel confident in asserting the plausibility of the basic model in accounting for observed variations in organizational culture.

In chapter 2, we motivated our use of simulation in part by claiming that although the individual components of the model were fairly well understood, their joint operation was not. Familiarity with dynamic processes led us to think that when these components were simulated together over time, the interactions would yield new insights. We believe that this chapter's finding that rapid growth and high turnover often aid in establishing cultural stability supports this motivation. We have already suggested that the effect of rapid growth is the result of the higher susceptibility of new employees to socialization. Conversely, the turnover effect could be the result of the exit of employees with greater resistance to socialization, particularly because employees with higher levels of alienation (lower enculturation levels) are somewhat more likely to exit and because newer employees—who have not been fully socialized—tend to constitute a larger proportion of the workforce and thus leave in higher numbers.

CHAPTER 6

Growth and Decline

6.1 INTRODUCTION

Chapter 5 examined the behavior of the basic cultural transmission model across organizational types defined by configurations of demographic features, including the organizational growth rate. It shows that types with low growth rates (namely, collectivist-democratic, governmental, and professional) take longer to reach equilibrium than do those with high growth rates (entrepreneurial, American, Japanese, and Z-type). Low growth does not, however, consistently produce homogeneous cultures in organizations, and high growth is sometimes (but not always) associated with homogeneous cultures.

Thus growth appears to affect organizational cultural systems but in ways that cut across the stylized organizational type groupings. Organizations vary significantly in growth rates, even though some types will display, on average, a higher growth rate than others. This observation implies that to understand the impact of growth, and how it trades off against other demographic components, it makes sense to unpack it from the type configurations—to study variations in growth within types as well as across them.

Such unpacking is also warranted by managerial considerations. Growth rates vary over time, even though other features of the organizational type remain stable. If management wants to keep the cultural system intact, it is important to know how these variations might affect the culture, and what other measures might be taken to counter any deleterious impact of growth. Then, too, organizations may decline in size over either short or protracted periods or show little growth over extended periods. What differences might this make for cultural transmission and persistence, and how can they be managed?

Accordingly, this chapter examines questions about how organizational growth and decline affect the cultural system.[1] We first investigate how the cultural transmission model behaves when growth rates vary while keeping the other parameter values constant for each of the seven stylized organizational types. We then turn to problems of cultural

---

[1]Parts of this chapter are adapted from Harrison and Carroll (1991).

management in the midst of growth. For this analysis, we focus on the three manipulable levers of the system examined in the previous chapter: recruitment selectivity, management socialization, and turnover. We next study the behavior of the system when the organization declines. Finally, we report a basic summary of the cultural transmission model by analyzing data from a wide-ranging set of simulated conditions.

Organizational Growth

We initiated the investigation of growth in straightforward fashion, by simulating each organizational type for a range of growth rates r_g, ranging from $-.02$ to $.02$ in increments of $.01$. In the negative growth condition, the decrease in the number of positions was frequently greater than the number of positions vacated through turnover. So, for decline, we first eliminated vacant positions up to the number decreased by decline; when this number exceeded the number of vacant positions, we randomly "laid off" incumbent employees to reach the targeted total decrease in positions. As in chapter 5, we ran each simulation for 100 iterations. We sought to understand whether variations in growth produced cultural differences, controlling for other aspects of the organization's demography.

Figure 6.1 presents the equilibrium outcomes for simulation runs in which the organizational growth rates are systematically varied for each organizational type. Compared with the figures at the end of chapter 5, where increasing parameter values produced unidirectional changes in either mean enculturation or time to equilibrium, the growth variations affect organizational types differently, so we first describe the patterns of effects for each type. For the Japanese and American manufacturing types, increasing growth rates (from negative, labeled as NEG in plots, to positive, labeled as POS) always decrease equilibrium time. For the professional and governmental types, equilibrium time rises and then falls as the growth rate increases; for the professional type, higher growth rates are always associated with higher mean enculturation, while for the governmental type, enculturation is highest at zero growth. For the entrepreneurial and Z-types, equilibrium time rises and then falls when the growth rate increases—as for the professional and governmental types—but mean enculturation increases and then decreases in step with time to equilibrium, with the highest equilibrium times and enculturation means found for a growth rate of $-.01$. Finally, for the collectivist-democratic types, both equilibrium time and mean enculturation rise as the growth rate increases, with the exception of a slight drop in equilibrium time for the highest growth rate.

These simulations clearly show that high growth rates produce shorter times to equilibrium, except for the collectivist-democratic and professional types. Since the speed with which equilibrium is attained

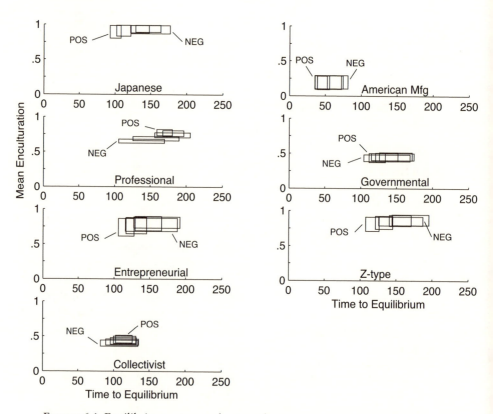

FIGURE 6.1 Equilibrium outcomes by growth rate

reflects a system's ability to recover when perturbed, this finding leads, in turn, to the rather paradoxical inference that high growth is actually conducive to cultural stability, not detrimental, as is commonly assumed (cf. Elster, 1989; Coleman, 1990). Perhaps the increased cultural stability results from the relative ease in socializing new rather than long-term employees. Except for the Japanese and American manufacturing types, all types also show cultural stability in decline, an issue we develop later. It is also interesting that several types (specifically, professional, governmental, entrepreneurial, and Z-type) show greater cultural stability in either growth or decline than they do in the no-growth condition.

6.2 CULTURAL MANAGEMENT AND GROWTH

Because managers often have some control over several of the main factors that affect transmission, cultural transmission in organizations rests potentially in managerial hands. As illustrated in chapter 5, a seemingly reliable way to maintain an organizational culture would be to establish each of the controllable factors in extreme form: highly selective recruitment, intensive management socialization, and strong alienation inducement processes. Managing these factors involves real costs to the organization, however. Research on organizations suggests that these costs may directly interact with growth trajectories. For example, selectivity in recruitment typically results in the slower filling of vacant positions, management socialization absorbs resources and managerial attention, and the use of higher pay to attract and retain desirable employees has budgetary consequences. These costs might be offset by the organizational advantages of a homogeneous culture, including increased efficiency and productivity. But because of the potential interdependencies of these costs and growth, it seems important to reexamine the ways investment in cultural management likely influences cultural direction and homogeneity under different growth scenarios.

To address this issue, we present a set of simulations conducted to examine the effects of selectivity, socialization by management, and turnover under differing growth conditions. We started these simulations with the organizational types in their equilibrium states, using the results of the earlier runs to determine the initial parameter settings for organizational size and for the enculturation scores and tenure distribution of employees. The parameters corresponding to base turnover (γ_0), selectivity ($\bar{C}_h$), management socialization (α_{mgt}), and alienation (γ_1) were then systematically varied for each type for each of three growth conditions—growth ($r_g = .02$), no growth or "steady state" ($r_g = 0$), and decline ($r_g = -0.2$) in organizational size.

The results are shown in figures 6.2 through 6.5, which plot the equilibrium mean enculturation levels against the values of the management-controlled parameters for the three growth conditions by type. Equilibrium points for each growth condition are connected by solid, dashed, or dashed-dotted lines, as indicated in the legends. The dotted lines indicate the initial equilibrium levels for the types.

Turnover

The turnover results (figure 6.2) are striking in that turnover appears to have little or no effect on mean enculturation for any organizational type, the only small exceptions being the no-growth or steady state condition for the Japanese, entrepreneurial, and Z-types. This finding is independent of the setting for the growth parameter and is contrary to the conventional wisdom that turnover rates have important consequences for organizations (Staw, 1980), at least as far as organizational culture is concerned.

For the Japanese, entrepreneurial, and Z-type organizations, the mean enculturation level drops slightly as the base turnover rate increases. The growth condition also shows a lower mean enculturation level for these

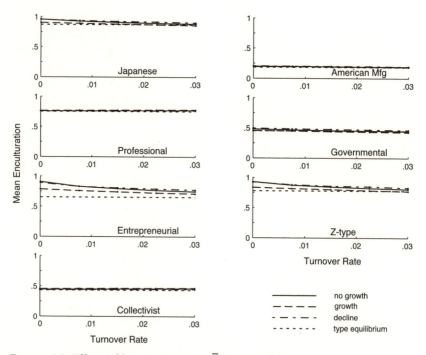

FIGURE 6.2 Effects of base turnover on $\bar{C}_e$ by growth

types, compared with the no-growth and decline conditions. Both of these effects are related to the fact that these three types are the only ones with high levels of management socialization. As turnover increases, the average time in the organization—and therefore the amount of time that employees are subjected to socialization by management—is reduced, leading to a decrease in mean enculturation. And for the growth condition, many new and less socialized employees are added to the organization over time, compared with the no-growth (steady state) and decline conditions, where employees reach higher levels of enculturation because they are subjected to management socialization for a longer period of time on average.

Recruitment Selectivity

The results for selectivity, shown in figure 6.3, suggest that the Japanese type is relatively insensitive to recruitment selectivity. Only in the growth condition does selectivity have even a small effect on average or mean enculturation in Japanese organizations. A similar but less pronounced effect can be seen in the entrepreneurial and Z-type organizations. By contrast, mean enculturation in the American manufacturing type rises

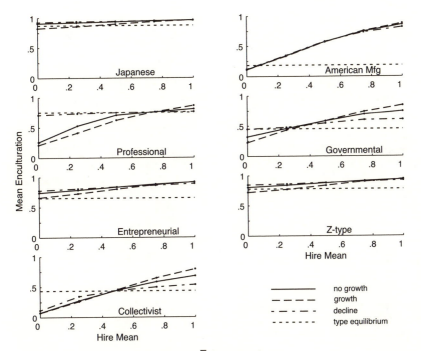

FIGURE 6.3 Effects of selectivity on $\bar{C}_e$ by growth

dramatically with increased selectivity for all settings. The other types have similar (although less severe) patterns, with the highest gains occurring in the growth condition.

As with the turnover findings, these effects are related to the high levels of management socialization for the Japanese, entrepreneurial, and Z-type organizations. In the other types, management socialization is low or nonexistent, so the level of enculturation depends more on recruitment selectivity. When recruitment selectivity plays a larger role, growth effects are more pronounced. In decline, there is almost no opportunity for selectivity to operate; in the no-growth or steady state condition, selectivity plays only a moderate role through replacement of those who exit; and in growth, where many new employees are being added to the organization, the role of selectivity is greatly enhanced.

Management Socialization

Changes in the intensity of socialization by management show the most dramatic effects for the American manufacturing type (see figure 6.4). Increased socialization leads to substantial increases in enculturation means

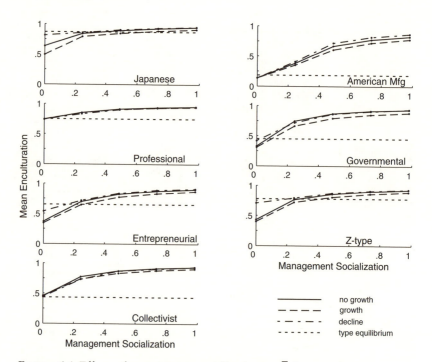

FIGURE 6.4 Effects of management socialization on $\bar{C}_e$ by growth

for all growth settings. To a lesser degree, the same effects hold for the other types. For the collectivist-democratic type, small increases in socialization from the natural level (no management socialization) lead to a more managerially preferred culture, but the effect levels off as socialization intensity continues to increase. The governmental, entrepreneurial, and Z-type follow a similar pattern. The professional and Japanese types show the least responsiveness to variation in socialization, although for the Japanese type the cultural intensity drops substantially at very low socialization levels for the growth and stability conditions but not for the decline condition.

Obviously, mean enculturation will be higher when management socialization is stronger, as the figure shows. And the general pattern in the figure is that the growth condition produces lower levels of mean enculturation than the no-growth (steady state) or decline conditions. Again, this is because there are more new (shorter-tenured) employees during growth, on whom management socialization has had less time to operate.

Alienation

The effects of the alienation coefficient on the enculturation means are shown in figure 6.5. For four types (Japanese, professional, entrepreneurial, and Z-type), variation in alienation produces no discernible

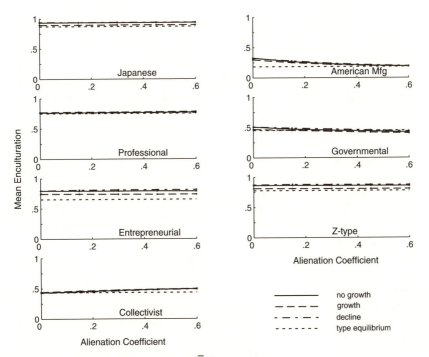

FIGURE 6.5 Effects of alienation on $\bar{C}_e$ by growth

effect on the outcomes; for the American manufacturing and governmental types, increases in the alienation parameter lower the mean level of enculturation, while the response in the collectivist type is the opposite. For the most part, outcomes here vary little by growth condition, the minor exceptions occurring for the Japanese, governmental, entrepreneurial, and Z-type, where differing growth conditions generate stable differences in the means.

These effects are related primarily to the demographics of entry and exit. In particular, since higher alienation produces higher levels of turnover and consequently entry when employees are less socialized, types with lower mean enculturation levels experience higher turnover of less socialized employees and higher entry around the mean recruitment selectivity level of enculturation. The three types that show the greatest sensitivity to alienation—American manufacturing, governmental, and collectivist—are those with the lowest mean enculturation levels. As exits increase with increasing alienation, more new employees enter around the recruitment selectivity level. For the American and governmental types, new entrants have on average a lower enculturation level than the mean for the organization, and so increasing alienation drives down the mean enculturation level for the organization. In contrast, for the collectivist type, the average enculturation level of new entrants is slightly higher than that for the organization, and so the mean enculturation level for the organization rises slightly as alienation increases. And as in the earlier figures, figure 6.5 shows a greater difference in growth compared with no growth (steady state) or decline at all levels of alienation for the types with the highest levels of management socialization, the Japanese, entrepreneurial, and Z-type organizations.

6.3 ORGANIZATIONAL DECLINE

Decline might be viewed as symmetrical to growth, where the process simply runs in reverse. Theory and research on organizational decline show, however, that the dynamics of decline might differ appreciably from growth. Freeman and Hannan (1975) found in empirical studies of school district organizations that adjustments to the administrative structure occurred much more slowly in decline than in growth. That is, growing organizations are much more likely to add administrative positions and units as the organizational workload (or demand) increases than are declining organizations to drop them as workload (or demand) declines. Thus, administrative overhead ratios are higher in decline than in growth. Similarly, ethnographic research shows that in declining organizations (those dying or suffering cutbacks), members often experience complex emotional reactions that intensify the culture. Because of these and similar studies, it is useful to explore in detail what happens to an organization's culture when it contracts in size.

To address questions about decline, we did not change the basic transmission model but instead set up the simulations in a different way. Rather than start with small organizations, we began with fairly large ones (i.e., 2,000 members). We then assumed a negative growth rate $(r_g = -.04)$ and a distribution of tenure appropriate for each organizational type at equilibrium (determined from the results described earlier). As before, employees with the lowest enculturation scores are the most likely to leave due to the alienation effect, although there is no explicit seniority rule associated with departure. The cultural transmission process was then simulated until it reached equilibrium and averaged across 100 iterations. Table 6.1 gives the equilibrium outcomes, as well as the values of the culture variables $\bar{C}_t$ and $\sigma_{c,t}$ at several other benchmark points in the decline trajectory. Figure 6.6 shows the simulated culture in declining organizations; it gives the mean of enculturation (solid lines) and the standard deviation from the mean (dotted lines) over time.

All organizational types reach cultural equilibrium while in decline. Moreover, in all instances except for the collectivist type (which has no

TABLE 6.1
Organizational culture during simulated decline

	Japanese	American manufacturing	Professional	Governmental	Entrepreneurial	Z-type	Collectivist-democratic
				Organizational type			
Start							
N_t	2,000	2,000	2,000	2,000	2,000	2,000	2,000
$\bar{C}_t$	.830	.179	.752	.453	.590	.730	.453
$\sigma_{c,t}$	.116	.095	.037	.057	.177	.128	.047
25% decline							
t	8	7	8	8	8	8	8
$\bar{C}_t$	.873	.194	.753	.465	.684	.780	.434
$\sigma_{c,t}$	.087	.094	.032	.047	.111	.094	.039
50% decline							
t	18	18	18	18	18	18	18
$\bar{C}_t$	.891	.199	.754	.475	.716	.803	.434
$\sigma_{c,t}$	.070	.094	.026	.038	.086	.076	.032
75% decline							
t	36	36	36	35	36	36	36
$\bar{C}_t$	.914	.202	.756	.488	.753	.831	.433
$\sigma_{c,t}$	.049	.093	.020	.028	.058	.053	.025
Equilibrium							
N_t	30	446	453	26	3	8	454
t^*	105.7	38.8	38	109.	164.3	139.5	38
$\bar{C}_e$	.956	.202	.757	.528	.861	.908	.433
σ_{ce}	.016	.094	.019	.024	.031	.029	.025

Note: $r_g = -.04$ for these simulations.

management socialization pull), the enculturation level is higher in decline than it was initially: at equilibrium, enculturation reaches its highest levels. The difference between start level and equilibrium is especially pronounced for the Japanese, entrepreneurial, and Z types.

6.4 DECOMPOSING TRANSMISSION

Table 6.2 presents regression models of the simulation data generated by 100 trials each for 3,888 experiments. These experiments consist of all possible combinations of three widely spaced values for each of the

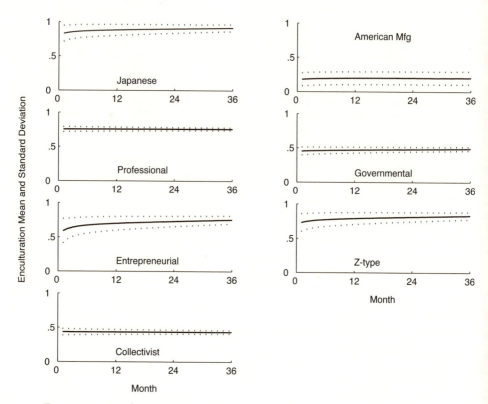

FIGURE 6.6 Enculturation in organization in decline

model parameters of primary interest, as well as conditions where the socialization error term e (see equation 4.3) is set to 0 and where susceptibility to socialization does not decline with tenure—that is, $B_{i,t}$ in equation (4.5) is constant at 1. The recruitment rate has been omitted because of its functional relationship to the selectivity mean. We focus on the equilibrium outcomes and regress these on variables representing the organizational parameters defining enculturation and the organizational types. Assuming only linear effects, these regressions provide a comparison of the effects of the various components of the model.[2]

The regressions show that the components underlying the types of organization all have significant effects on equilibrium outcomes. The

[2]Regressions of the outcomes on dummies for the various organizational types simply summarize the findings shown earlier in graphic form. Although we have estimated such models, we do not report them here, since they are redundant with results already presented. Our goal is to decompose the outcomes on the finer-grained differences in parameter settings.

TABLE 6.2
Regression models of cultural outcomes

	Equilibrium outcome		
	Mean level of enculturation C_e	*Standard deviation in enculturation* σ_{ce}	*Time to equilibrium* t^*
Constant	.296[*]	.045[*]	77.3[*]
Decline dummy[a]	−.020[*]	−.013[*]	−8.70[*]
Growth dummy[a]	−.001	.025[*]	−8.15[*]
Turnover parameter	.057[*]	1.25[*]	−398.[*]
Alienation parameter	.098[*]	.023[*]	−63.1[*]
Management socialization	.599[*]	.020[*]	−10.6[*]
Socialization decay	.002	−.004	4.92
Noise in socialization	−.037[*]	.280[*]	15.8[*]
Reduced susceptibility to socialization with tenure (dummy)	−.028[*]	−.010[*]	56.9[*]
Recruitment selectivity mean	.241[*]	−.063[*]	14.8[*]
Recruitment selectivity std. dev.	.026[*]	.056[*]	3.19[*]
R^2	.697	.400	.342
N	379,440	379,440	379,440

[*]$p < .05$.
[a]Omitted condition is no growth.

directions of these effects agree roughly with the effects of individual components on enculturation levels and time to equilibrium (shown in figures 5.3 through 5.6). Variations in two model components previously held constant also show significant effects. First, eliminating noise in the socialization process raises the mean enculturation level, lowers the standard deviation of enculturation, and shortens the time to equilibrium, as we would expect. Second, if individuals did not develop resistance to socialization with tenure, then the mean and standard deviation of enculturation would be higher, and the time to equilibrium shorter. But the socialization decay term does not show significant effects.

The growth effects differ by outcome. Enculturation levels tend to be higher in the growth and no-growth or steady state conditions than in the decline condition, after all other variables are controlled. Cultural heterogeneity increases with growth, being lowest in the decline condition and highest in the growth condition. Time to equilibrium is lower in both growth and decline than in no growth. Of these estimates, the most curious is the effect of decline on the enculturation mean: it is the reverse of the pattern observed earlier in the data with no controls. Why does the effect change when other conditions are controlled? Deeper investigation shows that this finding is a consequence of our procedure of starting with a $\bar{C}_0$ of 0: C does indeed go up in decline, as shown earlier, just not quite as much as in the other conditions when started from 0.

Perhaps the most interesting patterns in table 6.2 come from comparing the effects of variables across outcomes. Confining attention to variables subject to management control, we see that turnover, alienation, and management socialization increase the mean enculturation level and reduce the time to equilibrium but also increase cultural heterogeneity. Selectivity increases the enculturation mean and reduces heterogeneity but increases the time to equilibrium. Management surely prefers the three-way combination of a higher mean enculturation level, lower heterogeneity, and shorter time to equilibrium, but the findings suggest that no single variable favorably affects all three outcomes in the preferred directions. In other words, the findings reinforce the general notion that management faces trade-offs in choosing how to design and influence the organization's cultural system.

The regressions in table 6.2 control for growth conditions using dummy variables. In estimating these models, we assume implicitly that growth conditions affect only the intercept, and the effects of the other variables do not depend on growth. For a model involving complex interactions, however, it seems unlikely that other model components would have effects independent of growth condition. So to extend the decomposition of cultural transmission, we estimated separate models for growth, no growth or steady state, and decline.

Table 6.3 shows these respecified estimates for effects on the mean level of enculturation. Note in particular that the variables subject to management control—turnover, alienation, management socialization, and selectivity—display effects that depend on the growth condition.

Table 6.3
Regression models of cultural mean ($\bar{C}_e$) by growth condition

| | Growth condition | | |
	Decline	Steady state	Growth
Constant	.247*	.292*	.323*
Turnover parameter	.285*	.109*	−.186*
Alienation parameter	.185*	.096*	.023*
Management socialization	.661*	.608*	.530*
Socialization decay	.005	−.000	.002
Noise in socialization	−.002	−.048*	−.064*
Reduced susceptibility to socialization with tenure (dummy)	−.046*	−.013*	−.025*
Recruitment selectivity mean	.187*	.226*	.304*
Recruitment selectivity std. dev.	.030*	.022*	.025*
R^2	.715	.689	.725
N	120,240	129,600	129,600

*$p < .05$.

Higher turnover and stronger alienation increase mean enculturation in decline, but the effect is weaker for no growth or steady state, and turnover actually lowers the enculturation mean in the growth condition. And management socialization is relatively less important and recruitment selectivity more important in maintaining a high level of enculturation for growing organizations compared with declining organizations. These findings illustrate how the roles of different demographic processes depend on growth conditions. In organizational decline, the enculturation level is driven primarily by the exit process, whereas during growth periods, the entry process assumes a more prominent role.

TABLE 6.4
Regression models of cultural heterogencity (σ_{ce}) by growth condition

	Growth condition		
	Decline	Steady	Growth
Constant	.026[*]	.038[*]	.084[*]
Turnover parameter	1.219[*]	1.801[*]	.721[*]
Alienation parameter	.019[*]	.025[*]	.025[*]
Management socialization	.000	.011[*]	.046[*]
Socialization decay	−.011	−.002	−.000
Noise in socialization	.338[*]	.290[*]	.220[*]
Reduced susceptibility to socialization with tenure (dummy)	−.005[*]	−.013[*]	−.012[*]
Recruitment selectivity mean	−.035[*]	−.054[*]	−.097[*]
Recruitment selectivity std. dev.	.046[*]	.049[*]	.071[*]
R^2	.218	.428	.579
N	120,240	129,600	129,600

[*]$p < .05$.

Effects on the standard deviation in enculturation by growth condition are shown in table 6.4. As in table 6.2, we see that turnover, alienation, and management socialization increase cultural heterogeneity while recruitment selectivity reduces it, but the effects vary by growth condition. Turnover has the greatest effect on heterogeneity with no growth or steady state and the least in the growth condition. Management socialization increases heterogeneity during growth but has no effect in decline. Selectivity reduces heterogeneity the most during growth.

Variability in effects across growth condition also appears when we analyze time to equilibrium (see table 6.5). Turnover reduces time to equilibrium

TABLE 6.5
Regression models of equilibrium time (t^*) by growth condition

	Growth condition		
	Decline	Steady state	Growth
Constant	54.9*	79.4*	79.2*
Turnover parameter	−215.7*	−509.4*	−449.5*
Alienation parameter	35.7*	−75.7*	−75.3*
Management socialization	12.1*	−11.1*	−31.5*
Socialization decay	15.1	−.400	1.48
Noise in socialization	16.0*	22.6*	7.18*
Reduced susceptibility to socialization with tenure (dummy)	51.0*	65.4*	54.3*
Recruitment selectivity mean	1.02*	13.6*	28.5*
Recruitment selectivity std. dev.	8.51*	1.27	.056
R^2	.284	.348	.471
N	120,240	129,600	129,600

*$p < .05$.

most in the no-growth or steady state condition and exerts the smallest effect in decline. Management socialization reduces time to equilibrium during growth and to some extent with no growth but actually increases time to equilibrium during decline. Recruitment selectivity increases equilibrium time the most during growth and the least during decline.

Some general observations based on table 6.2 still hold for the extended decomposition. The effects of noise in the socialization process, resistance to socialization with tenure, and decay in socialization all remain essentially the same as before. And the variables subject to management control do not have consistently favorable affects on all cultural outcomes, reinforcing the earlier conclusion that management faces trade-offs in attempting to influence the cultural system of the organization.

6.5 MANAGERIAL IMPLICATIONS

What do the findings imply for cultural management? To explore this issue, it is helpful to focus on the two organizational types of comparative interest—the Japanese and American manufacturing types (cf. Cole, 1990). The Japanese type shows a high degree of cultural intensity and stability across all parameter variations and under all growth settings. This suggests that the Japanese reputation for managerially preferred homogeneous organizational culture is well deserved and provides support for the model's validity. It also suggests that once a homogeneous culture is established, it develops an inertia that is resistant to a wide variety of subsequent variations in management policy and organizational growth rates. The most significant implication for Japanese managers is that once the culture of the organization is established, managerial efforts directed toward maintaining recruitment selectivity and socialization and minimizing turnover may be relaxed without fear of a noticeable impact on the organization's culture. While the cultural impact would not be noticeable, the savings accruing to the organization because of reduced costs could be.

By contrast, the cultural preferredness of the American manufacturing type is highly responsive to changes in recruitment selectivity and management socialization. In practice, this type is characterized by the lack of concern for both of these processes. The advantages to be gained from investment in organizational culture may explain why culture has become such a popular topic with American managers. More managerial attention to recruitment and socialization could pay big cultural dividends. The advantages of managerially preferred homogeneous organizational cultures could well outweigh the costs of the extra effort.

The findings also suggest foci for cultural management in other organizational types. For example, the governmental, entrepreneurial, and collectivist-democratic types show strong cultural responsiveness to recruitment selectivity. Based on these findings, it seems important for these organizations to maintain their selection standards, and they could improve the managerial desirability of their cultures by raising the standards.

The simulation runs indicate that the dynamics of cultural transmission vary substantially across the different types. In circumstances for which greater recruitment selectivity is suggested, we assume that more desirable candidates exist in the labor market and can be found and recruited, given sufficient effort. It is possible that societal cultural constraints may restrict the candidate pool to the point that this assumption is not valid—for example, the American labor market may contain a scarcity of candidates with desirable cultural traits, in which case management must rely more on socialization after hiring to improve the desirability of the organizational culture. At the other extreme, the Japanese labor market may contain an abundance of desirable candidates, so that selective recruitment may not entail significant costs. Given appropriate techniques, socialization by management is controllable by the organization, but its costs are likely to be related to the characteristics of the societal pool from which new workers are drawn. The turnover findings imply that organizational emphasis on retention policies and the management of turnover may be misdirected, at least with respect to cultural management. Overall, the findings provide potential guidance for managerial decisions by showing which parts of the cultural transmission process are likely to show the highest returns to investment in managing organizational culture for different organizational types.

6.6 Conclusion

As with chapter 5, this chapter shows again that commonly observed variations in organizational culture correspond to plausible variations in demographic regimes. These findings increase our confidence in the basic model.

This chapter finds further that organizational culture becomes more managerially preferred as organizations decrease in size. We interpret this finding as indicating that culture intensifies in declining organizations because employees with short tenure are the most likely to exit, partly due to the alienation effects, and partly because short-tenured employees typically constitute a high proportion of the organizational workforce. These employees have not been exposed to organizational socialization processes for as long as long-term employees and, as a consequence, have relatively low levels of enculturation.[3] Once said, this explanation seems obvious, yet it is rarely invoked in discussions of organizational decline, which often view the changes observed during these periods as emotional reactions (Sutton, 1988). The simulated

---

[3]Careful readers may note that earlier we discussed the cultural susceptibility of new members as a reason for high enculturation levels in growing organizations. The difference is that in growing organizations, new members are likely to be exposed to socialization forces for a longer period of time, where as in declining organizations they are more likely to depart before the full effects of socialization can be realized.

declines make it clear that such an explanation is not necessarily needed and that the effect can be produced by a decline in the number of employees without considering organizational psychology. The effect could be enhanced by explicit seniority-based or enculturation-based retention policies.

Another interesting observation noted earlier is that several organizational types show greater cultural stability in either the growth or decline conditions than they do under no growth or steady state (see figure 6.1). In static organizations, the mechanisms that promote enculturation in growth (susceptible entrants) or decline (turnover of less culturally desirable employees) are weaker. The special problems of managing culture in static organizations have not previously been recognized, but the demographic perspective suggests that extra managerial efforts may be called for. These problems are likely to be pronounced for the collectivist type, which does not grow, and to a lesser extent for the professional and governmental types, which grow slowly.

The simulations have therefore demonstrated that the fairly simple demographic model developed here can reproduce outcomes consistent with those previously ascribed to behavioral processes (Pfeffer, 1983). Such findings are best regarded as hypotheses, and considerably more analysis and research needs to be done before they should be considered as anything more. Nonetheless, we are pleased that the model generates such conjectures and think this illustrates its potential value as a research tool.

PART III

Applications and Extensions
of the Model

The five chapters in this part of the book apply or extend the model to a variety of contexts and research problems. Chapter 7 applies the model to study the plausibility of a key assumption made in research on organizational demography. Chapter 8 extends the socialization component of the model; it specifies and examines variations in a person-by-person intraorganizational network of cultural influence. Chapter 9 uses the extended model to address an important public policy issue, namely, the cultural stability of network-based terrorist organizations when confronted with different governmental intervention strategies. In chapter 10, the model is applied to mergers, in particular to study cultural integration following a merger. Chapter 11 extends the model to macro concerns; it studies the relationship between cultural heterogeneity and organizational growth and mortality. Finally, chapter 12 concludes the book with a review of findings and several brief remarks.

CHAPTER 7

Heterogeneity in Tenure

7.1 INTRODUCTION

In this chapter, we demonstrate the potentially powerful explanatory value of organizational culture. We do so by using the basic model of cultural transmission developed in chapter 4 to examine a popular research problem in organizational demography. Inspired by Pfeffer's (1983) arguments, numerous researchers have examined the consequences of demographic distributions within organizations in a variety of contexts and outcomes. Much of this research focuses on the demographic distribution that Pfeffer emphasized, the tenure or length of service (LOS) distribution in an organization or its top management team.[1]

Researchers examining the LOS distribution have advanced an impressive set of empirical findings over the last two decades. Outcome variables found to be associated with it include turnover (McCain, O'Reilly, and Pfeffer, 1983; Pfeffer and O'Reilly, 1987; Bantel and Wiersema, 1992; Wiersema and Bird, 1993), innovation (O'Reilly and Flatt, 1986; Flatt, 1993), diversification (Wiersema and Bantel, 1992), and adaptiveness (O'Reilly, Snyder, and Boothe, 1993). Despite this progress, an awkward number of different theoretical processes have been advanced to explain the observed associations. Many of these explanations are based on questionable and unstudied assumptions, and several studies have failed to find the expected relationship between the LOS distribution and organizational outcomes. For these reasons, probing beneath the surface of the issues seems warranted.

As we explain later, a synthetic but parsimonious recasting of various theoretical ideas used in this research program implies a major role for organizational culture, specifically a strong link between the demographic (LOS) heterogeneity of an organization and the heterogeneity of its culture. Despite the role this link plays in designing and evaluating empirical research on the effects of LOS distributions, it (or any other

---

[1]A great deal of research focuses on various other demographic characteristics and their distributions within organizations. This work falls outside our concerns here, which deal exclusively with the LOS distribution. We concentrate on the LOS distribution because it has been the subject of more sustained efforts.

theoretical association playing a similar role) has for the most part not been investigated directly. Instead, researchers typically assume—often implicitly and perhaps unwittingly—that the link between demographic heterogeneity and cultural heterogeneity is highly plausible under a wide variety of conditions and organizational contexts.

In this chapter, we adapt the basic model of cultural transmission to explore this issue.[2] The adapted model allows us to clarify the theoretical processes involved in the assumed link, to examine the logical structure of the theory implicit in the usual research, to explore the general plausibility of the assumed link, to identify contexts (demographic and organizational) where the link would be more or less strong, and to design new approaches to studying organizational demography. In our view, this exercise generates insight into the research program on internal organizational demography and thereby shows how a formal model can sometimes generate unexpected benefits.

7.2 LOS DISTRIBUTIONS IN ORGANIZATIONS

Although several earlier minor contributions can be found, most contemporary research on organizational demography stems from Pfeffer's (1983) theoretical essay on the topic. In his essay, Pfeffer made a persuasive general case for the study of organizational demography. He also laid out a number of specific theoretical propositions about the causes and consequences of demographic phenomena in organizations. Most of these specific arguments concentrate on the properties of demographic distributions, especially the LOS distribution of members of the organization or its top management team. The number of subsequent empirical studies examining this distribution shows that organizational researchers are especially intrigued with Pfeffer's arguments about the consequences of the LOS distribution on organizational outcome variables, including (1) innovation, adaptation, and performance; (2) administrative succession or turnover; (3) organizational control structures and processes; (4) interorganizational relations; (5) career trajectories; (6) cohort identity and conflict; and (7) the distribution of power within organizations.

How do LOS distributions affect these outcomes? Although the substantive details of the theorized process depend on the particular outcome, a common general theoretical formulation holds that unevenness or heterogeneity in the LOS distribution is the demographic variable of primary interest. Consider, for instance, the theoretical argument of

[2]Parts of the chapter are adapted from Carroll and Harrison (1998).

Wagner, Pfeffer, and O'Reilly (1984: 77) about LOS distributions and turnover:

> Time of entry distributions that characterize a group will tend to predict similarity of members and frequency of communication. These, in turn, will affect the extent to which the group is integrated and cohesive, or the extent to which it is split by intercohort conflicts. Groups whose members are tightly linked and integrated are less likely to experience turnover than less integrated groups, and individuals who are less tightly linked to the group than are other members would be expected to turn over.

In fact, the idea that unevenness or heterogeneity in the LOS distribution should affect organizational outcomes such as turnover is the modus operandi for research on organizational demography.

Carroll and Harrison (1998) summarize the twenty-one major empirical studies conducted within this framework.[3] By most social science standards, it is an impressive set of studies. The set includes studies of public and private sector organizations, studies of a variety of different industries, and studies in two major national economies (the United States and Japan). The most frequently studied dependent variable is turnover; however, a variety of other variables have also received attention. Over time, the focus of this research has shifted from entire organizations to work groups within organizations—especially top management teams. The coefficient of variation (CV) in tenure has also become the most common measure of LOS heterogeneity. This measure is calculated as the standard deviation of tenure over the mean of tenure.

Most of the evidence presented in these studies supports theory about the LOS distribution. By our count, eleven of the studies present solid supporting evidence, another four contain soft supporting evidence, and six provide no support. Overall, the record for this research program is very good, but it is not without its anomalies. One would like to know, in particular, if there is not some way to account for the studies that do not support the theory (even though we believe not every study should be weighted equally). Unfortunately, the program currently has no concise explanation for these nonfindings. Moreover, because the studies differ in sample size, team size, observation period, and organizational context, analysts often resort to ad hoc and idiosyncratic arguments to reconcile the pattern of findings. Obviously, a more principled and systematic way to evaluate and compare these studies would be beneficial.

---

[3]This review covered studies published up to 1998.

7.3 THE IMPLICIT LINK

Taken at face value, the operational framework used in empirical research on organizational demography is theoretically stark. It relies essentially on the association between two variables, the homogeneity/heterogeneity of the LOS distribution and an organizational outcome. The framework derives more from a research strategy than from an attempt to explicate fully the theoretical ideas involved. This strategy, advocated by Pfeffer (1983) and adopted by most of those studying organizational demography, involves looking only at observable variables and estimating the strength of relationships between them. For instance, Hambrick, Cho, and Chin (1996: 663) note that direct psychological measures are "very difficult to obtain for senior executives in major firms and are unavailable for past, disbanded top management teams."

As with much science, unobserved variables and processes are either assumed or inferred by the logic of this approach. In this case, the unobserved variables involve the implied link between LOS heterogeneity and outcomes. Virtually every study investigating LOS effects assumes some kind of social process to justify theoretically the operational empirical framework. For example, Wagner, Pfeffer, and O'Reilly (1984: 76) justify investigating the relationship between variation in LOS and turnover with the following explanation: "Similarity in time of entry into the organization will positively affect the likelihood of persons communicating with others who entered at the same time. . . . the more frequent the communication, the more likely it is that those interacting will become similar in terms of their beliefs and perceptions of the organization and how it operates."

Empirical Status

A major problem with the demographic research program concerns the empirical standing of the explanations that have been offered. To our knowledge, only three studies have attempted to examine any intervening process between organizational demography and outcomes. Taken together, the three studies constitute a questionable empirical foundation for the demographic research program. Two of them (O'Reilly, Caldwell, and Barnett, 1989; Smith et al., 1994) found supporting evidence—but both used small, nonrandom convenience samples with low response rates. Although both constitute notable contributions, neither would classify as a benchmark empirical study of the kind found in more developed areas of social science (e.g., status attainment, personality, education). The other study (Glick, Miller, and Huber, 1993), perhaps the most ambitious empirical project, found no supporting evidence.

Alternative Explanation

The questionable empirical support for these theoretical stories is problematic because a very simple alternative explanation exists for many of the established findings. Although not commonly recognized by LOS researchers, simple aggregation of individuals with negatively declining turnover rates generates—in the cross section—a positive association between the coefficient of variation in tenure (for the set of socially unconnected individuals) and turnover. Table 7.1 illustrates this built-in cross-sectional relationship by showing the correlation between LOS heterogeneity (measured by the coefficient of variation in tenure) and turnover for simulated sets of socially unconnected individuals with tenure-dependent quit rates. It reports findings from simulations of the turnover process with two closely related tenure-dependent functions, both of which are commonly used in studies of individual turnover and mobility, the Gompertz and Makeham processes. For the Gompertz

TABLE 7.1

Cross-sectional correlations between heterogeneity in LOS (*CV*) and turnover in simple aggregates of individuals with simulated negative tenure-dependent rates of turnover

Number of persons	*Observation window*	$\hat{\rho}(CV, dummy)$	$\hat{\rho}(CV, event\ count)$
		Gompertz model	
5	3 months	.30	.29
5	12 months	.41	.34
20	3 months	.27	.25
20	12 months	.42	.38
		Makeham model	
5	3 months	.22	.25
5	12 months	.37	.29
20	3 months	.18	.28
20	12 months	.08	.30

Source: Carroll and Harrison (1998). Copyright © 1998 by Cornell University. Used by permission.

Note: Simulations were run for 120 time periods with 1,000 trials for each condition. All correlations are statistically significant at .005 level or less.

process, the simulated model for the turnover rate of person i as a function of his or her tenure (u) is

$$h_{i,u} = 0.20 \exp(-0.15u). \tag{7.1}$$

For the Makeham process, the simulated model is

$$h_{i,u} = 0.025 + 0.20 \exp(-0.15u). \tag{7.2}$$

The cross-sectional correlation between LOS heterogeneity and two turnover variables (a dummy indicating turnover in the first instance, and a count of turnover events in the second) is positive for all simulations and estimates. (Estimates with other parameter settings support similar conclusions.) Moreover, the effect is of a magnitude similar to that of many of the empirical studies reviewed in Carroll and Harrison (1998), thus calling into question the validity of the purported explanations. The effect occurs because an uneven LOS distribution implies some individuals with short duration, and these are the individuals most likely to leave in a duration-dependent turnover process. Presumably, any duration-dependent process might have a similar built-in spurious relationship with aggregated LOS measures of heterogeneity, but the built-in link between LOS and turnover is especially problematic because turnover is a frequently studied outcome.

Theoretical Issues

Another general question about the research program on demography concerns theory, in particular, the theory used to explain the estimated relationships between LOS distributions and organizational outcomes. Typically, these explanations are cast in the form of causal chains with unobservable intervening variables. Some explanations we have read about the issue point to psychological processes of similarity and attraction, to social psychological processes of homophily and group dynamics (including especially communication patterns), and to sociological processes about norms (see Lawrence, 1997; Boone and van Olffen, 1997).

The most commonly used explanation relies on social integration as the intervening variable (O'Reilly, Caldwell, and Barnett, 1989), although cognitive diversity is also widely used (Glick, Miller, and Huber, 1993). In attempting to develop comprehensive theory about organizational demography, Finkelstein and Hambrick (1996) used both social integration and cognitive diversity. They view demographic heterogeneity (of all kinds) as "a proxy for cognitive heterogeneity, representing innovativeness, problem-solving abilities, creativity, diversity of information sources and perspectives, openness to change and a willingness to challenge and be challenged" (Finkelstein and Hambrick, 1996: 125). Social integration, by their view, is an effect of demographic heterogeneity—it lowers the level of social integration. The two processes are negatively related because "social integration is facilitated when group members are more similar, while many of the effects of demographic heterogeneity, such as greater diversity of perspectives and willingness to challenge others, can create conflict that detracts from team cohesiveness and social integration" (Finkelstein and Hambrick, 1996: 126). In this theory, both heterogeneity and social integration are held to affect consensus (the former negatively, the latter positively), and this in turn affects organizational behavior and performance.

Admirable as these efforts are, we believe that they fall short of full theoretical unification. The problem is that the processes involved are inextricably tied together, especially in an ongoing group or team. The complexity of simultaneous feedback and interaction effects needs to be taken into account, and this is a daunting task. There is also the complexity of working at several levels of analysis simultaneously (individual, group or team, and organizational—see Lawrence, 1997).

An alternative theoretical strategy entails reconceptualizing the processes involved into a global overarching macro concept. Such reformulation is justified when a valid macro concept exists and when underlying micro processes are not yet fully understood, perhaps because of their complexity (Hannan, 1992). Reformulation potentially makes the macro theory robust with respect to details of the micro processes (Hannan, 1992). It also has the potential to enhance parsimony and to minimize levels-of-analysis problems.

Reformulation

We submit that in this context an appropriate intervening theoretical construct supporting this kind of reformulation is organizational culture. Culture is widely thought to be the "natural outgrowth of the social interactions that we call organizations" (Trice and Beyer, 1993: 2). As reviewed in chapter 1, organizational culture is generally regarded as consisting of both beliefs and social practices, including communication, socialization, and shared experience. Beliefs and social practices, of course, constitute the underpinnings for concepts of cognitive diversity and social integration, respectively. Moreover, because culture is frequently conceptualized in terms of homogeneity-heterogeneity across a social system, there is an easy connection to demographic homogeneity-heterogeneity (O'Reilly and Chatman, 1996; Koene, Boone, and Soeters, 1997).

This reformulation allows us to relate demographic heterogeneity to organizational outcomes by specifying cultural heterogeneity as the intervening variable in a three-variable causal chain. Demographic researchers usually estimate only the overall relationship between heterogeneity in LOS and an outcome. Assuming the three-variable chain is correct and the usual causal assumptions hold, the strength of the overall relationship should be the product of the relationships of the two links in the chain (see Duncan, 1975). Letting the second link in the chain be fairly positive, say .40, and then calculating the expected overall relationship between LOS and outcomes across the range of estimates of the first link of the chain (say .02 as the low estimate and .54 as the high one) yields an expected range of .008 to .216. At the low end, it would take a very large sample to detect a statistically significant effect on the overall relationship that is usually estimated, and it would have almost no explanatory power.

7.4 MODELING TOP MANAGEMENT TEAMS

We chose to adapt the model of cultural transmission laid out in detail in chapter 4 to resemble a top management team (TMT) because that is the social unit examined by most empirical research on LOS demography. TMTs are social organizations in and of themselves, and they are thus subject to similar processes of entry, socialization, and exit. Enculturation is defined in reference to the CEO or the board of directors' preferences. New team members are chosen from a candidate pool with a distribution of values on desired characteristics, although in this context candidates may be viewed as hired from the outside or selected from other parts of the organization. Peer socialization represents socialization by other team members, and size and growth rate refer to the team rather than the entire organization. Because the TMT constitutes a distinctive cultural milieu, the tenure terms in the socialization and turnover functions indicate tenure with the team. This means that all variables, including tenure and enculturation, are defined in terms of the TMT.

How should the CEO be represented? Because the CEO is usually a member of the TMT, we fixed one position with this status. As discussed later, we then used two different approaches to setting the CEO's initial enculturation score. After entry, the CEO is treated exactly like any other member of the team; the CEO is thus subject to all the forces in the model. Using this interpretation makes the management pull factor in the socialization function ambiguous, so we set the parameter to zero, leaving peer socialization as the primary influence on cultural change.

Adapting the model to TMTs shows several problems with some of the empirical studies (and, hence, discrepancies between the studies and the model). First, the TMT is assumed by researchers to be a social group, with membership criteria and collective responsibility. Too often researchers assemble data on executives without specifying or scrutinizing sufficiently the team definition—in other words, the executives may or may not constitute a distinct social unit. Second, the relevant clock for most processes theorized to operate within the TMT is tenure or length of service with the team, not the firm or organization. Too often researchers use another clock without justification (Boone and van Olffen, 1997).

Possible Expectations

Under what conditions will LOS and culture be tightly linked? Finkelstein and Hambrick (1996) made several arguments suggesting that team size plays an important role. They hypothesized that larger TMTs exhibit greater cognitive heterogeneity, less social integration, and less consensus. Their reasoning is consistent with the observation that in smaller teams, individuals are more likely to recognize and reinforce interpretations of common experiences than in larger teams or organizations. Alternatively, a minimum critical size may be needed to generate and sustain an organizational culture in the first place. That is, larger TMTs—which are still relatively small social organizations—may exert stronger normative pressure precisely because they will be less informal and personalistic than very small teams. This latter argument is buttressed by the empirical findings of the research tradition. As Carroll and Harrison (1998) observe, studies that report strong support for demographic theory about LOS distributions investigate larger teams than those with marginal or nonsupportive findings. Thus, we conducted simulations organized by team size; we simulated small teams with size of five and large teams with size of twenty. Because TMTs do not grow in any predictable fashion, we conducted all simulations with the growth rate set to zero. This means that for any given simulation, the size of the TMT is fixed and unchanging, except for stochastic delays in filling vacancies.

There is little or no theory specifying other conditions likely to generate a positive relationship between heterogeneity in LOS and culture, although there is ample theory about the conditions generating homogeneous organizational cultures (see O'Reilly and Chatman, 1996). In terms of the model, this theory suggests there will be more homogeneous cultures when there is (1) high selectivity, (2) a strong alienation effect, and (3) strong peer socialization (predictions supported by the model's performance—see chapter 5). Perhaps the operation of these factors strengthens any relationship between LOS and culture. High selectivity, for instance, might mean that tenure scores are more closely linked to enculturation scores. Alienation and peer socialization might produce similar effects. Put another way, this logic implies that if selectivity is low, alienation effects are weak, and peer socialization effects are weak, then culture is likely to stay distant from management's preferences and fragmented, no matter what the LOS distribution looks like. Yet it is also not entirely obvious that factors producing homogeneous cultures necessarily produce strong relationships between LOS heterogeneity and cultural heterogeneity. For example, weak alienation could produce a stronger LOS-culture association than strong alienation by subjecting less culturally fit members to peer socialization for longer periods of time before turnover, during which the coefficient of variation in tenure and variation in culture will both decrease. So expectations here are ambiguous.

7.5 DESIGN OF EXPERIMENTS

We designed and evaluated simulations that vary systematically six components of the basic model detailed in chapter 4:

- *Size of TMT.* We conducted simulations for two different team sizes, labeled large and small. The large teams have an expected size of twenty persons; small teams have five members. This variation coincides roughly with the sizes of teams used in the empirical studies.

- *Selectivity.* We varied the level of selectivity in choosing new members to TMTs by adjusting the mean enculturation of the recruitment pool from which new managers are selected randomly and the rate at which vacancies are filled. We use two settings, one labeled in the tables high selectivity (with mean of .80 and expected probability of filling a vacancy in one time period of .33), the other low selectivity (with mean of .10 and expected probability of .85).

- *Peer socialization.* Peer socialization on top management teams is often intense, yet there are undoubtedly teams where it is low—consider a team composed of divisional managers, each jockeying for the upper hand. To simulate these variations, we set the peer socialization parameter α_{peer} at two levels: .98 and .18, which we refer to as strong and weak peer socialization, respectively.[4]

---

[4]To ensure a meaningful comparison of the two peer socialization conditions, the denominator for socialization change intensity $A_{i,t}$ in equation (4.4) is set to 1.0 when $\alpha_{peer} = .18$, the same value it has when $\alpha_{peer} = .98$.

- *Alienation.* Alienation affects turnover in the model in that the further an individual's enculturation score is from the management ideal of unity, the more likely he or she is to depart. In our simulation, we set this parameter (γ_1) at two levels, .60 and .15, to reflect high and low alienation effects, respectively.

- *Base turnover rate.* We simulated the base turnover rate at two levels, reflecting a low rate ($\gamma_0 = .015$) and a higher rate ($\gamma_0 = .030$).

- *CEO modeling.* We used two different approaches to setting the initial enculturation level of the CEO. In a first approach, we set the CEO's score initially at the mean level for the team. In a second, we let it start at a value of unity. The first approach might be interpreted as the case where although the CEO may value the cultural ideal, he or she does not meet it exactly; he or she is only as culturally fit as the average team member. In the second set, the CEO exemplifies the cultural ideal. After the CEO's score is set at the mean or to unity, it is then subject to change from other forces in the model, just as for any team member.

In conducting the simulations, we varied all the theoretically relevant dimensions of the model systematically to obtain a total of sixty-four different simulation conditions. The parameter settings are summarized in appendix B. These parameters are calibrated so that one time period in the simulation represents one month in real time. We ran each simulated condition for 120 time periods, and we replicated each run for 1,000 trials, changing only the seeds of the random number generators. Statistics for each condition are calculated across the trials at simulation's end, period 120. In reporting findings, we focus on the statistic of primary relevance to the demographic research program—the correlation between the coefficient of variation in tenure (CV) and the standard deviation of enculturation ($\sigma_{c,t}$). The operating assumption of LOS demographers is that this correlation will be positive and of substantial magnitude given the implied causal chain.[5]

One question some colleagues have raised about our simulation design concerns the extent to which it incorporated lumpy rather than incremental changes in the composition of TMTs. As is well known, TMTs sometimes change dramatically in short periods of time as a new CEO ushers out the old team and replaces it with his or her own selections. Do we need to simulate this condition explicitly, or is it already generated within the simulation setup? Inspection of simulation time trajectories

---

[5] We also calculated statistics in a variety of other ways, including averaging coefficients across multiperiod windows near the end of the simulation. The findings from these efforts are broadly similar; hence, we report the simplest method.

revealed that the current framework does produce occasional multiple turnovers in the team in a single period and that, on occasion, for small teams the entire team turns over without overlap in the tenure of individuals. Although these events are infrequent, we believe that this is an appropriate setup because such lumpy changes do not occur frequently in the real world, and it is best to examine them in relation to the whole range of management team changes, as our simulation allows. Our simulation treats instances of complete turnover in the team as a regular part of the demographic process that continues through the restaffing period.

7.6 Findings

By Condition

Table 7.2 presents the primary findings from the simulations.[6] It shows the correlations between the coefficient of variation in tenure (CV) and the standard deviation of enculturation ($\sigma_{c,t}$). Each estimated correlation coefficient is based on 1,000 simulated trials. In other words, we simulated 1,000 TMTs and used these data to calculate correlation coefficients.

The first column of correlation coefficients in table 7.2 shows the relationship between heterogeneity in LOS and heterogeneity in culture for large teams with initial CEO enculturation scores set at mean values across the sixteen variations of selectivity, peer socialization, alienation, and turnover. The correlations are all positive and statistically significant, thus suggesting that the demographic program's usual assumption is generally plausible. The strength of these positive associations does vary widely, however. The coefficients range from a low of .10 to a high of .61. There is no obvious pattern in the variation as a function of the conditions.

---

[6]We subjected the model used to generate the correlations in table 7.2 to a wide range of sensitivity and stability tests. Three alternative CEO specifications were simulated for all conditions: no CEO; a strong CEO (exerting a dominant pull on enculturation scores toward the ideal); and cultural change with CEO turnover (in which the culture metric was rotated with each CEO turnover event to reflect the possibility that different CEOs may embrace different cultural values). Further, fixed parameters were varied; the parameters varied in the table were set to other values; and correlations at earlier points in simulation time and across various windows of time were examined. These tests convinced us that the findings reported in table 7.2 are broadly representative of the model. Specifically, the resulting correlations are almost always positive, and they vary by condition in complex interactive ways.

TABLE 7.2
Correlations between heterogeneity in LOS (CV) and heterogeneity in culture ($\sigma_{c,t}$) for simulated top management teams

Select-ivity	Peer social-ization level	Alien-ation level	Turn-over effect	Large team w/CEO first at mean	Small team w/CEO first at mean	Large team w/CEO first at unity	Small team w/CEO first at unity
High	Strong	High	High	.29	.31	.26	.32
High	Strong	High	Low	.34	.31	.35	.37
High	Strong	Low	High	.31	.38	.37	.36
High	Strong	Low	Low	.38	.37	.37	.41
High	Weak	High	High	.13	.11	.17	.11
High	Weak	High	Low	.22	.20	.22	.22
High	Weak	Low	High	.14	.10	.15	.14
High	Weak	Low	Low	.21	.12	.26	.20
Low	Strong	High	High	.14	.08	.00	−.00*
Low	Strong	High	Low	.10	−.06	.03	−.00*
Low	Strong	Low	High	.21	.25	.15	.27
Low	Strong	Low	Low	.23	.32	.16	.24
Low	Weak	High	High	.36	.36	−.43	−.33
Low	Weak	High	Low	.61	.57	−.43	−.31
Low	Weak	Low	High	.37	.32	−.26	−.17
Low	Weak	Low	Low	.61	.60	−.25	−.24

Source: Carroll and Harrison (1998). Copyright © 1998 by Cornell University. Used by permission.
*Not significant at $p < .05$.

The second column of coefficients in table 7.2 displays the correlations for the small TMTs with initial CEO scores set at mean levels. These estimates, too, are positive and significant in all cases but one, again supporting the demographic researcher's typical assumption. Here again there is ample variation in the estimates, with fluctuations in the correlations corresponding to those for large teams.

The third and fourth columns show the correlation coefficients for large and small teams, respectively, when the initial CEO enculturation score is set at unity. A strong majority (22 out of 32) of these estimates are also positive and significant. In ten of the conditions, however, the estimated correlations are negative. The eight significant negative relationships all occur in the conditions with low selectivity and weak peer socialization.

Our summary conclusion from the simulation tests is that the model generally supports the assumption of a positive relationship between heterogeneity in LOS and heterogeneity in culture. In the sixty-four separate demographic conditions that we explored, the model produced the expected positive correlation in fifty-three of them. These correlations range from lows near 0 to highs over .60. Generally speaking, the most consistently strong positive correlations are found in contexts where both high recruitment selectivity and strong peer socialization occur (the top four columns of table 7.2). Eight of the negative correlations are isolated to a specific set of conditions: those with low selectivity and weak peer socialization, and when the initial CEO enculturation score is set at unity. Interestingly, however, low selectivity and weak peer socialization with the initial CEO enculturation score set to the mean produced the highest positive correlation observed (for the low-turnover setting). Team size has no obvious effect.

Assessing Patterns

To partition the effects of various factors in the model, we used the simulation data to construct what simulation analysts call a "meta model" (Law and Kelton, 1991). We proceeded in this task by pooling the data from all the sixty-four conditions and calculating the correlation between heterogeneity in LOS and heterogeneity in culture for each of the last 100 simulated time periods.[7] We then fitted a series of hierarchical linear regression equations using as dependent variables the correlation coefficients and as independent variables dummy variables representing the various conditions and their interactions, as well as a variable measuring the time period. These regressions, which we do not report in detail here, show that the factors in the basic model we use combine in significant two-way and three-way interactions to produce correlations. There are also differences in these relationships across the CEO representation method. These complex effects of the model explain why it is not easy to see or comprehend straightforward patterns in table 7.2. It appears that even our relatively simple model cannot provide clear insights into the

---

[7] We did not use the data for the first twenty time periods because their stability is affected by the initial conditions.

influence of various organizational conditions because the interaction of the processes in the model surpasses the complexity threshold. This threshold is imposed by the complex ways that correlations of distributional (heterogeneity) measures vary as the characteristics of the underlying processes producing the distribution change.

In attempting to develop better intuition about the pattern of correlations produced by the model, we conducted numerous analyses of the underlying simulation data. The most insightful of these efforts involved examining the simulated time trajectories of individual TMTs. This view shows that entries and exits of individuals strongly influence cultural heterogeneity, but in a manner inconsistent with their influence on LOS heterogeneity. Because virtually all previous studies of LOS heterogeneity are cross-sectional (or at least treated like cross-sectional data in analyses), this is a perspective on the problem that has not received attention. Yet our investigations led us to believe it is critical to understanding what is going on in LOS heterogeneity studies, as we demonstrate in the following.

7.7 DECOMPOSING LOS HETEROGENEITY

Diversity and Disruption

Table 7.3 shows a typical TMT over time; it is a realization (sample path) taken from the simulation study. Note that whenever a demographic event of hiring or exit occurs, the coefficient of variation in LOS changes sharply in the next time period (we have confirmed this simple observation with regressions on the simulated data). For example, in table 7.3 the coefficient of variation in tenure jumps from .383 to .665 between periods 21 and 22 when a single individual leaves and is replaced. Of course, the new individual has a tenure score of 1 and replaces an individual with a score of 17.

Stated generally, individual TMTs show a strong relationship between demographic events of entry and exit to the team, on the one hand, and measures of LOS heterogeneity, on the other hand. This relationship implies that effects of diversity are inextricably tied up with effects of disruption (caused by the coming and going of team members), making interpretation of the conventional heterogeneity measures and their estimated effects on organizational outcomes problematic. To further complicate matters, we observed in data generated from the model (not shown here) that increases in LOS heterogeneity often do not lead to increases in cultural heterogeneity—the peer socialization process tends to produce mean enculturation levels close to the entry mean, and some exits are cultural outliers, causing disruption often to decrease cultural

TABLE 7.3
Coefficient of variation in tenure (CV) for a team over time with
demographic events

Period	Tenures at start of period	CV of tenure at start of period	Members departing in period	Tenure of leaver	Members hired in period
11	1,4,5,7,9	.583	0		0
12	2,5,6,8,10	.489	1	6	1
13	1,3,6,9,11	.687	1	1	0
14	4,7, 10,12	.424	0		1
15	1,5,8,11,13	.628	1	1	1
16	1,6,9,12,14	.611	0		0
17	2,7,10,13,15	.546	0		0
18	3,8,11,14,16	.493	0		0
19	4,9,12,15,17	.450	0		0
20	5,10,13,16,18	.414	0		0
21	6,11,14,17,19	.383	1	17	1
22	1,7,12,15,20	.665	0		0

Source: Carroll and Harrison (1998). Copyright © 1998 by Cornell University. Used by
permission.

heterogeneity when alienation is high. To be sure, disruptions do produce large fluctuations in cultural heterogeneity:[8] it is just that the directions of change in LOS heterogeneity show no obvious relationship to
the directions of change in cultural heterogeneity.

Social Processes

Given the distribution of tenure before and after the events, it might
seem reasonable to infer that the increase in LOS heterogeneity corresponds to a lower level of social integration or lessened cultural homogeneity. This view implies strongly, however, that a major source of this
cultural diversity comes from the disruption caused by newly entering
individuals. These individuals are presumably not socialized to the

[8]See figure 11.2 in chapter 11, which is typical of patterns we observed here, although it
is based on a reformulated model.

organization, and they replace individuals who were socialized. Pfeffer's (1983: 331) discussion of McNeil and Thompson's (1971) analysis of organizational newcomers and socialization shows clearly that he had in mind socialization processes when developing demographic theory. Of course, demographic theories of tenure-based diversity do not focus exclusively on socialization processes, and this is a serious drawback for a measure that weights all entry and exit events so heavily.

A second major theoretical focus is with group dynamics and social processes that produce integration, solidarity, and group cohesiveness (see Finkelstein and Hambrick, 1996). Consider Pfeffer's (1983: 328–29) statements about what happens when a group works together for a long time:

> This longer period of close association would tend to develop more stable, predictable, and shared expectations and behaviors. . . . Additionally the shared and stable expectations that had developed would tend make conflict less likely and less severe. People who are used to working with each other over a long period of time will have developed more consonant interaction patterns through years of association.

The relevant clock for this type of process would seem to be the length of time the group has been together as a functioning social entity.

A third major focus of many demographic theories is on the effects of common historical experiences. These are often cast in the form of cohort effects as when Pfeffer (1983: 335) proclaims that "in organizations, cohorts produce two important effects—potential conflict across groups, and sponsorship, solidarity and mutual choice within groups." Cognitive or belief diversity is frequently linked to ideas about the extent to which individuals were members of the organization when it experienced particular periods or events (Glick, Miller, and Huber, 1993).

By many organizational demographers' views, the widely used coefficient of variation of tenure (or any similar measure) is supposed to represent the effects of all these processes (and perhaps others—see Sørensen, 2002b). The validity of that view is virtually impossible to assess in any given context because all three processes operate simultaneously, in different directions (with respect to tenure), and with unknown weights. In other words, the combined or aggregated effect of all three processes might produce any pattern of diversity, and it is not possible to check the measure with any confidence.

Measures

One potentially promising way around this conundrum would be to decompose the combined diversity measure into separate measures, each corresponding to a single process showing a more straightforward relationship with tenure. For focus, we restrict our attention to the three processes discussed previously (socialization, group dynamics, and common historical experiences), which we believe to be dominant in the literature. We also constrain ourselves to measures that do not impose significant additional requirements on data collection in empirical research (i.e., measures based on tenure times).

SOCIALIZATION

Because the coefficient of variation of tenure heavily weights entry and exit events, we believe it is a good basis for diversity based on socialization. Organizational socialization operates forcefully on new entrants and then attenuates, however. The coefficient of variation measure of tenure does not display this property—it continues to change for much longer than we expect socialization processes to effect change. In other words, this component of tenure-based diversity should be transitory, and its effects should diminish rapidly. To represent this, we propose modifying the coefficient of variation of tenure by placing an upper bound on individual tenure scores, the bound representing the time when socialization effects will be negligible. That is, for purposes of this calculation, an individual tenure score cannot increase beyond the upper bound. For illustration, we set the bound at twelve months (researchers may wish to calibrate the measure otherwise), meaning that we calculate the coefficient of variation in tenure using $u_i' = \min(u_i, 12)$ instead of u_i. This implies that diversity from socialization will go up as new entrants appear, will decline as they stay in the organization, and will reach zero when everyone has been in the organization for at least a year. Table 7.4 provides some illustrations of this calculation, labeled CV_{12}, for various tenure distributions.

GROUP COHESIVENESS

To represent diversity from processes involving group cohesiveness, we use time since last entry event to the group or organization. This time variable gives the maximum duration that the team might have been operating as a unified functioning social entity. We also believe, however, that this process is stronger initially than it is with a long-standing team. That is, the returns of integration and solidarity to a given length of time together should be greater at the team's inception than after it has been operating for a while. Thus, we propose measuring diversity from group dynamics as

$$u_{last} = \exp(-u^*),\qquad(7.3)$$

where u^* is the tenure of the most recently entered member. Table 7.4 also offers some illustrations of this measure (again, calibrations may be in order).

TABLE 7.4
Illustration of tenure-based measures of heterogeneity

Tenure values of team in months	Combined hetero- geneity (CV)	Heterogeneity from socialization (CV_{12})	Heterogeneity from team cohesiveness (u_{last})	Heterogeneity from common experiences (u_{olap})
1,7,12,15,20	.665	.553	1.00	12.8
2,8,13,16,21	.610	.476	.368	14.8
3,9,14,17,22	.563	.407	.135	16.8
4,10,15,18,23	.522	.346	.050	18.8
5,11,16,19,24	.488	.293	.018	20.8
1,12,17,20,25	.609	.502	1.00	18.8

Source: Carroll and Harrison (1998). Copyright © 1998 by Cornell University. Used by permission.

COMMON HISTORICAL EXPERIENCES

Finally, we propose measuring diversity among teams members' common historical experiences by looking at the overlap in individual tenure times. We suggest examining the tenure times of every pair of individuals on a team and calculating the length of the overlap. We then propose averaging the overlap times for all pairs of team members. Formally, the measure is

$$u_{olap} = \frac{1}{N} \sum_{i \neq j} \min(u_i, u_j),$$ (7.4)

where N is the team size and u_i is tenure of the ith member. Again, table 7.4 shows illustrations of this measure (which also could be calibrated).

EVALUATION

How should these measures be evaluated? Two standards seem appropriate. First, each measure should be correlated with cultural heterogeneity. Second, the measures should contribute uniquely to the variation in cultural heterogeneity if they do indeed tap different social processes. Also of interest is the performance of the measures relative to the LOS coefficient of variation used as a combined measure.

TABLE 7.5
Correlations of tenure-based measures with heterogeneity of culture ($\sigma_{c,t}$)

Variable	Sample with initial CEO enculturation set at mean	Sample with initial CEO enculturation set at unity
Combined heterogeneity: CV	.30[*]	.28[*]
Heterogeneity from socialization: CV_{12}	.35[*]	.56[*]
Heterogeneity from team cohesiveness: u_{last}	.28[*]	.35[*]
Heterogeneity from common experiences: u_{olap}	.15[*]	.41[*]

Source: Carroll and Harrison (1998). Copyright © 1998 by Cornell University. Used by permission.
[*]$p < .05$; $N = 32,000$.

Table 7.5 presents some relevant analysis on this question. It reports correlations of each of the tenure-based diversity measures on heterogeneity in culture using the simulation data. Each of the proposed measures is positively correlated with cultural heterogeneity. Moreover, in four out of six instances, the alternative measures are more highly correlated than the conventional combined measure. We regard these estimates as encouraging.

We also conducted a series of ordinary least squares regressions of cultural heterogeneity on the various tenure-based measures of diversity (see Carroll and Harrison, 1998, for complete details). The most telling estimated equation uses all four diversity measures simultaneously along with a control for mean group tenure, $\bar{u}$. Strikingly, all three new measures are significant, and the combined (conventional) measure is not, suggesting that each taps a unique source of variation. The socialization diversity measure, CV_{12}, and the common experience diversity measure, u_{olap}, both show positive effects in the midst of controls for the other processes. The group cohesiveness diversity measure, u_{last}, shows a negative relationship. Thus, the proposed single-process diversity measures appear to be more strongly related to cultural heterogeneity than the conventional combined measure in data generated by our model. Most impressively, when considered together in analysis of the simulation data, these alternative measures seem to replace it entirely.

7.8 SUMMARY

Organizational demographers study the influence of LOS distributions on organizational outcomes, operating through intervening social processes that we view macroscopically as organizational culture. Although many empirical studies invoke this or a similar assumption, only three have tried seriously to examine its plausibility. Collectively, the results of these studies are subject to different interpretations, leaving the otherwise impressive research program on organizational demography on a soft foundation.

In this chapter, we adapted the basic model of chapter 4 to examine the plausibility of an assumption about heterogeneity in LOS and culture. Our simulations show that the assumption holds for the model under a very wide range of conditions, a finding that supports the common demographic research framework. Among various conditions, we found the assumption to be most plausible in organizational contexts with both high recruitment selectivity and strong peer socialization. Yet many of the positive correlations we observed between heterogeneity in LOS and culture are fairly low. Given the logical causal chain typically used in argumentation, the association between cultural heterogeneity and outcomes would need to be very strong in these cases to generate a meaningful relationship between LOS heterogeneity and organizational outcomes.

It would be a mistake, however, to conclude from the findings that all is well within the existing demographic framework. Current research on organizational demography typically does not incorporate considerations of organizational context in a serious way, meaning that many estimated effects likely combine several underlying processes. We believe that researchers would gain from comparative considerations of how strongly demographic factors might operate within the organizational units and industries that they study. Such considerations not only would clarify the status of estimated effects but also would enhance theory in our view.

The discipline imposed by our modeling efforts led us to uncover a number of methodological and conceptual shortcomings of typical research practice that deserve attention if the program is to sharpen its contributions. In particular, the model developed here helped us to discover the disruption effect, which confounds the association between LOS heterogeneity and cultural heterogeneity. It made clear the built-in relationship between turnover and the LOS distribution, impugning studies using LOS variation as a predictor of turnover without adequate controls. It also highlighted the importance of a well-specified theoretical model for the construction of empirical measures. To be sure, much of this might have been deduced from more specific considerations without the full model, but it had not been despite a great deal of research activity on this topic. Accordingly, we cannot help but think that the model's structure provided an insightful perspective that allowed us to see these problems and that it imposed a discipline on our thinking that facilitated analysis. In some cases, the full model was necessary to understand the effects of complex interacting processes—for example, the disruption effect requires the simultaneous operation of entry, exit, and enculturation processes. In other cases, once effects are deduced from the model, it becomes apparent that these effects are immediately applicable to real-world phenomena rather than simply being properties of the model (e.g., the built-in turnover relationship).

Based on the insights and findings of the simulation analysis, our recommendations for organizational demographers include the following:

1. Control for the built-in effect of LOS heterogeneity in studies of outcomes such as turnover where the underlying processes are duration dependent at the individual level. The best way to do this is to disaggregate—to collect and analyze event histories at the individual level with appropriate control variables (see, for example, O'Reilly, Caldwell, and Barnett, 1989). If this is not possible, then perhaps calculations similar to those reported in table 7.1 could provide a baseline or null hypothesis for this potentially spurious effect.

2. Control for potential sources of organizational and industrial heterogeneity to the extent possible so as to minimize the possible spurious effects of unobserved heterogeneity. The demographic tradition relies heavily on research designs involving random or representative sampling of diverse sets of organizations in the cross section; the industry-based longitudinal design advocated by Hambrick and Mason (1984) and used most fully by Sørensen (2000b) shows great promise for allowing researchers to measure and control for a variety of other factors. Note that eight of the ten studies of TMTs reviewed in Carroll and Harrison (1998) using industry-based designs found significant effects for the LOS distribution, compared with only one of six studies using broad cross-industry samples of Fortune 500, Compustat, or manufacturing firms (and this single study examined the built-in turnover relationship).

3. Use meaningful definitions and measurements of the TMT (when it is the relevant social unit), ideally based on theoretical principles and involving assessment of authority or decision-making behavior (Finkelstein and Hambrick, 1996) and social interaction as a group. The lists of officers routinely published by companies may or may not constitute the TMT of a given firm.

4. Construct tenure-based measures based on length of time in the theoretically relevant social unit, not just the unit for which data are readily available.

If the theory is about the social integration of a TMT, then the appropriate variable is usually time in the team, not the whole organization.

5. Decompose the theoretically central tenure-based measure of heterogeneity currently in wide usage—the coefficient of variation in tenure (and its cousins). It combines the effects of too many hypothesized processes with potentially inconsistent effects (Sørensen, 2002b). We believe that the three measures proposed here (based on theories about socialization processes, group cohesiveness, and common historical experiences) will assist in this task. Each shows a simpler relationship between tenure and an underlying process than does the combined measure. Each also shows promise in empirical analysis based on the simulated data. As a result, we believe that all three measures merit consideration and exploration in empirical studies on organizational demography. However, we are also certain that they can be improved upon, as well as complemented with other theoretical ideas and associated tenure-based measures, which we look forward to other researchers developing.

6. Address disruption processes, which appear to be the most important confounding effect in the commonly used aggregate measures of LOS heterogeneity (such as the coefficient of variation in tenure). We believe that we have made a start here with the proposed three measures, but we also recognize that fuller theoretical treatments are required. To what extent is cultural heterogeneity (or other intervening constructs) actually influenced by the arrival and departure of individuals? How are these cultural variations theoretically linked to organizational outcomes? How do organizational factors influence these links? How should empirical studies be designed to minimize or isolate the influence of disruption? The empirical study by Sørensen (2000b) demonstrates that the size of the disruption effect may be substantial. Using data on management teams of television stations, he shows empirically that failure to control for entry and exit events in investigating LOS effects can generate spurious findings.

Although this chapter contains criticism of organizational demography, our goal is not criticism itself. We have great appreciation for organizational demography's accomplishments to date, and we think observers who assess this area negatively by focusing only on its deficiencies or by making unrealistic suggestions for future research are misdirected. Organizational demography is one of a few genuinely new and exciting areas of organizational research. It is also an area with potential to unify the increasingly disparate micro and macro ends of the field. Consequently, the purpose of our criticism is not to destroy but to lay bare some problems that need attention if the full promise of the area is to be achieved. For this reason, we have tried to temper our criticisms of demographic research with constructive and realistic proposals. Our alternative tenure-based diversity measures, for instance, are proposed in this light. Yet it may be difficult, because of disruption effects, to capture fully the resilience of organizational culture with static tenure-based measures. Measurement, design, and theory all present challenges and opportunities to organizational demographers.

CHAPTER 8

Cultural Influence Networks

8.1 INTRODUCTION

The basic model of cultural transmission described in chapter 4 implies a fairly simple process of person-to-person influence. In the socialization component of the model, members of an organization influence each other's enculturation in the aggregate: individuals are pulled toward the mean level of enculturation of all persons in the organization according to some weighting parameter. In behavioral terms at the individual level, this specification implies that all individuals exert equal influence upon each other, probably as a result of equal levels of communication and interaction (French, 1956).

While equal influence represents a good baseline assumption in our view, it obviously does not allow for examination of the many variations in influence patterns commonly observed in organizations and other social settings. In reality, some individuals exert more influence than others, and influence patterns often develop on the basis of individuals' similarity to each other, and through processes of interaction. Looked at as a whole, influence networks that develop in these ways display an unequal distribution of influence ties or connections among individuals.

The structure of influence patterns within an organization surely affects the intensity of socialization pressures experienced by individuals. The location of an individual within an influence network, the characteristics of others in the network, and the influence of each network member all combine to produce socialization intensity. Over time the system also possesses high feedback: one's participation alters the influence network and affects the characteristics of others.

Inequality in the influence network relates to broad theoretical issues about the optimal design of social networks. Burt (1992) argues for informationally efficient networks, those with minimal redundancy in ties and information. Such networks are characterized by "structural holes," in his terminology; a network with large structural holes also usually possesses a high level of inequality of influence. Podolny and Baron (1997) accept this assessment when it concerns social networks where the purpose is to find and identify reliable information (e.g., locating job opportunities). But they argue that for purposes of identity and normative sanctioning such a network is not effective; instead, they suggest that for these purposes a dense network with overlaps and redundancies is more effective. By this reasoning, the less hierarchical network may be better for producing solidarity and homogeneity in an organizational culture.

The goal of this chapter is to enhance our understanding of how influence structures operate and what difference they make for organizational culture and its maintenance over time.[1] Accordingly, this chapter extends the basic model of cultural transmission to allow variations in the structure of the influence network. We do so by refining the model's representation of person-by-person influence patterns. Specifically, we draw from theory and research about social cohesion, influence processes, and small-group dynamics to specify a dynamic interaction process—one representing how pairs of individuals interact and subsequently change culturally over time. The model allows the strength of influence to vary in a number of ways, involving processes based on aggregate characteristics of all members, as well as some based on the similarity of individuals.

A central tenet of the research on internal organizational demography reviewed in chapter 7 holds that individuals who enter an organization at similar points in time will typically be closer to, and more influenced by, each other than by those who enter at distant points in time. This occurs because individuals who enter the organization at similar times have shared socialization experiences, join and help develop common groups, and experience common historical events within the organization (Pfeffer, 1983). Thus, timing of entry or hiring constitutes one plausible basis for unequal influence among individuals in an organization. When social influence is a function of proximity in hiring, we call it *cohort-based influence*. In the following experiments, we model cohort-based influence and compare it with cases without it, which we refer to as *random influence*.

As demonstrated later, the extended model generates a range of network influence structures, including much variation in levels of inequality in influence. These variations appear "naturally" at various occasions within each simulation condition, allowing us to explore the consequences of network inequality without generating additional simulation conditions. This situation also allows us to examine the effects of network inequality within and across the variety of other simulation conditions on enculturation and its dispersion. The findings give a broad picture of how structural holes and cohort-based influence might operate.

---

[1]This chapter uses and adapts sections from Harrison and Carroll (2001b, 2002).

8.2 Networks of influence

In the basic model of cultural transmission detailed in chapter 4, peer socialization occurs in a simple manner: the average enculturation of others in the organization exerts a pull on the individual that moves his or her score toward the average (the strength of the pull is given by the parameter α_{peer}). Using the average of others' scores in this way implies that each peer has equal influence at every point in time. The communication network typically associated with such a structure is one where all individuals have equally strong ties to all other individuals (see French, 1956; Friedkin, 1998).

While using this simplified representation made sense in developing the model's general structure, it clearly leaves room for further development. After all, full and equal access (let alone influence) to all individuals in an organization rarely occurs, even in small organizations. Obviously, variations in the structure of influence have the potential to produce major differences in cultural systems and their outcomes.

In initiating here an extension of the model in this direction, we work with the influence processes directly and do not deal with the communication patterns that produce them.[2] We first develop a general framework for modeling influence among individuals in a cultural system. We then describe how we envision influence processes changing over time. The resulting model specifies a much more dynamic and interactive process of cultural influence, including socialization, than in the basic model.

8.3 Modeling framework

The basic model of cultural transmission in chapter 4 sets an individual i's enculturation score at time t, $C_{i,t}$, based on three factors: (1) his or her previous enculturation level; (2) the individual's susceptibility to socialization (a decreasing function of tenure); and (3) the intensity of socialization forces he or she faces (which combines pulls from management, peers, and decay).[3] Before incorporating explicit person-by-person influence considerations, we simplify this general structure. We drop the susceptibility factor entirely because the widely observed pattern of decreasing susceptibility is itself likely an outcome of direct influence processes. We also disregard the socialization pulls from management

---

[2]The relationship between influence and communication is important but not central to our concerns here. We believe that for socialization and other cultural processes, influence is primary.

[3]See equation (4.4).

and decay in order to better isolate effects from the influence network. These simplifications leave us with a model with the general form

$$C_{i,t+1} = f(C_{i,t}, I_{i,t}), \qquad (8.1)$$

where $I_{i,t}$ is another function giving the effects of the influence network structure at time t between i and each of the other j members. So, as with the collectivist-democratic type of chapters 5 and 6 and the top management teams of chapter 7, the influence network model contains only peer influences on socialization. But, unlike the collectivist-democratic type, in this model we now specify fully a differentiated influence network structure with internal dynamics.

To describe the influence process, we start by defining the variable $S_{ji,t}$ as the influence that person j exerts on person i at time t. We fix $S_{ji,t}$ to be a continuous variable that ranges from 0 to 1 ($0 \leq S_{ji,t} \leq 1$). Thus, when $S_{ji,t} = 0$, person j has no influence on i; when its value is 1, j has maximum influence. Of course, the actual cultural change that j might induce on i likely depends not only on the amount of influence he or she exerts but also on how culturally similar or dissimilar the two of them are. Let cultural similarity be given by the difference in their enculturation scores, $(C_{j,t} - C_{i,t})$. Although absolute cultural similarity can be defined as the absolute value of this difference, we use here directional cultural similarity by retaining the sign of the difference. Then, the cultural effect of j on i can be given by the product of influence and similarity, $S_{ji,t}(C_{j,t} - C_{i,t})$. If $C_{j,t} > C_{i,t}$, then the effect of j on i is positive, tending to increase $C_{i,t}$; if $C_{j,t} < C_{i,t}$, then j tends to decrease $C_{i,t}$.

With these elements in place, we can set the intensity of cultural change from the influence network with the function $I_{i,t}$. This function lets individual i be influenced by all other members j in the organization or team. It does so by averaging their proportional contributions:

$$I_{i,t} = \sum_{j \neq i} S_{ji,t} (C_{j,t} - C_{i,t})/(N_t - 1) \qquad (8.2)$$

where N_t is the number of persons in the group or organization at time t. Making the function for the enculturation score at time $t + 1$ a linear combination of $C_{i,t}$ and $I_{i,t}$, so that the new culture score for i is given by the previous score plus an adjustment due to influence, yields

$$C_{i,j+1} = C_{i,t} + aI_{i,t}, \qquad (8.3)$$

where a is simply a weighting parameter with values between 0 and 1 and is inversely associated with cultural inertia; that is, cultural change occurs more slowly for lower values of a, which we set to .05.

8.4 DYNAMIC INFLUENCE

Influence patterns clearly change over time in a group or organization. The source of this change may be exogenous, but it may also be a function of cultural similarity and previous influence patterns—in other words, it might be endogenous. A novel aspect of the model we explore here is the manner in which such dynamic influence occurs.

We start with the general modeling assumption that cultural change is relational, meaning that it depends on the specific relations one has with other particular individuals (Friedkin, 1998). We further assume that how much influence a person exerts on another depends in large part on the cultural similarity of the two individuals involved—a behavioral assumption generally referred to as *homophily* (McPherson, Smith Lavin, and Cook, 2001).[4] When two individuals are culturally similar, they likely interact more and have more influence on each other than on other, less similar individuals. The increased interaction likely causes them to recognize and appreciate their similarity even more fully, thus leading them subsequently to assign even greater significance to each other's opinions and behavior. In this dynamic influence process, other individuals who have lower cultural similarity have less influence on one another. These individuals likely get less interaction time and have less influence; even if there might be a limited common cultural basis, it often does not get recognized and appreciated. And, known differences likely get heightened and exacerbated with decreased interaction. So, individuals who are highly dissimilar relative to available others tend to have less and less influence over time.

Overall, in a group or organizational setting, each individual experiences homophily-based influences, to a greater or lesser degree, from every other individual. This means that even though absolute similarity may still matter, individuals nonetheless drift toward those closest to them culturally. Without hard evidence to determine the functional form for the relative influence dynamics, we make the simplifying assumption that the relative influence of each other person on an individual is related to the mean level of cultural similarity among those available as interaction partners. That is, we specify that when the cultural similarity between an individual and another person exceeds the mean level of similarity between that individual and all other persons in his or her network, then the influence of that person will increase over time. Conversely, when the cultural similarity between an individual and another person falls below the mean level of similarity between that

---

[4]Homophily is often used to refer to sociodemographic rather than cultural similarity, although it typically implies the latter.

individual and all other available persons, then the influence of that person will decrease over time. In both cases, the exact magnitude of change in the other person's influence depends also on the absolute cultural similarity between the two individuals.

The model to generate these processes is given by the following. We first construct the mean cultural difference between i and all individuals j in the organization:

$$D_{i,t} = \sum_{j \neq i} |C_{j,t} - C_{i,t}| / (N_t - 1), \qquad (8.4)$$

where N_t represents the number of persons in the group or organization at t. We next calculate the weighting for the change in influence of each person j on i as

$$W_{ji,t} = (1 - |C_{j,t} - C_{i,t}|)^4 - (1 - D_{i,t})^4. \qquad (8.5)$$

In the first term on the right-hand side of equation (8.5), the absolute value of the difference is subtracted from 1 so that the highest weighting occurs when $C_{j,t} = C_{i,t}$; in the second term, the mean distance is also subtracted from 1 for comparability. Both terms are taken to the fourth power to increase the weighting for more similar individuals and to decrease it for less similar individuals, relative to the mean difference.

Changes in influence over time are then given by

$$S_{ji,t+1} = S_{ji,t} + b W_{ji,t}(1 - S_{ji,t}) \text{ if } W_{ji,t} > 0 \qquad (8.6)$$

and

$$S_{ji,t+1} = S_{ji,t} + b W_{ji,t}S_{ji,t} \text{ if } W_{ji,t} < 0, \qquad (8.7)$$

where the weighting parameter b varies from 0 to 1 and is inversely associated with inertia in the network's influence change process; we set b to .075. The multiplier of $W_{ji,t}$ in the first equation, $(1 - S_{ji,t})$, causes influence to change in the direction of 1 (maximum influence) when $W_{ji,t} > 0$, and the multiplier of $W_{ji,t}$ in the second equation, $S_{ji,t}$, causes influence to decrease toward 0 (no influence) when $W_{ji,t} < 0$.

Figure 8.1 illustrates how the influence of individual j on individual i changes in this model from time t to time $t + 1$ as a function of the cultural distance between two individuals for the case when $S_{ji,t} = .5$ and $D_{i,t} = .25$. Note that despite the smoothness of the curve, the direction in which influence moves depends on whether cultural similarity falls above or below the mean (i.e., whether cultural distance is above or below .25). The dotted line shows that when the cultural distance

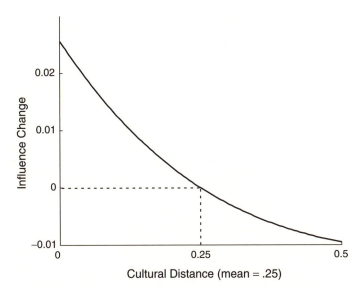

FIGURE 8.1 Influence change as a function of cultural distance

between i and j equals the mean distance between i and all others, no change in influence will occur. Note also that when individuals are more similar than the mean cultural distance, the increase in influence is greater than is the decrease in influence when they are less similar than the mean by the same amount. In other words, very similar individuals (relative to the mean cultural difference) experience stronger increases in influence on one another, whereas very dissimilar individuals experience much weaker decreases in influence. We believe this asymmetry is sensible, since we expect that more similar individuals interact more regularly and more intensively.

Model Comparison

Many network-based models of influence rely on binary representations of influence or tie strengths among individuals in a group or organization (for a review, see Wasserman and Faust, 1994). These models also typically contain fixed, or at least exogenous, influence processes. By contrast, the model proposed here represents influence with continuous variables and posits an endogenous process of influence change over time. We find both of these features highly attractive because they reflect

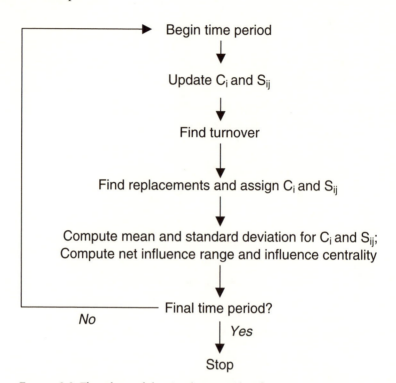

Begin time period

↓

Update C_i and S_{ij}

↓

Find turnover

↓

Find replacements and assign C_i and S_{ij}

↓

Compute mean and standard deviation for C_i and S_{ij};
Compute net influence range and influence centrality

↓

Final time period?

No

↓ *Yes*

Stop

FIGURE 8.2 Flowchart of the simulation with influence networks
Source: Harrison and Carroll (2001b). Copyright © 2001 by John Wiley and Sons Ltd. All rights reserved. Used by permission.

realistic assumptions about the processes involved in the formation and transmission of organizational culture.[5]

Flowchart of the Network Model

Figure 8.2, which presents a flowchart of the extended transmission model with influence networks, shows how the model operates.

[5]It is worthwhile to note that a major reason we can depart from conventional paths and incorporate these features is because of our use of simulation. Although other analysts commonly recognize the value of these approaches, they do not implement them because they are mathematically intractable or empirically overdemanding. Simulation methods allow us to overcome these otherwise formidable obstacles.

8.5 Demography and network structure

We report here simulation experiments with the extended model designed to examine the effects of variations in five factors on the cultural system of a formal organization. The first three factors can be characterized as primarily demographic: turnover rates, hiring processes, and organizational size. The final two concern primarily the structure of influence processes: cohort-based influence and inequality in influence. The first four of these variations are controlled by specification in the simulation program; variations in inequality arise as a consequence of the processes modeled. In examining these factors, we focus on both the cultural and the influence patterns of a team or organization. We now describe each set of issues and how they are treated in the simulation.

Turnover, Hiring, and Size

Turnover, hiring, and organizational size are potentially important factors because such demographic conditions set the stage for the operation of influence in a cultural system. Although it is commonly thought that turnover undermines stability and thereby causes culture to deteriorate, two previous analyses show that this need not be the case. In a model of organizational learning, March (1991) demonstrated that limited turnover aids in learning by introducing new information to the organization. Similarly, Harrison and Carroll (1991) found that turnover allows an organization to flush itself of relatively unencultured members faster, thus raising levels of enculturation and propelling the system toward equilibrium (see also chapter 4; and Krackhardt and Porter, 1985). In both cases, turnover assists in adaptation of the system over time. However, it is also clear that turnover can be detrimental to culture, as when whole generations of individuals depart, erasing the collective memory of the system.

How might these different views be reconciled? The effects of turnover may be nonlinear; they may also be confounded with size and hiring selectivity. Small organizations are much more susceptible to wholesale departures. But large organizations typically preclude intensive interaction among all members on a regular basis. Moreover, turnover effects are mediated by the characteristics of the replacement members. The issues are potentially very complex. So, we investigate these factors by designing simulation conditions that systematically produce variations in each.

We model turnover here using a slightly different specification than previously. Recall that in the basic model developed in chapter 4, individual-level turnover is given by the hazard rate for individual i as

$$r_{i,t} = \gamma_0 + \gamma_1[1 - C_{i,t-1}]^3, \tag{8.8}$$

where both γ_0 and γ_1 are parameters, the first indicating a baseline rate of departure and the second associated with alienation (an individual's distance from the perfect culture score). We use here a modified formulation, one that bases alienation on cultural distance from the other members of the organization rather than from a perfect score. We do this by making alienation a function of an individual's squared distance from the cultural mean $\bar{C}$. This gives an individual hazard rate of

$$r_{i,t} = \gamma_0 + \gamma_1 [C_i - \bar{C}]^2, \tag{8.9}$$

where the culture variables are again measured at $t - 1$ but the subscripts have been dropped for convenience. This new formulation is consistent with our focus in the chapter on peer influence and our exclusion of management influence from the model.

The simulation experiments vary the strength of the baseline turnover rate, including a condition for no turnover; the alienation effect is held constant except in the no-turnover condition, where it is zero. Appendix B provides the exact parameters used for each; in reporting our findings we simply refer to the levels as high, low, and no turnover.

The hiring policy variations address the cultural selectivity of the hiring process. Members of the labor pool from which new entrants are selected vary in their cultural fit with the organization because of prior socialization, and the organization may put more or less effort into selecting entrants with a good fit. The selectivity of the hiring process is simulated by assigning each new entrant i an enculturation score C_i given by

$$C_i = \bar{C}_h + \sigma_{ch} v, \tag{8.10}$$

where $\bar{C}_h$ is the mean enculturation level of new entrants, σ_{ch} is the standard deviation of the hiring pool, and v is a standard normal deviate drawn from $N(0, 1)$. We keep σ_{ch} fixed at .15 and vary hiring selectivity by setting $\bar{C}_h$ to either .3, .5, or .7 to represent low, intermediate, and high hiring selectivity.

We also vary organizational size. We do this simply by setting the number of persons in the organization at different fixed levels of either 5, 15, 25, or 50. Size does not vary over time: there is no growth mechanism in the model, and when a person departs from the organization he or she is immediately replaced.

Network Inequality and Cohort Dependence

As mentioned previously, the extended model produces much variation in levels of inequality in the influence network. In the simulations, these variations occur naturally within each condition. Thus, instead of developing new simulation conditions to examine the effects of inequality, we examine the issue within and across the variety of other simulation conditions. We do this by calculating two measures of influence network inequality for each simulated organization at each point in time. The first, the net influence range (S_R), is computed as the difference between the individual with the highest net influence (average influence on others less the average influence of others on him or her) and the individual with the lowest net influence. The second, influence centralization (S_C), indicates the extent of influence dominance by a single individual. To calculate this measure, we first create an influence score for each individual at each time point by taking the average of that person's influence on all others. We then divide the influence score of the person with the highest influence by the average influence score for everyone in the network. For both measures, the higher the score, the greater the inequality in the influence network.[6]

The network inequality measures can be interpreted straightforwardly. The network influence range measures the span of influence scores S_{ij}. When all individuals have equal influence (as in the basic model in chapter 4), there is no inequality in influence and the net influence range is zero. At the other extreme, when the net influence range is high, there are large differences in the amount of influence exercised by individuals in the organization, with some individuals having a great deal of influence and others very little. The network centralization measure captures the degree to which the most influential individual's cultural influence exceeds the mean influence level for the organization. When influence centralization is zero, all individuals have the same amount of influence, equal to the mean (as in the basic model of chapter 4), but when influence centralization is high, one individual exercises substantially more influence than the average amount of influence exerted by others in the organization. In a sense, compared with the basic model in chapter 4 (where there is no influence inequality), the net influence range measures horizontal differentiation in influence, while influence centralization measures vertical differentiation in influence. That is, the constructs correspond to two different dimensions of influence inequality. In the simulation data generated for this chapter, the two constructs have a correlation of .47—that is, about 22 percent of their variance is shared.

In examining the effects of cohort-based influence, we compare simulated organizations where there is no cohort basis of influence with those

---

[6]In an earlier analysis of the influence network model (Harrison and Carroll, 2001b), we called the net influence range and network centralization variables "inequality of influence" and "maximum influence," respectively; since both variables measure inequality, we have chosen more descriptive terms here.

where such influence operates in a particular way. In modeling cohort-based influence, we focus on the time of entry. We do this by setting the strengths both of influences on a new entrant and of the new entrant's influence on others as functions of recency of entry (or, inversely, tenure) of incumbent organizational members. In other words, a person entering an organization with many long-tenured individuals will not be heavily influenced by them and will also not exert much influence on them (Pfeffer, 1983). By contrast, a person entering an organization with many others who have recently entered will be greatly influenced by them and will also have a large impact on them. In the more typical situation, a person entering an organization will find both short- and long-tenured individuals, and he or she will be more influenced by, and exert more influence on, those who entered more recently or at the same time.

The presence or absence of cohort-based influence processes is modeled by the manner in which the person-by-person influence scores S_{ij} between incumbent members and new entrants are set at the time of entry of the new members. In the model without cohort-based influence, each new entrant i is assigned a full set of influence scores S_{ij} drawn randomly from a uniform distribution, $U(0, 1)$. The influences of each incumbent j on the new entrant i (S_{ji}) are also drawn from this distribution.

In modeling the cohort-based influence process, we set influence to be a function of absolute similarity in tenure. More precisely, in setting the influence of an incumbent j on the new entrant i we use the following rules. We first draw a random uniform deviate and square it, producing an influence score that is, on average, less than in the noncohort setup; we label this value as P_{ji}. We next calculate a cohort-based influence score $Q_{ji} = 1 - \theta_1(u_j + \epsilon)$, where θ_1 is simply a weighting factor (set to .01 in the simulations reported here), u_j denotes the tenure of person j, and ϵ is a disturbance drawn randomly from $N(0, 1)$, the standard normal distribution. We then finally set the influence of each incumbent j on the new entrant i to be the larger of the two. That is, $S_{ji} = \max(P_{ji}, Q_{ji})$. The reason for using the maximum is to provide a floor level P_{ji} of influence that is greater than zero but less than the noncohort influence level as u_j becomes very large, but most of the time—when $u_j < 100$ in this case—Q_{ji} will dominate.

We set the new entrant's influence on incumbents in a similar way. That is, we start by drawing a random uniform deviate and squaring it; we label this value P_{ij}. We next calculate a cohort-based influence score $Q_{ij} = 1 - \theta_2(u_j + \epsilon)$, where θ_2 is a weighting factor (set to .02 in the simulations reported here rather than .01 as earlier, since the influence of new members on incumbents is likely to be less than the influence of incumbents on new entrants), u_j denotes the tenure of person j, and ϵ is a disturbance drawn randomly from the standard normal distribution

$N(0, 1)$. We then set the influence of new entrant i on each incumbent j to be the larger of the two values. So, $S_{ij} = \max(P_{ij}, Q_{ij})$.

Finally, we allow new entrants i and k to influence each other by $S_{ik} = 1 - |0.05|\epsilon$, with a minimum of 0, where ϵ is a disturbance drawn randomly from a standard normal distribution $N(0, 1)$. In general, persons entering the organization at the same time will strongly influence one another under this process.

Taken together, these specifications define the condition that we call cohort-based influence.

8.6 Design of experiments

Exploring the preceding factors together gives us seventy-two basic simulation conditions. These come from the combination of three variations in turnover (no turnover, low turnover, high turnover); three variations in hiring selectivity (.3, .5, and .7); four variations in size (5, 15, 25, and 50); and two variations in cohort-based influence (random and cohort-based). The variations in network influence inequality arise naturally as a result of the simulated influence process and thus are not built in directly as design conditions; instead, these variations appear spontaneously within each of the seventy-two basic conditions.

We simulated each basic condition for 100 trials. Each of the trials represents a simulated organization; each is initiated at time 1 with initial C and S values drawn as random deviates from normal, $N(.5, .15)$, and uniform, $U(0, 1)$, distributions, respectively (the seeds for random number generation vary across trials, of course). Each trial organization operates for 300 time periods (representing months) before it is stopped. We save the data from the entire history of the trials, not just the ending time. We report here analyses based on pooled periodic snapshots of the data. Specifically, we combine data from each trial taken at every 60-period time point (representing every five years); the outcome variables of interest at each time point are average values for the preceding 24 time periods. Thus, each trial contributes 5 observations to the data set. The total number of observations in the file equals 36,000, resulting from 5 periodic observations of each of 100 trials for each of seventy-two conditions.

8.7 Findings

In exploring the extended model, we focus on the mean enculturation level, as well as on the heterogeneity of culture among members of a team or organization. To give an overview, we report figure 8.3, which

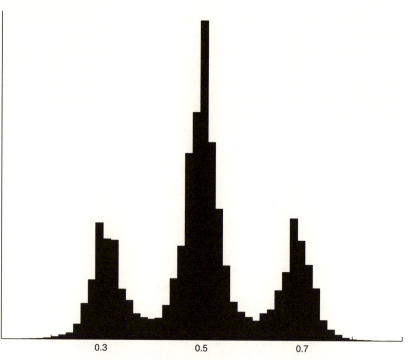

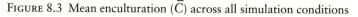

FIGURE 8.3 Mean enculturation ($\bar{C}$) across all simulation conditions

depicts visually the distribution of the mean enculturation level $\bar{C}$. Clearly, the distribution looks symmetric. It is also somewhat polymodal, with .500 representing an overall mode and two smaller peaks falling above and below. The two smaller peaks correspond to hiring selectivity settings of .3 and .7, respectively; the central peak is higher because selectivity does not come into play in the no-turnover condition, and because the influence process tends to pull new hires entering with enculturation scores of .3 or .7 toward the center of the distribution under some conditions.

What accounts for the variation in mean enculturation levels? Inspection of the data shows that variability in the mean level of enculturation apparently increases as a function of time and turnover—in both cases, the standard deviation of mean enculturation drifts upward. Variability in mean enculturation also increases for more extreme selectivity values (.3 or .7 rather than .5). Although the effects are less dramatic, it also

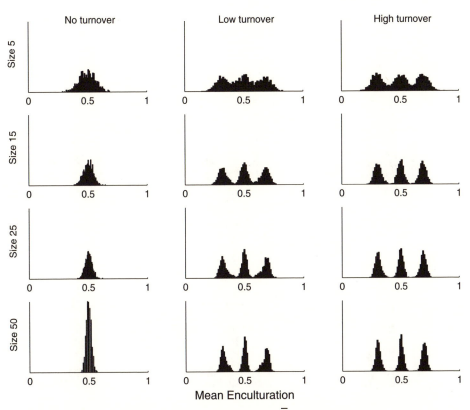

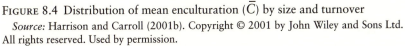

Mean Enculturation

FIGURE 8.4 Distribution of mean enculturation ($\overline{C}$) by size and turnover

Source: Harrison and Carroll (2001b). Copyright © 2001 by John Wiley and Sons Ltd. All rights reserved. Used by permission.

appears that variability in mean enculturation decreases with cohort-based influence and with organizational or group size.

Because the means are so stable across conditions, it makes no sense to analyze mean enculturation with statistical methods predicting the mean, such as ANOVA (analysis of variance) and regression analysis. Instead, we conducted informal analyses of the relative frequency distributions of mean enculturation by condition: we graphed by condition and compared the shapes visually.[7] The two strongest and most interesting breakdowns involved comparing the frequency distributions across, first, combinations of size and turnover and, second, variations in the net influence range. Figures 8.4 and 8.5 show these distributions, respectively. In figure 8.4, the mean of enculturation is graphed by twelve

[7]This is an exercise that is possible only because the simulation generates so much data.

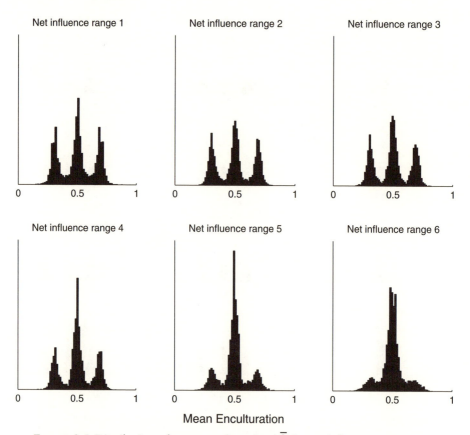

Net influence range 1 Net influence range 2 Net influence range 3

Net influence range 4 Net influence range 5 Net influence range 6

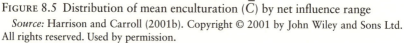

Mean Enculturation

FIGURE 8.5 Distribution of mean enculturation ($\overline{C}$) by net influence range
    Source: Harrison and Carroll (2001b). Copyright © 2001 by John Wiley and Sons Ltd.
All rights reserved. Used by permission.

categories of a cross-classification of the size (four levels) and turnover (three levels) settings. In figure 8.5, mean enculturation is graphed by six intervals of the net influence range labeled from 1 to 6 as the range increases, chosen to facilitate comparison by putting approximately equal numbers of cases (6,000) in each graph.[8]

The turnover effect seen in figure 8.4 appears to be dominant. The leftmost four graphs (associated with zero turnover) show much tighter distributions (in part because there are no new entrants) than either of

[8]The range labels on the graph correspond to the following values: .0765 to .3314 for net influence range 1; .3314 to .3818 for net influence range 2; .3818 to .4216 for net influence range 3; .4216 to .4629 for net influence range 4; .4629 to .5238 for net influence range 5; and .5238 to 1.0245 for net influence range 6.

the other sets (associated with low and high turnover). However, a size effect is still apparent: within each column (same turnover level), the distributions tighten as you move down (corresponding to increases in size). Thus, turnover and size appear to affect jointly the distribution of mean enculturation. Higher turnover produces more variation in the mean; greater size produces less variation.[9]

Comparisons across levels of the net influence range suggest that the effects of this variable on variation in mean enculturation are not as strong as those of size and turnover, except for high values of the range. The graphs in figure 8.5 show that the frequency distribution changes shape slightly as the net influence range rises. It is most normally shaped when the net influence range is greatest. It is also most dispersed for the three lower levels of the net influence range (compare the top row with the bottom one). Thus, even though the relationship looks complex, it also appears as though lower values of the net influence range are associated with higher variation in the mean level of enculturation.

Figure 8.6 shows the distribution of the variance in enculturation across the 36,000 observations. Obviously, the distribution is skewed. So, in conducting statistical analyses of variance in enculturation, we work with a transformed variable, the natural logarithm of the variance in enculturation.

Table 8.1 reports an analysis of the natural log of the variance in enculturation. It shows regressions of the log variance in enculturation on the relevant demographic and influence network variables. Model a uses all available observations in estimation[10] and incorporates a set of dummy variables for the simulation time period of the observation (we omit the period 1 dummy, so effects are contrasts to the first period); it shows that as simulation time increases, the variance in enculturation declines. Model b uses only the last observation (end of period 5) for each trial when available.

It is encouraging that the two sets of estimates basically agree with each other despite some differences in significance. Selectivity and the cohort effect are not significant in the final time period; additional analysis shows that the cohort condition has its strongest effect on cultural

---

[9]We also looked at these distributions for the last observation period only and found the same patterns, but the effects of size and turnover appear to diminish as a function of simulation time.

[10]We lose cases for this analysis when the variance is zero, since the log of zero is undefined and gets assigned a missing value. The only instances of zero variance are for the no-turnover condition, where the organization becomes culturally homogeneous over time due to socialization without entry or exit. In the no-turnover condition, there are no cases of zero variance in the first two time periods, 449 for period 3, 736 for period 4, and 952 for period 5.

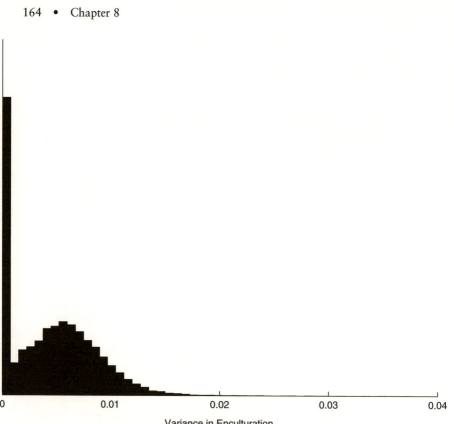

Variance in Enculturation

FIGURE 8.6 Distribution of variance in enculturation ($\sigma^2_{c,t}$) across simulation runs

variability in earlier time periods. Influence centrality becomes significant only for the final time period. The inequality findings suggest that a broad range of influence generally dampens cultural variability but that when a single individual has undue influence, cultural variability increases.

How do demographics, cohorts, and other factors affect an organization's influence structure? To address this question, we conducted a series of regression analyses using the four key influence variables as outcomes: the mean level of influence effects $\bar{S}_{ji}$; the variance in influence effects σ^2_S; the range of influence effects S_R; and influence centralization S_C. The findings are reported in detail in Harrison and Carroll (2002), but they can be described simply as follows:

- For the influence mean model, moderate selectivity is significant, showing that the influence mean is higher under the two extreme selectivity

TABLE 8.1
Regressions of log $\sigma^2_{c,t}$ on covariates

	Model a	Model b
Constant	−10.6	−16.3
Period 2[a]	−.862	
Period 3	−1.47	
Period 4	−1.92	
Period 5	−2.21	
Low turnover[b]	6.77	10.0
High turnover	5.99	9.77
Moderate selectivity[c]	−.039	.016*
High selectivity	−.016*	−.005*
Log size	.990	.754
Cohort[d]	−.116	−.018*
Net influence range	−1.84	−3.13
Influence centralization	.085*	1.35
Log size × low turnover	−.812	−.594
Log size × high turnover	−.875	−.647
R^2	.748	.957
N	33863	6248

Source: Harrison and Carroll (2001b). Copyright © 2001 by John Wiley & Sons Ltd. All rights reserved. Used by permission.
*Not significant at $p < .05$
[a]Omitted category is period 1.
[b]Omitted category is no turnover.
[c]Omitted category is low selectivity.
[d]Omitted category is no cohort-based influence.

conditions. In the no-cohort (random) condition, turnover makes little difference, but in the cohort condition, higher levels of turnover produce substantial increases in the influence mean. Intuitively, turnover brings inflows of new members to the organization, providing the opportunity for cohort formation and the development of high influence within cohorts.

- In the regression for influence variance, both the demographic variables (with the exception of selectivity) and the cohort variable are significant, but the demographic variables account for most of the variation. Influence variance increases with size and decreases with turnover, and is highest for maximum size and no turnover. The influence variance increases with size more quickly for lower turnover. The cohort condition enhances turnover's effect of reducing the variance in influence, relative to the random condition.

- In the net influence range model, all variables except selectivity and the interactions are significant. But the explanatory power of the models is weak, and so we hesitate to make too much of these findings.

- The influence centralization regression shows that except for selectivity, the demographic variables are all significant, as is the cohort variable. Size and turnover show significant interactions with cohort. The demographic effects are strongest, but the demography-cohort interactions also contribute substantially. Once again, the cohort condition enhances the effects of turnover; higher turnover reduces influence centralization more in the cohort condition. The cohort condition also moderates the negative effect of size on influence centralization.

8.8 DISCUSSION

In this chapter, we extended the basic model of cultural transmission to explore the consequences of demography and structural variations in the cultural influence network. The extensions we incorporated into the model possess two attractive novel features: (1) continuous measures of network tie strength or influence and (2) endogenous dynamic influence processes.

Our simulation experiments with the extended model show that over time the cultural influence network evolves to a robust configuration, fluctuating around a stable dynamic equilibrium as individuals enter and leave the organization. Although entry and turnover can both disrupt enculturation and influence, cultural influence network dynamics appear to mitigate this disruption and help to explain the cultural stability of organizational systems.

Mean enculturation levels in the extended model are fairly stable. However, turnover rates and organizational size appear to affect jointly the distribution of mean enculturation levels: higher turnover and larger size combine to reduce variation in the enculturation mean. It also appears that a lower range of influence is associated with higher variation in the mean level of enculturation.

Cultural variability within the organizations generated by the extended model differs by demographic and influence network conditions.

The findings show that as time increases, the variance in enculturation is significantly lower when influence is cohort based. By contrast, high turnover produces significantly higher cultural variablity. Perhaps the most intriguing effects on cultural variability concern the influence inequality variables. In general, we find that a greater range of influence lowers cultural variability within the organization, but that when a single individual has very high influence, cultural variability increases (after the overall structure of influence has been controlled).

Both demographic factors and cohort-dependent influence processes affect the influence network structure. In particular, cohort-based influence shows an important interaction with turnover. Turnover provides for a flow of new entrants, creating the possibility for cohort formation and the development of high intracohort cultural influence; with low levels of turnover, cohort-based processes have less opportunity to operate. As turnover rates rise, cohort-based influence affects the influence network by increasing the influence mean and decreasing influence variation and influence centrality. In other words, cohort-based influence strengthens the influence network (promoting cultural stability) and reduces inequality in the network. We believe this finding provides insight into the role of cohort dynamics in promoting cultural stability in organizations.

The influence network appears to be fairly robust with respect to organizational size. The influence mean is essentially constant across organizational size. Influence variance rises somewhat with size, but this effect is attenuated with turnover. In addition, cohort-based influence stabilizes the size effect on influence centrality.

We did not examine organizational growth using the extended model, but growth, like turnover, creates the opportunity for cohort formation by providing a flow of new members into the organization. Thus, we would expect cohort-based influence processes to play an important role in stabilizing the influence network and reducing network inequality as organizations grow. Conversely, we would expect organizations declining in size to be characterized by weaker influence networks and greater network inequality. But, as chapter 6 shows, decline need not result in lower enculturation levels.

What do these findings imply for management practice? Coupled with our previous work with this model (Harrison and Carroll, 2001b), we think the findings lead to one clear suggestion for strengthening organizational culture. It is to pay particular attention in the hiring process to whether job candidates possess cultural characteristics desired by management, and to hire culturally desirable candidates at approximately the same time to capitalize on the cohort effect; the effectiveness of this strategy can be enhanced if accompanied by turnover of less culturally desirable employees. We would expect this strategy to be most effective when concentrated on specific subunits deemed to be culturally problematic by management because the interaction of the new cohort with incumbent workers is likely to be more intense with others in the same subunit. For example, in an academic department with a faculty subgroup needing an upgrade in research emphasis, the implication is that the most effective strategy would be to make multiple hires of research-oriented faculty to the group within a one- or two-year period.

CHAPTER 9

Terrorist Networks

9.1 INTRODUCTION

In January 2002, the coordinator of an antiterrorism project sponsored by the U.S. Department of Defense called one of us. The coordinator requested attendance at a project meeting in the Washington, D.C., area to discuss how the cultural transmission model might provide insight into the fight on terrorism. The project focused primarily on consideration of ways to destabilize terrorist networks, and Al Qaeda in particular, following the terrorist attacks of September 11, 2001.

Prior to the call, we had not considered applying our model to this problem, but upon reflection it became clear that cultural and demographic processes could affect terrorist network organizations, much as they affect other types of organizations. Accordingly, a speculative presentation was developed and made at the meeting, suggesting how the model might be relevant for understanding terrorist networks and what modifications might be required to make it more relevant. Subsequent to adapting the model successfully, the author was invited to return to a second meeting to present findings that might stimulate discussion and inform antiterrorism policy.

In this chapter, we present the findings of this work and subsequent extensions. The adapted model builds on the network model of chapter 8, in which each person in the network has some (perhaps very small) influence on every other person. In this analysis, we model an influence network with a particular (restricted) structure, that of a stylized terrorist organization. We then conduct simulations to examine some of the model's consequences for organizational viability. In particular, we explore the terrorist organization's vulnerability and resilience when confronted with intervention strategies commonly considered by governmental counterterrorism units.

Beyond the possible substantive interests, we include this material in the book to illustrate the flexibility of the model and simulation methods. Many organizations, of course, display restricted influence structures, where individual influence is confined to a subset of other members. This chapter shows that such influence patterns can be readily incorporated into the model and analyzed.

The chapter proceeds as follows. The next section provides some background on terrorist organizations. After that, we turn to a more general discussion of underground network-based organizations, attempting to isolate some of the distinctive features of terrorist networks. We then discuss the general kinds of antiterrorism policies typically implemented by governmental agencies charged with counterterrorism. With these notions in mind, we describe the adapted model and the simulation designed to examine its behavior under the different policy environments. We present the findings of the analysis and explore what they imply for effective policy.

9.2 BACKGROUND ON TERRORIST ORGANIZATIONS

Terrorist organizations have traditionally been viewed as possessing hierarchical cellular structures with clear command and control apparatuses (Encyclopedia of World Terrorism, 1997; Hoffman, 2001). In this view, the terrorist organization consists of units or cells (as they are often called) arranged in a hierarchical chain of command. In the past few years, a new terrorism paradigm emerged, in which terrorist organizations are viewed as loosely connected networks of cells that are more adaptable and less subject to central authority and control (Hoffman, 2001; Tucker, 2001; Rothenberg, 2002). Such views apparently receded when, following the September 11, 2001, attacks, disclosures about Al Qaeda revealed an organization with a clearly identifiable central authority, a chain of command, formal training regimens, and other characteristics of the traditional form.

Given these shifting views, it seems sensible to us to assume that terrorist organizations typically possess hierarchical cellular structures, but that the extent of top-down control exerted through these structures might vary by organization. Whatever the degree of central control, the hierarchical structure seems well suited for the usual activities of terrorist organizations. It permits organizing activities to be carried out with a minimum of intra-organizational interaction, which is important for security reasons; if a cell is identified by government authorities, the cell members will have little or no knowledge of other cells in the network. It also provides a measure of resilience: as Simon (1962) observed, hierarchies have stable intermediate forms and near decomposability, making them less likely to suffer catastrophic disruptions than other forms of organization. We will assume strong central control of the hierarchy, consistent with the current perspective on Al Qaeda's structure, when we explore the potential effectiveness of antiterrorism strategies.

A hierarchical organizational structure does not necessarily imply a hierarchical influence structure; rather, the need for secrecy does. For security reasons, terrorist organizations constrain communications to what is needed for coordination purposes—the "need to know" principle. Interaction is limited to those individuals within a cell and, across hierarchical links, to those cells above and below it in the hierarchy. So, while some variation in the command structures of terrorist organizations seems evident, the security dictates shaping the influence network are enduring and are enforced by selective survival (Gibbs, 1989). We will refer to the resulting influence network as a hierarchical network, or simply a terrorist network. It is this influence structure that we suggest might be characteristic of terrorist organizations, and it is of particular importance to our modeling cultural influence in such organizations.

It is important to emphasize that we are concerned here only with the operational component of terrorist organizations. Operations refers to the part of the organization that actually conducts terrorist acts, such as bombings, hijackings, and assassinations, and can be considered as the technical core of the organization. Terrorist organizations engage in a variety of other activities—for example, recruiting, financing, supply, intelligence, and public relations—in addition to operations. Each activity can have its own organizational structure and influence network; these other activities typically face a less severe security threat than operations, and consequently their influence structures are less constrained. Since operations is the part of the organization that delivers terror and has the greatest impact on the public, we will focus exclusively on the operational side and ignore the other parts of the organization. Thus a terrorist network, as we use the term here, refers to the network associated with the operational component of the organization.

9.3 UNDERGROUND NETWORK-BASED ORGANIZATIONS

Of course, organizations other than those used for terror also operate clandestinely or covertly. So, before proceeding with the analysis, we describe the terrorist network more fully and highlight its distinguishing features.

Underground organizations or networks engage in activities that require them to operate with some degree of secrecy or concealment. Their activities usually involve illegal behavior and are subject to governmental suppression or retaliation if discovered. Examples of underground organizations, in addition to terrorist networks, include drug distribution networks, other criminal organizations, espionage networks, and political resistance movements.

Underground organizations typically display a hierarchical command and control structure with cells comprising the structural elements.

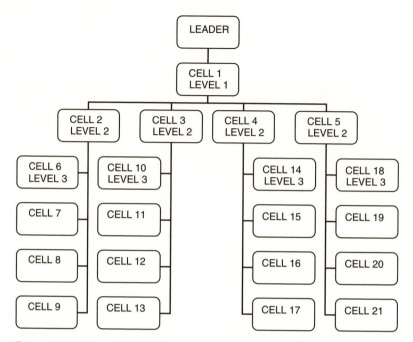

FIGURE 9.1 Hierarchical cellular structure

Figure 9.1 shows a stylized hierarchical cellular structure. The degree of control of the top command may vary, however, because of ideological or strategic conflict within the ranks or simply because there is a more decentralized control system in place. We have already mentioned variation in tight central control for terrorist organizations; Klerks (2001) makes a similar observation for criminal organizations, and Useem (1975) for Western Communist parties, which he classifies as protest movements. Cell size can vary from three to six persons in terrorist organizations to a hundred or more in urban drug gangs (Wolf, 1978; Horgan and Taylor, 1997; Levitt and Venkatesh, 2000; Rothenberg, 2002).

Underground organizations differ, however, in the structures of their communications (and thereby influence) networks. Any communication path creates some security risks. To communicate, individuals must know about (if not know) one another. There is the possibility that communications will be observed, and also the possibility that a captured individual will reveal knowledge of other organizational members. From the standpoint of security, the perfect communication network is complete isolation: no communication at all. This could be the case for a lone sleeper agent with a predefined mission activated, say, by an exogenous event such as a presidential inauguration.

Interaction Within Cells

		No	Yes
		Isolated Node	**Integrated Cell**
	No	Espionage	Terrorists
Interaction Across Cells		Drug rings	Political resistance
			Cross-linked
	Yes		Organized crime
			Urban drug gangs

FIGURE 9.2 Communication patterns in underground organizations

But usually coordination of the organization's activities requires some level of communication. Communications can also occur for social reasons unrelated to the organization's purpose. Underground organizations vary on two basic network dimensions: (1) within-cell communications, the degree to which individuals within a cell communicate with one another, and (2) across-cell communications, the degree to which individuals within cells communicate with those in other cells (except through the hierarchical chain of command). Simplifying the situation somewhat by assuming that both within-cell and across-cell communications are binary variables leads to the typology of underground organizations shown in figure 9.2. Although criminal organizations include drug networks, we have listed the drug operations separately because of the special attention they receive in the literature. Drug organizations divide further into two categories, drug rings and urban drug gangs, because of differences in their network structures.

As discussed earlier, terrorist organizations typically display interaction within their cells but no cross-cell interaction except through the chain of command. Coordination of the cell members' activities (say, a hijacking to be carried out by the cell members) requires within-cell communications. But as self-contained operational units, the cells do not need to communicate with members of other cells, and these organizations tend to avoid this activity for security reasons; ideally members do not even know of the existence of other cells, let alone their makeup. Many political resistance networks follow a similar pattern: their self-contained tasks require within-cell coordination, but interaction with other cells presents unacceptable risks. We label this type of structure an *integrated cell network structure*. An apparent example is the Weather Underground, which carried out politically motivated bombings in the early 1970s.

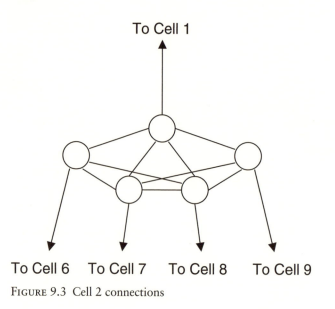

FIGURE 9.3 Cell 2 connections

Figure 9.3, which is an elaboration of cell 2 in figure 9.1, shows the interaction patterns for individual members of the integrated cell network. The nodes represent individuals and the lines, communication links. The downward links shown in the figure are not present for members of the lowest-level, or frontline, cells, which are the ones that actually engage in terrorist acts (level 3, cells 6–21 in figure 9.1).

Another type of underground network consists of cells that communicate internally to coordinate cell activities but that also know about and communicate with other cells in the network. Organized crime networks often fit this pattern, as do urban drug gangs in particular (Levitt and Venkatesh, 2000). Here cross-cell communication is not for coordination purposes; it often arises simply because members of different cells know one another and interact socially. This type of interaction poses some risks for the network, and the fact that it occurs suggest an attitude of defiance toward government agencies. We call this an *integrated cross-linked network structure.*

A third type of underground network uses minimal communications. Except for interaction with the cell leader, cell members do not contact one another; in fact, they do not even know one another's identities and perhaps not even of their existence. Further, they know nothing about other cells and so obviously have no communications with them. This type of structure provides maximum security and is possible when tasks can be carried out by individuals and do not require coordination among cell members. Examples here include espionage networks and the more traditional drug distribution networks, which we refer to as drug rings to distinguish them from urban drug gangs. We call this type of structure an *isolated node network structure*.

A fourth type of communications pattern, communication across cells but not within cells, is an abstract possibility. But we know of no organization that fits this pattern, although it may be characteristic of some individual roles in cells that are otherwise integrated.

9.4 ADAPTING THE NETWORK MODEL

Cultural transmission processes are highly relevant for terrorist network cells for two major reasons. First, the level of enculturation of cell members relates to the levels of trust among members, to the level of commitment to the cell's mission, and to the degree of shared tacit understanding. These factors are crucial in the hostile environments in which terrorist cells commonly operate. Second, enculturation processes interact with cell demographics, according to the models we presented in earlier chapters; the enculturation characteristics of cells are related to the enculturation distribution of the recruitment pool, the rate of filling vacancies, and the likelihood of turnover of cell members.

To analyze terrorist organizations, we modified the network model presented in chapter 8 in several respects to make it appropriate for this context:

1. *Integrated cell structure.* In the network model of chapter 8, each person can influence every other person to some extent. Because of the restricted interaction patterns in the integrated cell structure of terrorist networks, many of these influence paths do not exist. Thus, in the modified model, only those links among members within cells and from the cell leader to the next higher level in the hierarchy are active, and they change according to the dynamics described in chapter 8. For all other dyads, $S_{ij,t} = 0$. These changes create a hierarchical influence structure.

2. *Lagged replacement.* In chapter 8, we assume that vacancies in the network are filled immediately. For a terrorist cell, it may take time to recruit and train a replacement member and to insert that person into the operational area of the cell. Thus, the adapted network model used here allows for lags in filling cell vacancies. We specify the replacement lag for a level k cell in figure 9.1 as L_k.

3. *External influences on network demographics.* Except for the enculturation level of entrants, all factors in the network model of chapter 8 are

endogenous. But many external factors may impact terrorist networks. Indeed, these external factors are likely linked to the policy alternatives available to counterterrorist agencies. They include disruption of recruitment, training, and insertion of new members; the possibility that turnover will be accelerated by capture; and the possibility that entire cells will be eliminated. Further, the consequences of these factors may vary with the hierarchical level of the network that they affect. Our analytical strategy involves introducing the various possibilities for external influence on the terrorist network as design variations; accordingly, we specify an exogenous probability of cell elimination, p_{cell}. Similarly, we view variations in the mean enculturation and standard deviation of the replacement pool ($\bar{C}_h$ and σ_{ch}), the replacment time lag (L_k), and the base turnover rate (γ_0) as due to exogenous influences—specifically, to counterterrorist policies.

4. *Noise in cultural transmission.* Finally, we have modified the cultural transmission process described in chapter 8 by adding a small natural decay term (α_{idecay}) of 2 percent to $C_{i,t}$ for cases of a completely isolated terrorist (the case where all interaction partners are missing due to vacancies). We also added small noise terms with standard deviations of .02 for changes in both $S_{ij,t}$ and $C_{i,t}$. In all other respects, the model used in this chapter is the same as that of the cohort condition in chapter 8. We use the cohort condition because terrorists entering the field at similar times are likely to have gone through similar training regimes (perhaps together) and thus to share a bond as new entrants to a hostile environment.

9.5 EFFECTS OF COUNTERTERRORISM STRATEGIES

We use the modified network model here to explore the possible impact of two general counterterrorism intervention strategies: (1) those that are directed toward removing terrorists from the network (i.e., influencing departures), and (2) those that are directed toward inhibiting replacement of vacancies in the network. We consider two specific versions of each strategy:

1. *Strategies for removal or departure of terrorists.* Of the two removal strategies considered, one involves incremental removal: when individual terrorists are identified, they are removed by capture or arrest one at a time. The other strategy involves removal of an entire cell. Once a terrorist is identified, surveillance could lead authorities back to the cell, or a cell may be discovered serendipitously or through infiltration. It would then be fully eliminated by arrests or other governmental actions.

2. *Strategies for inhibiting replacement of terrorists.* When vacancies occur in a terrorist network, the terrorist organization typically attempts to fill the

vacancies quickly with qualified replacements. One strategy that could be used to inhibit this process involves making it more difficult to obtain qualified replacements; possible actions include interfering with the recruitment and training activities of the terrorist organization. The expected outcome is that less qualified replacements will be used. A second strategy entails increasing the time it takes the terrorist organization to fill the vacancy. Interfering with recruitment and training and maintaining stricter border controls are possible actions that might produce this effect.

In evaluating the potential effectiveness of these strategies, we look at the consequences for various aspects of the operational capabilities of the terrorist network. Because cells at the lowest hierarchical level of the organization (e.g., level 3 in figure 9.1) typically carry out terrorist acts, we focus on outcomes manifested on cells at this level. Five types of outcomes are examined, each of which is plausibly associated the capabilities of the terrorist network:

1. *The mean enculturation level $(\overline{C}_t)$ of terrorists in the cells.* The mean enculturation level relates to the commitment of cell members to the cell objectives and to identity with the cell. Higher levels of enculturation are produced partly through selective recruitment and training. According to Atran (2003: A23), "Intense indoctrination, often lasting 18 months or more, causes recruits to identify emotionally with their terrorist cell, viewing it as a family for whom they are as willing to die as a mother for her child or a soldier for his buddies." Additional enculturation takes place through the socialization process after terrorists have joined a cell. The mean enculturation level is also related to cell viability because less enculturated individuals are more likely to turn over through alienation.

2. *The standard deviation of enculturation $(\sigma_{c,t})$ of terrorists in the cells.* The standard deviation of enculturation, or cultural heterogeneity, is related to cell cohesion. Lower heterogeneity promotes similarity of views and also increases intracell influence, since in the network model, interpersonal influence is a function of cultural similarity. And high heterogeneity increases turnover through alienation because a broader distribution of enculturation scores within a cell is associated with more members with lower enculturation levels.

3. *The mean cell size.* The capabilities of a cell are related to the number of members in the cell. A smaller cell is weaker because it is understaffed. To the extent that cell members are specialized—for example, if some are pilots, some are explosives experts, some are expert marksmen, and so forth—a cell that has lost members may also have lost expertise valuable to carrying out its mission.

4. *The mean number of cells with breaks in the chain of command.* Cells are connected to the organizational leadership through a hierarchical chain of

command, through which operational instructions are passed down to the cells. When this chain is broken through vacancies in positions at any higher hierarchical level linking the cell to the top of the hierarchy, the cell becomes isolated in terms of contact with the organizational leadership, and the organization is unable to direct and coordinate cell activities.

5. *The mean cultural influence of cell leaders.* Cell leaders with less influence are less effective in producing and maintaining high enculturation levels in the cell, with consequences described earlier. And since influence is associated with cultural similarity, less influence means that on average the leader has less cultural similarity with other cell members. When other cell members have less in common with the leader, they likely identify less with him or her, creating potential problems for the leader in controlling and coordinating cell activities.

9.6 SIMULATION DESIGN

We designed the simulation study to focus on variables in the model that would likely be influenced by the four governmental actions under consideration. For the removal or departure strategies, we consider both incremental and whole-cell tactics. Because incremental removal corresponds in the model to a higher base turnover rate, we adjust this parameter (γ_0) in experiments to study possible consequences. For elimination of an entire cell, we specify in the model a fixed probability that a cell will be eliminated in any given time period (p_{cell}).

We also model two strategies for inhibiting replacement. In the first, we make it more difficult to obtain qualified replacements. In the model, this corresponds to using replacements who are less culturally fit or less enculturated to the organization's ideals. That is, this strategy is operationalized as lower selectivity in hiring (a lower $\bar{C}_b$), and since the replacements have had less time to be socialized, we also use a higher dispersion (σ_{cb}) around the mean. The second inhibition strategy, increasing the time it takes the terrorist organization to fill vacancies, is examined by increasing the delay in the rate at which the model fills vacancies (L_k).

For comparison purposes, we also model a baseline condition with a low turnover rate, a zero probability of cell elimination, high selectivity, and a short delay in filling vacancies. We then systematically examine the effects of changing each of these settings in the simulation; in other words, we study conditions with all possible combinations of higher turnover, a nonzero probability of cell elimination, lower selectivity, and a longer delay in filling vacancies. The parameter settings for these conditions are given in appendix B.

We report findings for certain combinations of the possible strategies for removal and for inhibiting replacement, along with the baseline findings. In each condition, all cells start with a size of five individuals, and the simulation is run for thirty-six time periods (months) with no interventions to permit the cells to evolve naturally; the various counterterrorism strategies are then introduced in period 37 except for the baseline condition. The simulation then proceeds for 120 months. Each condition is run 100 times for the full network, and the averages across all sixteen level 3 cells for the 100 runs are reported.

9.7 Findings

We present findings for each of the five outcomes, broken down by effects of the two general types of intervention strategies, removal and replacement. For each strategy type, we examine the effects of each particular tactic, as well as both tactics combined. For comparison, we also report the baseline of no intervention.

Figure 9.4 displays the effects on the mean enculturation level ($\bar{C}_t$) of the level 3 cells in the simulated organization. The top half of the figure

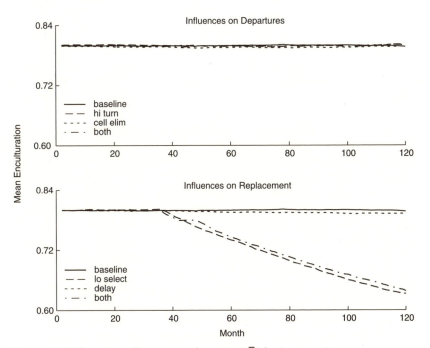

FIGURE 9.4 Terrorist cell mean enculturation ($\bar{C}_t$) by intervention strategy

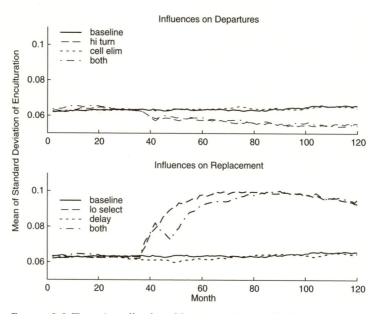

FIGURE 9.5 Terrorist cell cultural heterogeneity $(\sigma_{c,t})$ by intervention strategy

shows the effects of the removal or departure strategies. Obviously, neither the incremental strategy of increasing turnover (the line labeled "hi turn") nor eliminating cells (the line labeled "cell elim") affects the mean enculturation level relative to the baseline, whether these strategies are used individually or together. Thus, removal strategies have no discernible effect on mean enculturation in the model.

The bottom half of figure 9.4 plots the effects of the replacement inhibition strategies. It indicates that lowering selectivity (the line labeled "lo select") affects enculturation when implemented in period 37. Combining this strategy with delaying replacement ("delay") does not increase the effect. In fact, the mean enculturation level is slightly higher with the combination; as we have seen in chapter 6, mean enculturation tends to rise in decline, so the delay actually raises mean enculturation a bit. By these findings, the most effective way to affect enculturation through influencing replacement, then, seems to be to make it more difficult for the terrorist organization to find and recruit qualified replacements.

The effects on cultural heterogeneity—measured by the standard deviation of enculturation—are given in figure 9.5. For removal or departure strategies, a small effect is shown for incremental removal, which actually reduces cultural heterogeneity due to the increased susceptibility to socialization of new entrants. Cell elimination has no effect, primarily

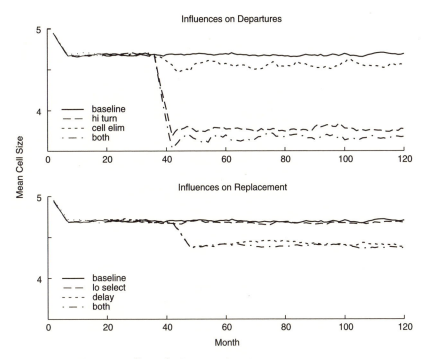

FIGURE 9.6 Terrorist cell size by intervention strategy

because there is no influence across cells in a cellular network (the eliminated cells are excluded from the calculation of the standard deviation because they are empty). The replacement inhibition strategy of delaying replacement has no effect. But lowering selectivity has a substantial effect in increasing the cultural heterogeneity of cells by adding less enculturated members to the cells.

The findings for the mean cell size outcome are shown in figure 9.6. The main effect of removal on cell size comes from increasing turnover. Eliminating cells yields a smaller effect when used alone, and also slightly increases the turnover effect when used in combination with it. Delaying replacement produces the obvious effect of reducing cell size, but lowering selectivity has no apparent consequence for cell size.

Figure 9.7 shows mean breaks in the chain of command. Increasing turnover creates more vacancies in positions linking cells and consequently more breaks. Eliminating cells has no apparent effect, but this is because empty cells at level 3 are excluded from the computation of mean breaks in the command chain. Replacement delays also contribute to the average number of breaks, but lowering selectivity does not.

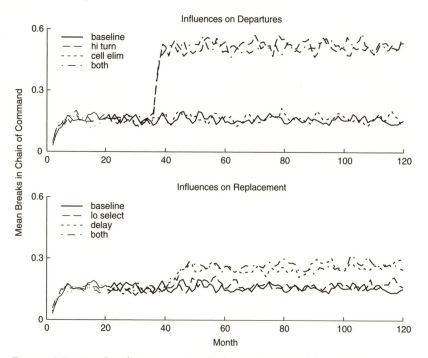

FIGURE 9.7 Mean breaks in terrorist cell chain of command by intervention strategy

Figure 9.8 shows effects of the various intervention strategies on the mean cultural influence of cell leaders. Increasing turnover actually strengthens the cell leader's influence, an interesting but nonobvious finding. High turnover promotes entry cohorts that may include a new leader; a similar effect of turnover on mean influence was observed in chapter 8 for the cohort condition. Cell elimination also contributes slightly to leader influence by mitigating the baseline tendency for leader influence to decline over time. Strategies to inhibit replacement have no noticeable effect on leader influence.

9.8 CONCLUSION

In this chapter, we modified the extended network model of chapter 8 to study the hierarchical cellular structure of terrorist networks. By manipulating model parameters, we illustrated how the model could be used as a tool to analyze the possible effects of various types of counterterrorism strategies on some characteristics related to the effectiveness of terrorist

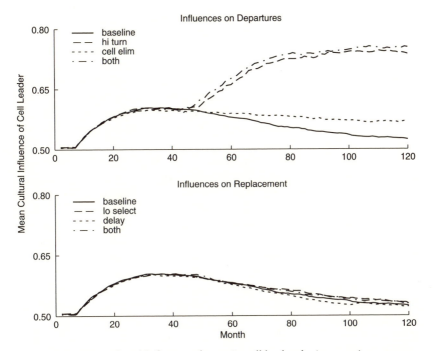

FIGURE 9.8 Mean cultural influence of terrorist cell leaders by intervention strategy

organizations. While some strategies apparently exert detrimental effects on terrorist capabilities, others seem to have little effect.

To be more specific, we summarize the findings from the terrorist network simulation as follows. For removal strategies, terrorist networks appear to be most vulnerable to the incremental removal of terrorists. Attempting to eliminate full cells has little apparent effect on the outcomes we examined and is also likely to be more difficult tactically; of course, it might still be a desirable action if the full cell membership is known, particularly if intelligence indicates that a terrorist act is imminent.[1] In terms of influencing replacement, delaying replacement of cell vacancies is the more viable strategy for reducing cell size and creating breaks in the chain of command. Efforts directed toward reducing the qualifications of terrorists, on the other hand, produce the expected

[1] Obviously, the effects of cell elimination can become dominant if the probability of cell elimination is set to a high enough level relative to the probability of incremental removal. The essential point here is that cellular networks are designed to be robust with respect to cell elimination—losses are compartmentalized—and they are effective in accomplishing this purpose. Incremental removal, by contrast, can have effects throughout the network.

effects of lowering the mean level and increasing the heterogeneity of cell culture. We had expected reducing qualifications (lower selectivity) to also reduce cell size and damage the chain of command indirectly by increasing turnover through alienation—and, to be sure, there are very small effects of this nature barely visible in the figures, but they are dominated by the effects of delaying replacement. Thus, the primary effect of reducing qualifications is the direct effect on cell culture, which can interfere with commitment to cell objectives, identification with the cell, and cell cohesion.

Perhaps the most striking inference to be drawn from this exercise is that while some actions can weaken terrorist networks, the networks still retain significant capabilities. These networks appear highly resilient and cannot be easily destroyed. We did not examine here the fast speed with which the networks recover when counterterrorism strategies are suspended. Nor did we explore how policies lose effectiveness when the terrorist organizations make their implementation more difficult through actions such as relocating training camps. When these factors are taken into account, it appears that persistence in the fight against terrorism is essential and that such an effort can at best reduce, but not eliminate, the terrorist threat.

More generally, this chapter illustrates how the cultural transmission model could be used for policy analysis. An important characteristic of the model is that it explicitly incorporates demographic processes that, in combination with internal organizational processes, produce outcomes that are sometimes not obvious and that can help sensitize policy makers to the complex dynamics of the consequences of potential actions.

This chapter further shows how the model can be adapted to specific organizational contexts. Organizational structure can be incorporated to develop a more fine-grained model; in this case, we adapted it to the structure of terrorist networks. By imposing constraints on the influence paths dictated by structural configurations of particular types of organizations, it could also be adapted for other purposes, such as examining cultural transmission processes in organizations with particular architectural structures, for example, the multidivisional organization (M-form) or the matrix organization. Model adaptations can also be based on environmental conditions, as we have done here in considering possible governmental counterterrorism policies. In other contexts, different exogenous factors could be built into the model. For example, the effects of changes or differences in labor markets could be considered through modifications in the selection and turnover processes designed for the situations of interest.

CHAPTER 10

Merging Cultures

10.1 INTRODUCTION

Corporate mergers and acquisitions usually occur because of the strategic or financial imperatives of one or both partner firms. For example, the merger between computer makers Hewlett-Packard (H-P) and Compaq was announced as "creating an absolute powerhouse in the market place" (Williams, 2001: A3). Similarly, when Daimler-Benz and Chrysler merged in 1999, the CEOs of both companies cited as motivation the increasing role of scale economies in a globalizing industry, as well as complementarities between the companies' products (Vlasic and Stertz, 2000). And the merger of hospitals between Stanford University and the University of California at San Francisco (UCSF) supposedly would "not only offer superior patient care but would provide financial stability that would ensure the medical centers' survival in a brutally competitive health care industry. Together, Stanford and UCSF would bargain more aggressively with insurance companies and suppliers, boosting revenues and saving money" (Feder, 2000: 1). Indeed, a recent academic review suggests that enhanced efficiency is the most common general motivation for mergers and acquisitions (Holmstrom and Kaplan, 2000).

Despite these market-based motivations, the success or failure of a merged corporation often depends on its ability to integrate effectively the two previously independent organizations and to operate as a coherent entity. Although integration may be thwarted by any number of factors, extant cultural differences between the organizations involved in a merger often prove problematic.[1] For instance, as the business press opined about Compaq's earlier merger with Digital Equipment Corporation: "The two cultures clashed as Compaq's high-volume, high-speed approach ran into Digital's low-volume system in which sales of big computers took time. The company was so distracted by the merger that it lost its long-standing crown as the largest seller of PCs to rival Dell" (McWilliams, 2001: A14). Likewise, the dismal performance of

---

[1]This is certainly not intended to say that cultural or other integration of two merger partners is always advisable.

DaimlerChrysler has been attributed to the difficulties of combining Daimler-Benz's hierarchical bureaucratic culture with Chrysler's free-wheeling creative culture (Vlasic and Stertz, 2000). And, after losing $176 million in twenty-eight months, the Stanford-UCSF hospital merger was dismantled because "the two hospitals had radically different cultures, which made the merger impossible in the end" (Pyati, 2000: 25).

Moreover, the increasing prevalence of cross-border mergers and acquisitions suggests that post-merger cultural conflict may be on the rise as national cultural differences may reinforce organizational differences. Certainly, the disappointing performance of contemporary high-profile cross-border mergers such as DaimlerChrysler suggests this possibility. Some observers predicted a similar fate for the European units involved in the Hewlett-Packard(H-P)/Compaq merger (Delaney and Woodruff, 2001).

Analyses such as these, which assess the compatibility or fit between two cultures to explain outcomes, focus on what we call in chapter 1 the content of culture.[2] Content-based cultural assessment is the dominant way that many observers, including social scientists, analyze the cultural aspect of mergers and acquisitions. In fact, this way of thinking is so engrained that some progressive firms such as Johnson & Johnson now use such analysis proactively: they systematically attempt to analyze cultural compatibility in assessing potential merger targets.[3]

Although not widely recognized, the post-merger integration of two cultures is a function of organizational demography as well as cultural content. To see the potential impact of demography, imagine two merger scenarios between hypothetical organizations with dissimilar and highly incompatible cultural contents. In the first merger, all members of both organizations possess lifetime job security; they cannot be terminated, and they are basically expected to remain in their positions until

---

[2]Cultural content may, in fact, be behind a broader set of reasons often offered for post-acquisition success and failure. For instance, a recent detailed economic analysis of two large mergers concludes that "in both cases, post-acquisition difficulties resulted because managers of the acquiring company did not understand deeply the target company. [For example,] despite the fact that [the acquirer] Cooper Industries had operations in [the target] Cameron Iron Work's industry (the petroleum equipment business), Cooper's management did not understand that its expertise in manufacturing technology and internal control would not translate into success for Cameron. As Cameron managers described it, Cooper did not understand that 'Cameron' was not a manufacturing business. It was a service business with a manufacturing component" (Kaplan, Mitchell, and Wruck, 1997). An objective post hoc analysis of this merger might regard its difficulties as arising from noncomplementary lines of business, which is true superficially, but ignores the fact that failure to understand something so basic likely reflects an impenetrable or deeply ingrained cultural difference.

[3]In the 1990s, Cisco Systems also used such analyses in assessing its many acquisitions.

retirement. In the second merger, organizational membership is fluid: members come and go with high frequency. In general, cultural integration should be easier to achieve in the second merger. Why? In our view, the cultural differences in the first merger will likely persist because they can be overcome only by transforming previously enculturated individuals. By contrast, the second merger can wash out extreme cultural differences through the departure of alienated individuals and their replacement with fresh ones more compatible with the preferred culture and more susceptible to enculturation. Underlying this conjecture is the presumption that it is easier to select and to socialize new organizational members than it is to resocialize existing members. In any event, it should be clear from these stylized scenarios that post-merger cultural integration involves demographic flows of personnel and associated socialization processes as much as it does the contents of the cultures being merged.

This chapter addresses the issue of cultural integration following mergers.[4] It does so by using the basic model, developed in chapter 4. In particular, we focus on demographic factors related to post-merger cultural integration and examine their implications for content-based factors such as cultural compatibility or fit. To apply the model to the cultural integration problem, we first simulate two separate organizations and then combine them into one post-merger organization. We next observe how the culture of the post-merger organization evolves over time. Simulation experiments vary the relative sizes of the merged entities and the growth rate, hiring practices, socialization processes, and turnover rates of the post-merger organization. We also look at the effects of cultural inertia in the acquired organizations, as well as any layoff policy used in dealing with the newly acquired employees. The primary outcomes of concern are the time paths of mean enculturation and cultural heterogeneity of the post-merger organization. Of particular interest are the conditions under which the post-merger organization quickly develops homogeneously and in the direction of management's preferred culture, or fails to do so in a reasonable time interval. In the conclusion, we consider the implications of our findings for the management of corporate mergers.

10.2 POST-MERGER CULTURAL INTEGRATION

The prevalence of unsuccessful corporate mergers presents a problem for many efficient market theories because strong versions of these theories hold that firms' officials and others involved in assessing the transaction

---

[4]Parts of this chapter are adapted from Carroll and Harrison (2002).

(e.g., financial analysts, underwriters) can make accurate cost-benefit calculations of the likelihood of success of the projected merger and then behave accordingly. That is, an efficient markets view might interpret a potential merger as a market opportunity that executives and financial people recognize, move to take advantage of it, and then reap ample rewards after consummation. Decisions and actions in this view of the world are forward-looking: current behavior is explained as a result of future expectations, which (in interpretations) are often assumed to be accurate (March, 1978).

Many reasons lie behind merger failure and the inability of markets to make full adjustments to the likelihood of merger failure (see Holmstrom and Kaplan, 2000). Although certainly not always the case, difficulties of cultural integration seem likely to be increasingly important as a cause of both problems.[5] As discussed in chapter 1, more and more firms today attempt to manage their cultures and to develop strong cultures. This implies that randomly chosen merger partners are more likely to include a strong-culture firm (or possibly even two such firms), which would presumably be more resistant to the changes required by integration than would a firm with a weaker culture.

Many observers note that despite the occasional lip service paid to cultural integration issues in a proposed merger, rarely do these concerns weigh heavily in decision making and firm valuation. A major factor behind such insufficient consideration is the lack of a precise, relevant theory about cultural content. Accordingly, there is no widely agreed upon way to assess content compatibility or incompatibility; and any kind of projected content combination can be plausibly argued as likely to bring about better performance (Weber, 1996). For instance, cultures assessed to be compatible can be pointed to in order to allay questions about integration difficulties, and cultures assessed to be incompatible can be seen as strengths of the merger because they will complement each other after integration.

Weber and Camerer (2003) emphasize a different potential problem of cultural integration. In their view, culture is local convention, whereby individuals develop highly idiosyncratic but efficient tacit communication skills, language, and knowledge (Kreps, 1990a). When persons following two such conventions are grouped together and required to communicate in a common way, those subscribing to at least one of the

---

[5]By searching the texts of business periodicals, we found some indirect evidence that culture is increasingly recognized as a major issue in recent years. We searched for articles containing the two words *merger* and *culture* in the Dow Jones list of selected publications, which includes major news and business publications, as well as the top fifty newspapers and wires. We found 1.95 percent of all articles contained these words in all years available. But from 1995 to 2003, 2.12 percent did, from 2000 to 2003, 2.50 percent did, and from 2002 to 2003, 2.83 percent did.

conventions will be required to drop their own (efficient) process and to learn another one. Moreover, the individuals who already know the dominant convention will be called upon to spend time and energy teaching it to the others. Thus, even if the cultural learning goes smoothly—and it may not—the process involves a transition period resulting in a temporary loss of efficiency, regardless of content compatibility. Weber and Camerer (2003) also argue that individuals will be more likely to ignore (or weight less heavily) hard-to-measure cultural factors than tangible and easily quantifiable features of a firm. This asymmetry in cognition means that the costs of integration fail to get fully considered and "leads to overestimation of the value of a merged firm at the time of the merger" (Weber and Camerer, 2003: 401).

An implicit assumption of almost all analyses of cultural integration is that individuals experience some sort of cultural inertia, in that they cannot instantaneously rid themselves of the values, norms, beliefs, and so forth of the prior culture and adopt those of the new one. Engrained habits and internalized values persist for some time, even when the context changes and incentives are amplified. Many observers report that identities and other prior cultural differences remain in merged companies years after the actual merger event. For instance, the cultural integration effort in the SmithKline Beecham merger of 1989 was still clearly in progress two years later (Burke and Jackson, 1991). Moreover, if the two cultures involved are each homogeneous, are intensely held, and display visible markers identifying respective members (with, say, different dress codes or speaking norms), the merger combination may be reactive itself, creating conflict and generating greater solidarity among members of the original cultures. For instance, one observer attending an H-P reception after the H-P/Compaq merger is reported by Tam (2003: A1) to have commented that he "'could tell the H-P folks from the Compaq folks right away.' The former Compaq employees, in suits and ties, huddled on one side of the room. Polo-shirted H-P staffers stood on the other."

Of course, structural conditions shape the extent to which integration might be problematic. Organizational size differences, in particular, seem to set the stage for the social interaction that drives much integration. Assuming random interaction among members of a post-merger organization means that the relative sizes of the two merger partners determine which group influences which the most, the members of the acquirer or those of the target.[6] With equal-sized partners, peer-based cultural influence would not necessarily favor any particular direction of change. With

---

[6]We do not intend to suggest that random interaction is likely to occur in a newly merged, or for that matter any, organization. Rather, we find this assumption useful in thinking about and isolating relative size effects. Obviously, other structural features such as geographic and hierarchical location need to be taken into account in any real setting.

unequal-sized partners, peer-based influence would be stronger from the larger group, creating a majority-minority influence pattern (Blau, 1977). Given that authority also rests with the acquirer, who can presumably use management-based influence tactics as well, the obvious expectation is that the greater the relative size of the acquirer, the easier and faster cultural integration should proceed in the combined unit.

Managers possess several direct levers that can be used to try to prevent cultural backlash and to facilitate integration. On the positive side, socialization efforts from management can be intensified, reducing peer-to-peer influence and increasing management influence. Managerial socialization activities might include seminars, cultural and behavioral training, incentives for desired behaviors, social activities such as beer blasts and parties, regular executive addresses and feedback sessions, personnel evaluations, and the like. On the negative side, managers can amplify the discomfort felt by those with do not fit well into the preferred culture, thereby making them more likely to leave the organization.

Anecdotes from the business world suggest that a period of confusion and uncertainty often plagues integration efforts that follow a merger, creating delays and long-lasting problems of resentment and identity as cultures clash. Currently touted best practice examples suggest that quick and decisive action regarding any post-merger reorganization, consolidation, and cultural change strongly facilitates integration. For instance, in the H-P/Compaq merger, the CEOs involved each appointed a senior executive to lead integration a month before the deal was even announced. These executives then assembled an integration team of thirty persons. The team studied past mergers, both successful and failed, to determine best practice: "The lessons: Offer rich retention plans and bonuses as Citigroup did to executives the company wanted to keep and create a unified culture to avoid the kind of divisions that have plagued AOL Time Warner. The H-P executives also realized that they had to choose swiftly between competing assets—departments, products and executives" (Tam, 2003: A1). When the deal closed, the team had already identified the stronger products in almost all categories. They also anointed 650 part-time internal cultural consultants to facilitate the integration of the culture. Although a definitive assessment on the integration process has yet to appear, the business press seems to think that H-P has done a better job with integration than most companies.[7]

---

[7]We speak here only of the organizational and cultural integration effort at H-P, not the strategic wisdom of the merger itself. Indeed, at the time of this writing most analysts claim the merger did not succeed strategically or financially. The contrast between the integration effort and the performance of the merged company led Loomis (2005: 56) to state: "If a thing is not worth doing, it is not worth doing well."

10.3 MODELING FRAMEWORK

To use the basic model of chapter 4 to study cultural integration, we begin by considering two separate organizations with different cultural ideals, each strongly embraced by their respective employees. We designate one of these organizations as the acquiring firm—its cultural ideal dominates after the merger—and the other the acquired, or target, organization. Because we are primarily interested in the cultural integration process, we designed a framework for the simulation experiments where the cultural ideals of the two organizations involved in the merger are essentially incompatible. Since the cultural representation scheme we use defines cultural fit according to an organization-specific scale, comparing across organizations requires positing a transformation rule between scales. Rather than tackle this issue generally, we focused on the condition of greatest substantive interest—high difference in content (a sort of inverse relationship between management cultural preferences in the two organizations where a high enculturation score on one implies a low score on the other). We designed the experiments to allow for the content differences of the two organizations to be at the same fairly high level for all experiments; thus, content differences are high but controlled. To simulate this context, we started two organizations each with high enculturation levels according to their pre-merger ideals, and then we reset the enculturation scores of all individuals in the target organization following the merger as follows: each individual in the target organization is randomly reassigned a new score drawn from a distribution with a (low) preset mean and standard deviation. We use random reassignment because we do not want to build in an exact relationship between the two culture scores of every individual in the target firm.

In some of the simulated conditions, we posit cultural inertia—a slow responsiveness of individuals in the target organization to the newly imposed cultural regime. We do this by specifying two versions of the socialization function so that the relevant set of peers operating through the peer socialization parameter is composed disproportionately of individuals from the target organization. In the case of strong, or full, cultural inertia, we restrict the socialization influence on members from the target organization to only those individuals who were also members of the target organization. In other words, despite the merger, these individuals are influenced only by their fellow survivors from the target organization with no management influence. In another condition, we let the peer influence of fellow survivors be proportional to the percentage of survivors from the target organization, with remaining peer influence coming from the full organization and additional influence from management.

Of course, these different inertia conditions might emerge naturally from the influence patterns of various employees in different interdependent locations in the two organizations, or they might be the result of staff assignments made by management in an attempt to control integration directly.

We treat the combined post-merger organization as a single organization and observe how its culture evolves over time. We pay special attention to the process of cultural integration in the three years (thirty-six elapsed months) following the merger. In particular, we examine two outcomes reflecting the extent of cultural integration: (1) average cultural fit of employees, indicated by the mean level of enculturation (with respect to the acquirer's ideal) in the merged organization; and (2) heterogeneity in the culture, indicated by the standard deviation of enculturation for the merged organization.

Because enculturation scores are immediately and accurately revised following the merger event, the modeling framework is consistent with a scenario where individuals experience a swift and clear understanding of cultural issues (as well as other possible scenarios). Thus, the best practice advice of quick and decisive action to reduce confusion and uncertainty can be seen as essentially implemented in all conditions. The framework therefore simulates conditions with great content differences in culture but no ambiguity about individuals' cultural standing.

10.4 Experimental design

Simulation experiments started by allowing each pre-merger organization to develop cultures independently for 120 simulation periods (ten simulation years), using hiring and management socialization strategies to achieve these outcomes. In these runs, the mean enculturation levels varied from .79 to .90 after ten simulation years, depending on demographic and cultural parameters. However, because enculturation is assumed to be based on different criteria in different organizations, the values are not comparable across organizations. Thus, we used a rule to reassign all values of one organization (the target) to the preference scale of the other. As explained earlier, our goal was to make the culture of the target unit incompatible with or very different from the acquiring organization (in terms of assessment of fit based on content). Thus, we reset the mean enculturation level of the target unit at .2 (with random assignment of enculturation scores to individuals based on a normal distribution); the tenures of the individuals in the target organization were preserved. We then combined the two organizations and let the new combined organization follow the previously set hiring practices, management socialization practices, strength of alienation, and turnover rates of the acquiring organization before the merger.

In these experiments, we attempt to identify the conditions under which the post-merger organization quickly develops a management-preferred homogeneous culture. The first outcome we examine is the mean level of enculturation ($\bar{C}_t$) in the post-merger organization. The second outcome we examine is cultural heterogeneity, measured as the standard deviation of the enculturation levels of the individuals ($\sigma_{c,t}$) in the organization. Given the general structure of the simulation experiments, the lower the cultural heterogeneity, the higher the level of cultural integration of the merged organization.

Experimental design choices here extend multiplicatively beyond our usual simulation setup. At least three sets of possibly varying parameters come to mind: those of the acquirer, those of the target, and those of the combined post-merger entity, which can contain new hires as well. To keep the analysis tractable, we use the same parameter settings for the acquirer and post-merger firm within a given variation—assuming continuity of behavior across the merger event. We use only several variations of basic model parameters such as the turnover rate, and we set these to be the same for the acquirer and the combined post-merger organization.[8]

We do, however, introduce variations for factors not in the basic model that potentially seem most important for cultural integration. These include (1) the layoff policy of the combined post-merger entity with respect to individuals from the target; (2) the extent and form of post-merger cultural inertia among individuals in the target organization; and (3) the organizational sizes of both acquirer and target, generating differences in the ratio of their sizes.

To be more specific, we examine the following variations:

Layoff policy. We simulate two different layoff policies imposed on the members of the target organization. In the baseline condition, there are no layoffs and target members are treated the same as other individuals with respect to turnover. In the layoff condition, we impose layoffs among target members such that three months after the merger event only 50 percent of these individuals will, on average, still be present in the post-merger organization. These layoffs occur to randomly chosen individuals from the target organization and are implemented monthly for three months with a constant rate.

---

[8]These settings are all consistent with research using the model reported in the preceding chapters and elsewhere. The settings for the variations used in the simulation are given in appendix B.

Cultural inertia in target. Recall from chapter 4 that the basic model of cultural transmission sets socialization-change intensity as

$$A_{i,t} = \frac{\alpha_{mgt}(1 - C_{i,t-1}) + \alpha_{peer}(\overline{C}_{t-1} - C_{i,t-1}) + \alpha_{decay}(0 - C_{i,t-1})}{\alpha_{mgt} + \alpha_{peer} + \alpha_{decay}} + e, \quad (10.1)$$

where e is a normally distributed error term with mean zero and α_{mgt}, α_{peer}, α_{decay} are parameters representing the pulls toward ideal socialization (from management), mean socialization level (from peer pressure), and zero socialization (from decay), respectively. Note that $\overline{C}_{t-1}$ in the peer influence component is calculated from all individuals in the post-merger organization, regardless of origin. We regard this specification as the baseline condition of no cultural inertia.

In the condition we call full inertia, we specify the peer influence component for individuals from the merger target as consisting only of other surviving members from the target and no management influence. That is, socialization-change intensity for these individuals becomes

$$A_{i,t}^* = (\overline{C}_{t-1}^* - C_{i,t-1}) + e, \quad (10.2)$$

where $\overline{C}_{t-1}^*$ is the mean enculturation of all individuals surviving from the target organization at $t - 1$.

In the condition we call proportional inertia, we specify the peer influence component for individuals from the merger target as pulled by both the full inertia process and the baseline process, with weights dependent on the proportion of target members surviving. Specifically, we let p_t represent the proportion of target members surviving at t relative to the target membership at merger time (i.e., $p_t = 1$ at the time of merger). To preserve the distribution of the error term in the ultimate socialization-change intensity function, we then redefine $A_{i,t}$ and $A_{i,t}^*$ to be exactly as previously, but without the error terms e added. Individuals from the target in this condition then experience socialization-change intensity as

$$A_{i,t}^{**} = (1 - p_t)A_{i,t} + p_t A_{i,t}^* + e, \quad (10.3)$$

where e is a normally distributed error term with mean zero and standard deviation σ_e.

Organizational sizes. We vary the sizes of the two organizations at the time of merger. Each organization is simulated with initial sizes of 50, 200, or 800 and no growth during the 120 pre-merger simulation periods, generating nine possible size combinations for the merger. In the analysis, we use the size ratio by dividing the merger size of the acquiring organization by the merger size of the acquired organization (target), so the size ratio varies from .0625 to 16.[9]

Hiring selectivity. Hiring selectivity is fixed for the target at an intermediate level by setting the mean of the hiring pool at $\overline{C}_h = .50$ (in terms of the cultural preferences of the pre-merger management of the target firm). For the acquirer and post-merger organization, hiring selectivity varies simultaneously across three conditions: high selectivity ($\overline{C}_h = .80$), medium selectivity ($\overline{C}_h = .50$), and low selectivity ($\overline{C}_h = .20$). In all cases, the recruitment rate varies simultaneously with the hiring pool mean, with $r_r = -\log(\overline{C}_h)$.

Socialization. In the target organization, socialization is fixed for all experiments as a mixed management-peer process with $\alpha_{mgt} = .49$ and $\alpha_{peer} = .49$. In the acquirer and post-merger organizations, socialization varies simultaneously at three levels: management dominated ($\alpha_{mgt} = .80$ and $\alpha_{peer} = .18$), mixed ($\alpha_{mgt} = .49$ and $\alpha_{peer} = .49$), and peer dominated ($\alpha_{mgt} = .18$ and $\alpha_{peer} = .80$).

Turnover. Baseline turnover for the acquirer and target organizations is fixed at $\gamma_0 = .015$ For the post-merger organization, we vary baseline turnover simultaneously from a low setting of $\gamma_0 = .005$ to a high setting of $\gamma_0 = .015$.

Alienation. The alienation level of the target is fixed with $\gamma_1 = .15$. We vary the alienation level simultaneously in the acquirer and the post-merger organization by setting the γ_1 parameter to either .15 or .6 for weak or strong alienation effects, respectively.

Growth rates. Before the merger, the growth rate for both organizations is set to zero. After the merger, we simulate three conditions for growth of the post-merger entity: (1) negative growth, a stochastic growth rate of $r_g = -.04$ per simulation period (month); (2) no growth, a growth rate of zero; and (3) positive growth, a stochastic growth rate of $r_g = .04$ per period.

Trials. Each simulation begins by running the two separate organizations for 120 periods. Then the cultural mean for the acquired organization is reset by generating new cultural scores from a normal distribution with a mean of .2 and a standard deviation of .1 (with a minimum of zero), the two organizations are merged, and the evolution of the merged organization using the pre-merger background conditions of the acquiring organization is observed for an additional 36 periods. The simulation is run separately for each of 5,832 different conditions, corresponding to all possible combinations of three growth settings, three cultural inertia settings, two alienation settings, two base turnover settings, two layoff policy settings, three management socialization settings, three hiring selectivity settings, and nine size settings

---

[9]We also analyzed the simulation output data using dummy variables for each size setting and using logs of size and their interactions; the findings did not differ substantively from the analysis using the size ratio, so we report only the size ratio findings.

(three for each pre-merger organization).[10] Each condition is simulated ten times, and the findings we present are averages across the ten runs.

10.5 SYSTEM DYNAMICS

Figure 10.1 helps to comprehend the demographic system generated by the simulation. It depicts visually the demographic flows in the combined post-merger organization. The post-merger organization consists of the union of three sets of people, defined by their relationship to the merger: those survivors originally from the acquirer, those survivors originally from the target, and those hired after the merger. Each of these sets is

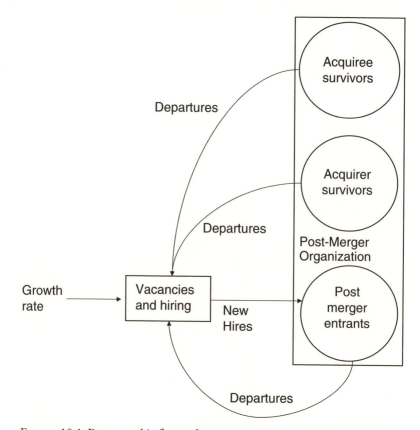

FIGURE 10.1 Demographic flows after merger

[10]In the full cultural inertia setting, the variations for socialization apply only to those individuals not from the target.

represented by a circle on the right-hand side of the figure. In terms of demographic flows of personnel, all three will experience outflows or departures after the merger. The levels of these departures depend on the base turnover rate of the model as well as the alienation rate. The number of people departing because of alienation is also affected directly by the enculturation mean of the post-merger organization and indirectly by the characteristics of the base of people available to socialize their peers. In addition to these effects, departures from the target people or acquirees also depend uniquely on the layoff policy of the merger, as well as the degree and form of cultural inertia among the target people. When a person departs from any of the three sets, it generates a vacancy so long as the organization is not contracting due to negative growth. Vacant slots would be filled more or less quickly depending on the hiring selectivity policy in effect. Newly hired individuals enter into the set of post-merger people; they may also depart at any time.

It should be obvious that if the system operates long enough, the post-merger entrants will dominate the newly merged organization and eventually be exclusively represented. Such an eventuality, however, may take a very long time. Among other things, peer socialization in the newly merged organization depends on the enculturation levels of individuals in all three sets. This means that newly hired post-merger people may serve to slow the departures of people from the other two sets, if they are hired selectively, by increasing their enculturation scores.

The figure should help one to appreciate how the dynamics of the system might lead to some unexpected occurrences. Consider, for instance, a condition of zero growth, layoffs in the target, and low selectivity in hiring. Here the many people laid off from the target will be balanced by new hires to keep the size of the organization stable. The remaining target people may have higher enculturation scores than the newly hired people, however, implying that it is possible the target people will contribute positively to the socialization of the post-merger set.

A detailed examination of the sample paths of the post-merger organization for various conditions shows, surprisingly, that in a number of situations the cultural heterogeneity of the merged organization actually rises for a period of time.[11] This tendency can be glimpsed in figure 10.2, which graphs the cultural heterogeneity (standard deviation of $C_{i,t}$) of the original target organization members across time for all conditions. Obviously, many sets of target individuals increase in heterogeneity, especially in the first twelve months. As we will see later, this can lead to increased heterogeneity in the whole post-merger organization. Note

---

[11]By contrast, the mean level of enculturation in the merged organization rises steadily throughout the simulation.

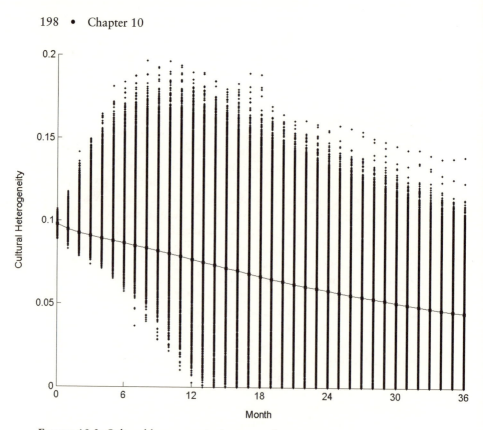

FIGURE 10.2 Cultural heterogeneity in target after merger

also that, in many instances, the heightened heterogeneity persists to month 36. Nonetheless, the dominant pattern in the simulations is of decreasing heterogeneity among the sets of target individuals. This can be seen in the figure by the solid line drawn through the points, which charts the median trajectory of heterogeneity among all the simulated conditions. Understanding the difference between these cases and those where heterogeneity rises may provide some clues as to when mergers go awry culturally. After analyzing the basic patterns in the simulated merged organization, we return to this issue by isolating these cases and examining the behavior of the three sets of people within them.

10.6 FINDINGS

The dynamics of demographic processes can be as important as any eventual equilibrium distribution (Sørensen, 2004). Thus, we analyzed the time paths of the cultural distributions in the simulated organization in depth.

We started by looking at plots of both mean enculturation and cultural heterogeneity in the combined post-merger organization over time by selected specific conditions. We then examined the differences in outcomes generated for variations in each parameter, looking at the median trajectory for a condition and collapsing the data across all other conditions (i.e., not controlling for any other variations). These plots revealed that some within-parameter variations produce big effects while others can hardly be detected. Among those showing small (barely) discernible effects are layoff policy, cultural inertia mechanism, growth, and turnover. We find it especially surprising that random layoffs and inertia show such little impact. By contrast, we see big effects across variations in size ratio, hiring selectivity, socialization, and alienation. Although there are complications, these generally show the intuitively expected effects: increasing the mean and reducing heterogeneity when the size ratio (acquirer/target) is big, hiring selectivity is high, socialization is primarily management based, and alienation is strong.

Figures 10.3 and 10.4 present these plots for variations in the alienation parameter (the low-alienation condition is denoted as "lo alien"; the high-alienation condition is "hi alien"). Obviously, for both the mean and the standard deviation of enculturation, the median for the low- and high-alienation conditions start at the same point and then diverge over time, only to begin to come back together somewhat near the ending time of the simulation. The maximal divergence appears

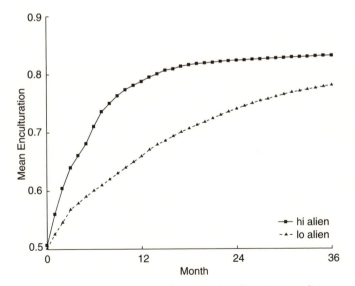

FIGURE 10.3 Post-merger enculturation by alienation condition

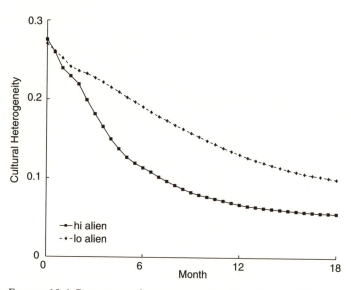

FIGURE 10.4 Post-merger heterogeneity by alienation condition

in both plots to be between five and eighteen months. Thus, these variations in the alienation parameter produce effects in dynamics and levels of the outcomes.

Of course, the patterns seen in such uncontrolled plots might be misleading, since the model processes are highly interdependent. In an attempt to isolate the effects of variations net of such interdependencies, we estimated regression models from the simulated data. In doing this, we first used all the data and introduced control variables both for the value of the dependent variable at time of merger and for the time elapsed since the merger (a log month variable works best). For ease of interpretation, with one exception, we also contructed dummy variables for each set of within-parameter variations and entered each set, minus an omitted contrast condition, into the equation. The exception is the size ratio variable, which contains nine conditions and is straightforward to interpret. Table 10.1 shows estimated equations for both outcome variables.

The regression estimates show that higher hiring selectivity, management-based socialization, strong alienation, a big size ratio, and layoffs in the target all serve to increase the mean level of enculturation, although the size ratio effect attenuates with time since the merger (see the interaction effect in the middle equation). Higher turnover, growth (positive or negative), and cultural inertia exhibit the opposite effects. Cultural heterogeneity is reduced with higher hiring selectivity (although in nonlinear

TABLE 10.1
Regressions of cultural outcomes in merged organization

	Mean level of enculturation $\bar{C}_t$	Mean level of enculturation $\bar{C}_t$	Standard deviation in enculturation $\sigma_{c,t}$
Constant	.102*	.049*	.285*
Dependent variable at merger	.448*	.448*	.056*
Log month since merger	.073*	.093*	−.055*
Selectivity[a]			
High	.129*	.129*	−.017*
Med	.076*	.076*	−.018*
Socialization[b]			
By management	.176*	.176*	.048*
Mixed	.123*	.123*	.031*
Turnover[c]			
High	−.002*	−.002*	.0004*
Alienation[d]			
High	.067*	.067*	−.052*
Growth[f]			
Negative	−.002*	−.002*	−.0002*
Positive	−.015*	−.015*	.009*
Size ratio (acquirer/target)	−.002*	.015*	−.004*
Layoffs in target[g]			
Yes	.004*	.004*	.001*
Inertia in target[h]			
Proportional	−.003*	−.003*	.006*
Full	−.004*	−.004*	.012*
Size ratio × log month since merger		−.0066*	
R squared	.848	.873	.699
N	209,952	209,952	209,952

Note: Data are across all conditions and times.
*$p < .05$.
[a]Omitted condition is low selectivity.
[b]Omitted condition is peer socialization.
[c]Omitted condition is low turnover.
[d]Omitted condition is low alienation.
[f]Omitted condition is no growth.
[g]Omitted condition is no layoffs.
[h]Omitted condition is no inertia.

fashion), strong alienation, negative growth, and a big size ratio. Heterogeneity rises with (surprisingly) management-based socialization, higher turnover, positive growth, layoffs in the target, and both mechanisms of cultural inertia. Overall, the most straightforward effect consistent with managerial goals of increasing mean enculturation and reducing heterogeneity as quickly as possible comes from the high-alienation condition. Other variables produce either undesirable effects on the two outcomes (e.g., turnover, growth, inertia), inconsistent effects across the two outcomes (e.g., management-based socialization, layoffs), or possibly time-dependent nonlinearities (e.g., hiring selectivity, size ratio).

Although all effects are significant because of the large sample size, these estimates generally reinforce the impressions gleaned from our inspection of plots not shown here, except alienation. Relatively small coefficients are associated with the turnover, growth, layoff policy, and inertia variables. Larger effects are associated with hiring selectivity, management-based socialization, alienation, and size ratio.

Table 10.2 shows estimates of very similar models for the simulated data cut into cross sections at two different points in time, six months and thirty-six months. The only difference in the models is that the elapsed time since merger variable and its interaction with the size ratio have been dropped. Comparing estimates across the two cross sections allows us to see more concretely how any time-dependent effects might be operating. For the most part, the estimates in this table agree with those reported in table 10.1. However, the source of the nonlinear effect of hiring selectivity now seems clear: high hiring selectivity actually increases heterogeneity in the short run. Undoubtedly, this is because the immediate post-merger organization is generally characterized by a low mean level of enculturation, and hiring very selectively (from a pool with a high mean) introduces more variability. Note also that the effects of hiring selectivity are greater in the later period, once the transition has eased. Further, note that again the single effect consistently producing managerially desirable effects on the outcomes at both times is high alienation.

Regression estimates track the central (mean) tendencies in the data, of course.[12] But as we see in figure 10.2, considerable variation occurs

---

[12] Although we do not report the estimates here, we have run regressions similar to those in table 10.1 with variables measuring directly the demographic flows of individuals into and out of the various sets of people demarcated in figure 10.1. We regard this as an attempt to control for the disruption effect identified in chapter 6. These demographic flow variables do show significant effects on the trajectories of both the mean of enculturation and its standard deviation. However, after controlling for these flows, we still see the same general pattern of effects for the experimental conditions shown in table 10.1.

TABLE 10.2
Regressions for merged organization at months 6 and 36

	Mean level of enculturation at month $t = 6$ $\bar{C}_t$	Standard deviation in enculturation at month $t = 6$ $\sigma_{c,t}$	Mean level of enculturation at month $t = 36$ $\bar{C}_t$	Standard deviation in enculturation at month $t = 36$ $\sigma_{c,t}$
Constant	.141[*]	.142[*]	−.435[*]	.124[*]
Dependent variable at merger	.710[*]	.199[*]	.238[*]	−.057[*]
Selectivity[a]				
High	.101[*]	.012[*]	.152[*]	−.042[*]
Medium	.061[*]	−.006[*]	.089[*]	−.030[*]
Socialization[b]				
By management	.107[*]	.062[*]	.226[*]	.035[*]
Mixed	.071[*]	.042[*]	.162[*]	.022[*]
Turnover[c]				
High	−.001[*]	.0004	−.003[*]	.002[*]
Alienation[d]				
High	.089[*]	−.048[*]	.040[*]	−.034[*]
Growth[f]				
Negative	.0000	.0013	.0004	−.006[*]
Positive	−.007[*]	.0011	−.027[*]	.021[*]
Size ratio (acquirer/target)	−.003[*]	−.006[*]	−.002[*]	−.002[*]
Layoffs in target[g]				
Yes	.0021	.004[*]	.003[*]	.0007
Inertia in target[h]				
Proportional	−.009[*]	.010[*]	.0003	.002[*]
Full	−.014[*]	.018[*]	.003	.007[*]
R squared	.929	.772	.741	.492
N	5832	5832	5832	5832

Note: Data are across all conditions and times.
[*]$p < .05$.
[a]Omitted condition is low selectivity.
[b]Omitted condition is peer socialization.
[c]Omitted condition is low turnover.
[d]Omitted condition is low alienation.
[f]Omitted condition is no growth.
[g]Omitted condition is no layoffs.
[h]Omitted condition is no inertia.

around the median trajectories. Of special substantive interest for post-merger cultural integration are those conditions where cultural heterogeneity actually rises over time, because this pattern reflects a situation where integration likely appears to organizational participants as failing. To identify these conditions and the ways in which they cause cultural heterogeneity to increase, we selected all observations where the standard deviation of enculturation rises between two points in time and calculated mean values for each of the parameters for the condition (plus the time period) for the acquirer and acquiree subsets shown in figure 10.1 and for the full organization. These means are shown in table 10.3.

The first thing to note about table 10.3 is that rising heterogeneity is not a rare occurrence. This can be seen by comparing the number of observations (shown in the last row) across the columns. The first column in table 10.3 shows the means for the full sample. It reflects exactly the experimental design of the simulation. For example, each of the three selectivity conditions shows a mean of .333 because these variations were run in equal proportions across all other conditions. The next three columns of means are calculated for each of the three subsets of people only for cases where cultural heterogeneity rises. By comparing the means in these columns with those in the first (the full sample), the over- or underrepresentation of a condition in the rising heterogeneity cases can be inferred. By comparing the means of these columns with each other, the locations of greatest increases in heterogeneity can be inferred. For instance, when selectivity is high, heterogeneity rises in all three sets of people because the means of .407, .366, and .860 all are greater than the design factor of .333. Also, in cases where the heterogeneity of the acquirer rises, high selectivity is especially prevalent.

Among the more interesting findings in table 10.3 is the comparison for management-based socialization, which shows that strong management socialization can lead to rising heterogeneity in the post-merger organization because of its effects on those individuals from the target. Likewise, we find it interesting that the no-cultural-inertia condition makes it less likely that heterogeneity will rise in the post-merger entity but more likely to rise among target-based people (but not those from the acquirer), while full inertia tends to produce the opposite effects. Finally, note that high alienation also tends to lessen overall heterogeneity in the post-merger organization but that it does induce higher heterogeneity in the group from the target. Obviously, even when heterogeneity is declining in the whole post-merger organization, it may be rising among the target people, suggesting that they are often in for a rocky experience.

TABLE 10.3
Comparison of means for various scenarios of increasing heterogeneity

	Full sample: all cases	Cases where heterogeneity of merged organization rises	Cases where heterogeneity of former target rises	Cases where heterogeneity of former acquirer rises
Month	18	8.7	15.3	7.96
Selectivity				
High	.333	.407	.366	.860
Medium	.333	.267	.336	.140
Low	.333	.326	.298	0
Socialization				
By management	.333	.454	.521	.002
Mixed	.333	.332	.358	.336
By peers	.333	.214	.121	.662
Turnover				
High	.500	.503	.502	.498
Alienation				
High	.500	.325	.580	.452
Growth				
Negative	.333	.359	.344	.306
Positive	.333	.344	.327	.338
Zero	.333	.297	.329	.306
Size ratio				
(acquirer/target)	3.0625	.997	3.575	.230
Size				
Acquirer at merger	350	117	393	107
Target at merger	350	661	315	602
Layoffs in target				
Yes	.500	.426	.489	.500
Inertia in target				
No	.333	.231	.830	.322
Proportional	.333	.329	.082	.336
Full	.333	.441	.088	.342
No. of observations	209,952	13,795	44,916	8,047

10.7 Discussion

It is widely recognized that achieving cultural integration in a newly merged organization is difficult and sometimes even impossible. Prior cultural differences between two merged entities often persist for months and years, possibly generating conflict and rendering the organization less effective. Indeed, the widespread inability of mergers to accomplish their goals frequently gets blamed on the failure to integrate the cultures of the merging organizations.

Cultural integration following a merger is almost always analyzed in terms of the contents of the organizational cultures involved. The basic question raised is, Are the cultures compatible or consistent? Analyses then focus on how the various elements of the cultures might be reconciled, compromised, or emboldened in an organization's operation. Both popular and scholarly assessments tend to use this mode of reasoning.

While clearly insightful, the content-based approach to studying cultural integration following a merger also has limitations (see chapter 1). First, these analyses are often conducted at a high level of abstraction, and it is difficult to know how much of an organization's culture is captured by simple characterizations such as hierarchical or freewheeling. Second, there is no developed theory guiding the assessments of cultural elements as compatible or not; the assessments tend to be intuitive and ad hoc (or post hoc) in most instances. Third, since many cultural phenomena are tacit, judging how people will react to their alteration is a daunting task for social science. It seems to us that such reactions likely depend on the particular phenomena involved, as well as the process by which their alteration is attempted.

A complementary way to assess cultural integration following a merger is to examine the demographic dynamics underlying the organizational cultures. When the demographics of two merger partners show fluid movement of individuals into and out of the organizations, then it seems that cultural integration might be achieved more quickly than if the two partners show stagnant demographics with little movement in and out. The primary assumption behind such a conjecture is that it is easier to recruit and socialize new individuals to the cultural ideals of the merged organization than it is to resocialize and retrain incumbents already inculcated in the ways of one or the other partner.

We examined post-merger cultural integration using the basic model of organizational cultural transmission from chapter 4. We began by setting up the research problem by assuming that the content differences among merging organizations are very strong. We then investigated how quickly cultural integration might be achieved under a variety of commonly seen demographic conditions.

In terms of outcomes, our simulation experiments looked at the mean enculturation level of individuals in the merged organization, reflecting management's cultural preferences, and the standard deviation of the enculturation levels of the individuals in the merged organization, reflecting cultural heterogeneity.

The findings suggest that while post-merger cultural integration is influenced by many demographic processes, the strongest effects are associated with hiring selectivity, management-based socialization, high alienation, and a large size ratio. Moreover, among these conditions only high alienation consistently across time produced the managerially desired goals of high mean enculturation and lower cultural heterogeneity. Other conditions showed either small or inconsistent effects in terms of likely managerial goals for post-merger cultural integration. These included the commonly used tactic of laying off individuals who came from the acquired (target) organization (unless layoff decisions are based on enculturation and thereby capitalize on the alienation effect). Furthermore, comparative examination of the cases where heterogeneity rises suggests that conditions such as high alienation that reduce overall heterogeneity in the post-merger unit often increase heterogeneity among the target people while accomplishing this task.

The implications of these findings for managerial policy are straightforward but should be treated with caution given their harshness. According to the model, the fastest and most consistent way to achieve cultural integration consists of ramping up the alienation effects, that is, making individuals who are a long distance from the cultural ideal feel so uncomfortable that they will leave (or simply removing these individuals). In the process, we expect that cultural heterogeneity among those from the acquired (target) organization may rise, possibly because some of them respond quickly while others do not. A transitory period of turmoil would not be surprising.

CHAPTER 11

Culture, Aging, and Failure

11.1 INTRODUCTION

In his classic discussion of the liability of newness, Stinchcombe (1965) anticipated a relationship between organizational culture and failure. Specifically, Stinchcombe observed that new organizations are typically peopled with strangers attempting to invent and learn new roles. He argued that socialization may be especially problematic under such conditions. A reasonable interpretation of Stinchcombe's argument holds that cultural heterogeneity will be high in new organizations and this makes it difficult to develop goals and routines. By this argument, the heterogeneity of culture should affect organizational mortality rates. Moreover, cultural variations might account in part for negative age dependence in organizational mortality, a common empirical pattern (see Carroll and Hannan, 2000).

Insightful as his effort is, Stinchcombe's analysis of socialization in new organizations relies on an overly simple model of the demographics of employment. Notice that Stinchcombe's arguments are based on what is essentially a cohort analysis of the initial employees of a firm: they start out as strangers attempting to do new things, and with time they become more familiar with themselves and their interdependent activities. The problem is that the employment base of a new firm typically changes quickly and sometimes even radically. The initial members often leave (at least some of them), and new members enter, perhaps in large numbers. Departures likely affect the established culture within the organization, and new members require socialization and mutual adjustment by incumbent members.

Given various demographic inflows and outflows, the changing mix of persons in the organization implies that the exact same arguments advanced by Stinchcombe might generate different forms of age dependence in mortality. Consider, for instance, a new small firm with high turnover and a growth trajectory of three phases: a first that starts slow, a second that accelerates rapidly, and then a third that stabilizes at a lower growth rate. It would seem that the high-growth second period would be characterized by the greatest cultural variability within the organization, and hence would possess the greatest instability in social relations and difficulty in learning and mutual adjustment. It would also possess the highest turnover rates and consequently the greatest probability of shrinking to zero size. If so, then the implied pattern of age dependence in mortality would resemble an inverted U: the chances of mortality would rise and then decline with organizational age, a pattern that has been described as a honeymoon effect (see Carroll and Hannan, 2000). Of course, it is not difficult to impose other conditions on this scenario that would seem to change the prediction (e.g., let the hiring be based on cultural fit with the initially established norms). In addition, there are many other growth scenarios to consider before we might arrive at a general prediction for a typical organizational population.[1]

This chapter can be viewed as a friendly follow-up to Stinchcombe's (1965) analysis. It allows for rigorous theoretical investigation of the role of culture in organizational aging and mortality under more complex and realistic demographic conditions.[2] It does so with a macro version of the cultural transmission model. The macro model allows for incorporation of appropriate variables—organizational age, size, and culture—into the organizational growth-decline process. We develop these model modifications in the chapter by linking to organizational culture the rates at which new organizational members are added to and dropped from the organization. We envision organizational death as occurring when the size of the organization shrinks to zero members. We use this setup to investigate questions about the relationship between organizational culture and the probability of death. Specifically, we investigate the relationships between cultural heterogeneity and age and size dependence in mortality rates.

11.2 MACRO MODEL FRAMEWORK

The basic cultural transmission model developed in chapter 4 is a multilevel model. It is macroscopic in that it represents an entire organization and the structure of the cultural system that develops within it. It is a micro model in the sense that individual behavior and processes such as socialization and turnover are modeled directly. The model is limited, however, in its representation of organization growth, where the model

---

[1] The potential complexity of the phenomenon might seem overwhelming and intractable. In our view, however, neither the complexity of the employment dynamics of new firms nor the mixing of growth scenarios in a population is intractable with a formal model and simulation techniques. This is again a case where the various parts of the processes seem to be understood well enough to describe mathematically—the complexity arises from their interdependence in the system, especially as it unfolds over time.

[2] Parts of the chapter are adapted from Harrison and Carroll (2001a).

specifies a constant rate of growth (r_g). The organizational size distribution implied by this specification does not correspond to observed size distributions of organizations. Given the importance of size and growth for many organizational characteristics, this limitation makes it difficult—if not impossible—to link the model of culture to other macro phenomena in plausible ways.[3]

To link internal cultural processes explicitly with macro phenomena, we develop here a macro version of the cultural transmission model. The macro model modifies the specification of organizational growth so that it produces realistic size distributions for a set of simulated organizations. This task is accomplished by using a new growth function and decomposing it into processes of individual arrivals and departures (as we explain in detail later). We also specify aggregate functions for the cultural system at the organizational level. These functions give the distribution of enculturation at any point in time for given demographic settings without using the individual-level hiring, socialization, and turnover functions in the basic model of chapter 4. The specified functions are not derived exactly from the basic multilevel model but (we believe) capture the essentials of the same processes. In this regard, the macro model should be regarded as a translation rather than a derivation or extension. A major advantage of the translation is computational efficiency.

Model Translation

To develop the macro version of the model, we start by noting the definitional relation between organizational size and demographic flows over time. Since the relevant clock in the growth model is organizational age rather than historical time, we designate organizational age as τ, noting that $\tau = t - t_f$ where t_f is time of organizational founding. As described in chapter 4, N_τ denotes organizational size at τ, $N_{D,\tau}$ the number of individuals departing between τ and $\tau + 1$, and $N_{B,\tau}$ the number entering the organization in the same interval. Then for any interval $N_{\tau+1} = N_\tau + N_{B,\tau} - N_{D,\tau}$.

Our modeling strategy is to use this relationship to find the number of persons entering the organization, after we have found realizations based on the specifications for growth and departures. (The initial size of the organization N_0 is determined by a draw from an exponential distribution with a median size of five.) Based on these variables and

---

[3]There are obviously other limitations to the model as well. For example, organizational age is not in the model, yet age places bounds on the tenure or length of service distribution of individuals.

other assumptions consistent with the multilevel model, we then calculate the organization's variation in enculturation and observe mortality events when the organization shrinks to zero size.

Turnover

Consider first turnover at the organizational level. Recall that in the basic model of chapter 4, individual-level turnover is given by the hazard rate for individual i in period τ as $r_{i,\tau} = \gamma_0 + \gamma_1[1 - C_{i,\tau-1}]^3$, where both γ_0 and γ_1 are parameters, the first indicating a baseline rate of departure and the second associated with alienation (an individual's distance from the ideal enculturation score). We work here with a specification that bases alienation on cultural distance from the other members of the organization rather than from some ideal score, as we did in chapter 8. We do this by making alienation a function of an individual's squared distance from the cultural mean $\bar{C}$, giving an individual hazard rate of

$$r_{i,\tau} = \gamma_0 + \gamma_1[C_{i,\tau-1} - \bar{C}_{\tau-1}]^2. \tag{11.1}$$

From this specification, we derive the expected individual turnover rate r^* as

$$r_\tau^* = E[r_{i,\tau}] = \gamma_0 + \gamma_1 \sigma_{c,\tau-1}^2, \tag{11.2}$$

where $\sigma_{c,\tau-1}^2$ is the variance in organizational culture. We can then calculate for any given time period the number of departures $N_{D,\tau}$ in the organization by using a binomial distribution with parameters n and p, where n is set as the number of individuals $N_{\tau-1}$ in the organization at time $\tau - 1$ and $p = 1 - e^{-r_\tau^*}$. For small values of r_τ^*, the binomial distribution behaves like a Poisson with an absorbing state. In simulations reported later in this chapter, we simultaneously vary γ_0 and γ_1 to represent conditions with high and low base turnover and alienation.

An interesting and attractive feature of this modeling framework is that the number of persons expected to depart in a period can equal the current size of the organization. This is especially likely for small organizations. In these instances, we regard the organizations as "shrinking" to their deaths and consider them as dying in that period. When this happens, we flag the mortality event, record the organization's relevant information, and move on to the next organization. The macro model thus represents organizational mortality as an absorption process that occurs when organizational size reaches zero.[4]

---

[4]There is a similarity in imagery here with that of Levinthal's (1991) model of organizational mortality.

Organizational Growth

Now consider organizational growth. Recall that one of the primary motivations for developing the macro model is to yield realistic portrayals of population size distributions. We do this by modifying the well-known Gibrat's law for organizational growth to incorporate information about organizational age τ and size N. In Gibrat's law, $N_{\tau+1} = N_\tau \exp \varepsilon$ where $\varepsilon = \sigma v$, σ (the stochastic growth standard deviation) is a constant, and v is a random normal disturbance with mean of zero and standard deviation of unity (Sutton, 1997). Because Gibrat's law does not represent many empirical size distributions of organizations accurately, we modify it to let the standard deviation in growth be a function of both age and size. Specifically, we set

$$\sigma_\tau = \lambda_0 + \lambda_1 \exp (\lambda_2 \tau) + \lambda_3 N_\tau^{\lambda_4}. \tag{11.3}$$

In the simulations reported in the following, we use parameter settings where $\lambda_0 > 0, \lambda_1 > 0, \lambda_2 < 0, \lambda_3 > 0$, and $\lambda_4 < 0$. Thus, the variance in growth decreases with both age and size.

We expect that the growth rates of organizations will vary more when they experience higher levels of turnover, since high turnover can disturb planning and hiring processes. To introduce this source of variation in growth, we further modify Gibrat's law by using size (N_τ) *plus* the expected number of departures as the base level for growth, rather than just N_τ. We then subtract the *actual* number of departures $N_{D,\tau}$ from the result to get the new size. The expected number of departures is found from the turnover function to be

$$E(N_{D,\tau}) = N_\tau [\gamma_0 + \gamma_1 \sigma_{c,\tau-1}^2], \tag{11.4}$$

and our modified Gibrat's law becomes

$$N_{\tau+1} = \{N_\tau [1 + \gamma_0 + \gamma_1 \sigma_{c,\tau-1}^2]\} \exp (\sigma_\tau v) - N_{D,\tau}. \tag{11.5}$$

Hiring/Entry

Now we turn to the final variable in the demographic system, the number of persons entering the organization at τ, $N_{B,\tau}$. Because the system is closed and $N_{\tau+1}$, N_τ, and $N_{D,\tau}$ are already determined, we can solve for this variable as $N_{B,\tau} = N_{\tau+1} - N_\tau + N_{D,\tau}$.

A potential complication arises when the relation yields a negative value for $N_{B,\tau}$, which is, of course, meaningless. In these (rare) occurrences, we set $N_{B,\tau}$ at its lower bound of zero and then increase $N_{D,\tau}$ accordingly so that the equality relation of the demographic system

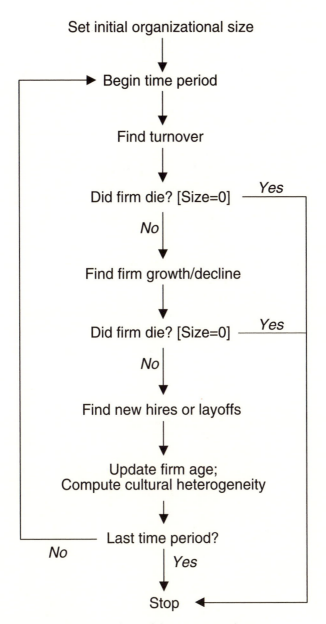

FIGURE 11.1 Flowchart of the macro simulation

holds. Substantively, these increases in $N_{D,\tau}$ might be regarded as layoffs of employees as the organization declines in size.

Figure 11.1 presents a flow chart of the translated macro model of cultural transmission. It shows how the simulation model operates.

11.3 DEMOGRAPHY OF THE SYSTEM

The level of demographic activity generated by the new macro model seems reasonable.[5] Young and small organizations have lower numbers of members arriving and departing, as we would expect. The arrival and departure means are also fairly low, and roughly comparable for the two processes at all ages and sizes, suggesting a certain stability in the organizations. However, the ranges of arrivals and departures at each observation point also show that it is possible for an organization to grow or contract rapidly. In our view, this combination of stability and occasional rapid change are broadly indicative of actual growth trajectories in organizational populations.

Table 11.1 gives summary statistics for the size-age distribution of a set of simulated organization at various ages. The data come from 1,000

TABLE 11.1
Organizational size distribution by age

	Size			
Age	Minimum	Maximum	Mean	Median
1	1	33	5.98	3
2	1	33	6.60	4
3	1	45	8.09	4
5	1	85	8.81	4
10	1	82	9.21	4
20	1	377	13.5	7
50	1	628	25.6	11
100	1	3030	55.9	17

Source: Harrison and Carroll (2001a). Copyright © 2001 by the MIT Press. All rights reserved. Used by permission.

Note: From 1,000 runs of conditions set for high growth, low selectivity, and high alienation.

[5]For more details, see Harrison and Carroll (2001a).

runs for a high-growth, low-selectivity, and high-alienation condition. To conform to empirical observations, the ideal here is a right-tailed skew distribution with a low mean size. These statistics show that to be the case for the simulated model; the median is substantially lower than the mean at all ages. More detailed inspection of these data reveals that the distribution does indeed have a long right tail, as suggested by the high maximums. The mean and median also increase slightly with age, as the table shows. Overall, we regard these simulated size distributions as fairly realistic (cf. Harrison, 2004); there is no doubt that they are more realistic than those generated by the basic model.

11.4 THE CULTURAL SYSTEM

What about culture? We now develop the organization's implied distribution of C_i, the enculturation variable. To accomplish this, we rely on assumptions about the distribution of the hiring pool and knowledge about the number of new members entering each period. We define the organization's variance in culture at τ as $\sigma_{c,\tau}^2$, the variance at equilibrium as σ_{ce}^2, the base variance of the hiring pool as σ_{cp}^2, and the maximum variance of the hiring pool as σ_{cm}^2. The initial set of persons in the organization is assumed to have a cultural variance of σ_{cp}^2. The organization's cultural variance changes as members enter and leave the organization.

We can now determine the variance in culture for specific sets of members and then aggregate to get an overall value. For new members, the cultural variance will depend on the proportion of new members entering the organization. If a relatively small proportion of new members joins the organization, their cultural variance will be close to the base variance of the hiring pool, σ_{cp}^2. When a larger proportion of new members enters, the organization cannot be as selective in choosing new members, so their variance increases from σ_{cp}^2 toward σ_{cm}^2. Specifically, we model the cultural variance of new members as increasing linearly from σ_{cp}^2 to σ_{cm}^2 as the ratio of new entrants to total members approaches one. Formally,

$$_b\sigma_{c,\tau+1}^2 = \sigma_{cp}^2 + \left[\frac{N_{B,\tau+1}}{N_{\tau+1}}\right](\sigma_{cm}^2 - \sigma_{cp}^2) \tag{11.6}$$

The organization's cultural selectivity in hiring can be varied by varying the base variance of the hiring pool σ_{cp}^2, with lower values of σ_{cp}^2 representing more selective hiring policies.

For members who survive from one period to the next, the variance in culture will move toward the equilibrium variance σ_{ce}^2, set to .05—well below the hiring pool variances used in the simulation. Since members exiting from the survivor group tend to be further from the cultural mean due to the alienation effect on turnover, the movement toward equilibrium will be greater when the proportion of surviving members is lower. For this group,

$$_s\sigma^2_{c,\tau+1} = \sigma^2_{ce} + a'\left[\frac{N_{s,\tau+1}}{N_\tau}\right](\sigma^2_{c,\tau} - \sigma^2_{ce}),\qquad(11.7)$$

where N_s is the number of survivors at $\tau + 1$, and a' is a constant in the interval [0, 1] (set to .95) representing resistance to change, or cultural inertia. With no new members entering the organization to increase the cultural variance, the cultural variance over time will approach σ^2_{ce} asymptotically.

The overall cultural variance at time $\tau + 1$ is given by the combination of these two groups. The formula is

$$\sigma^2_{c,\tau+1} = \frac{_b\sigma^2_{c,\tau+1}N_{B,\tau+1} + _s\sigma^2_{c,\tau+1}N_{s,\tau+1}}{N_{\tau+1}}(1+\epsilon),\qquad(11.8)$$

where ϵ is a small disturbance term (variance of .0001) to introduce stochastic fluctuations into the variance. Figure 11.2 shows the time paths of the cultural variance for examples of runs under two different simulation conditions. The asymptotic path for the case of an organization with no entry and no exit is also shown. The disruption effect (see chapter 7) is more pronounced for the condition reflecting high growth, low selectivity, and high alienation but is also noticeable for the condition of low growth, high selectivity, and low alienation. The two conditions also differ in the average level of cultural variance.

11.5 DESIGN OF EXPERIMENTS

We now use the macro model to examine the possible nature of relationships between organizational culture and organizational mortality. Recall that the liability of newness story advanced by Stinchcombe (1965) implies that the heterogeneity of culture should affect organizational mortality rates but that it relies on a stable cohort analysis of employees. In our view, Stinchcombe's analysis of this particular issue is fine as far as it goes—it just does not go far enough, especially in terms of the employment dynamics of new firms. Specifically, we want to examine the relationship of culture to organizational aging and failure under a variety of demographic conditions where employees come and go.

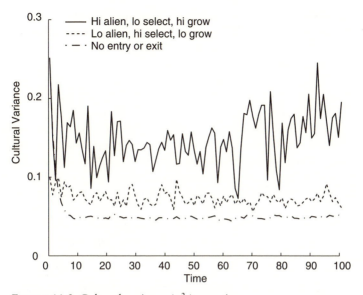

FIGURE 11.2 Cultural variance ($\sigma^2_{c,t}$) over time

The macro model allows us to examine these issues because it considers mortality as an absorption process that occurs when organizational size falls to zero. That is, we run simulations of culture in a set of organizations and then analyze the mortality process across the set using the simulated data on organizational lifetimes and their characteristics. We examine first the condition of high growth, low selectivity, and high alienation, for which the size distributions were reported in Table 11.1 (parameter settings are found in appendix B for this and all conditions reported here). We simulated 1,000 organizations and followed each until its death or until the end of the simulation, which corresponds to fifty years. Each simulation period represents one month of time. Thus, the simulation potentially runs for 600 periods for each organization, at which time, if it survives, it becomes a right-censored case in the data. The simulated data represent event histories of organizational lifetimes, with mortality as the ending event. We record each organization's values on the covariates of age, size, growth, cultural heterogeneity, arrivals, and departures at each point in time. In preparing the simulated data for analysis, we follow convention in splitting the lifetimes into spells of one month, linking the associated values of the covariates with the spell and treating all but the spells ending in mortality events as right censored.

The split-spell data with time-varying covariates are then analyzed with the estimation program TDA (acronym commonly used for the program name Transition Data Analysis; Rohwer and Potter, 1998).

11.6 FINDINGS

Table 11.2 shows estimates of the effects of covariates on the mortality rate for 1,000 simulated organizations with settings of high growth, low selectivity, and high alienation. The models estimated are constant-rate models with a log linear specification of the covariates. Model a shows that age and cultural heterogeneity each contribute uniquely to the mortality rate, but the negative effect of the culture variable is surprising. Model b shows that age is unimportant in these data once size differences have been taken into account: the significant negative size effect swamps the previous age effect, rendering it nonsignificant. But the strong effect of size does not eliminate the effect of cultural heterogeneity, as model c indicates; adding cultural heterogeneity also improves overall fit. Moreover, the specification in model c makes the significant effect of cultural heterogeneity turn positive, thereby agreeing with Stinchcombe's arguments. Thus, for this condition, the simulation model generates age dependence in organizational mortality, but this age dependence can be accounted for by the effects of small size and cultural heterogeneity.

TABLE 11.2
Estimates of mortality hazard functions

	Model a	Model b	Model c
Constant	.976*	3.41*	3.54*
Size		−3.98*	−4.20*
Age	−.005*	−.0002	
Cultural heterogeneity	−31.8*		1.51*
ln L	−3638.9	−1720.1	−1713.1

    Note: From 1,000 runs of conditions set for high growth, low selectivity, and high alienation.
    *$p < .05$.

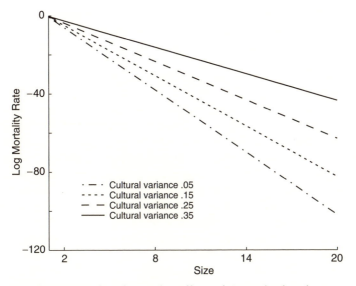

FIGURE 11.3 Predicted mortality effects of size and cultural heterogeneity

In fact, the relationship between size and cultural heterogeneity is even more complex. For this condition and others (but not all) that we have simulated, the data support a statistically significant interaction term between size and cultural heterogeneity. Harrison and Carroll (2001a) report the mortality models with the interaction terms across a variety of simulated conditions. In some simulated conditions, the interaction term is significant, whereas in others it is not (although the signs of the coefficients are the same across all models). It seems that the combinations of (1) low growth and high alienation and (2) high growth and low selectivity drive the interaction effect.

What do the interactions look like? Figure 11.3 plots the interaction effect estimated in a model for a condition highlighted by Harrison and Carroll (2001a)—the high-growth, low-selectivity, and high-alienation condition—by plotting the log of the mortality rate as a function of size for different values of the cultural variance.[6] The mortality rate falls more rapidly with increasing size for smaller values of cultural heterogeneity, showing that mortality decreases with size more quickly for organizations that develop and maintain more homogeneous cultures. That is,

[6]The estimates on which this plot is based are from model 8 of Harrison and Carroll (2001a: 60) table 6.

organizations that grow without developing homogeneous cultures experience greater chances of failure. All in all, it appears that cultural heterogeneity mediates size and growth effects on organizational mortality.

11.7 IMPLICATIONS

This chapter has explored the link between cultural heterogeneity and age and size dependence in organizational mortality. To facilitate pursuit of this question, it was first necessary to develop a macro translation of the model, one incorporating a more realistic growth process that generates reasonable distributions for organizational size and longevity. Once that task was completed, we were able to show that cultural heterogeneity can play a significant role in organizational mortality processes often linked to organizational aging and known as the liability of newness.

Specifically, the simulations using the macro model show that it generates age dependence in organizational mortality, but that in some conditions this age dependence can be accounted for by the effects of small size and cultural heterogeneity. Thus, observed age dependence in failure might be a spurious relationship masking an effect of cultural heterogeneity. The simulations suggest that organizations that grow without developing homogeneous cultures continue to experience higher risks of failure than those that do. Overall, it appears that cultural heterogeneity mediates size and growth effects on organizational mortality. This general finding suggests that Stinchcombe's classic arguments about the liability of newness imply a complex relationship between organizational growth, size, and culture—a relationship that is not obvious from purely age-based considerations. Essentially, the extent to which problems caused by interactions with strangers declines with time (Stinchcombe's thesis) depends on the flow of people into and out of the organization. Under some conditions, an organization can continue to maintain a high proportion of new employees, and associated problems persist.

The implications of this finding have yet to be explored in any systematic fashion either theoretically or empirically. Current analyses of organizational aging often attend to external organizational processes to the neglect of internal organizational processes such as cultural formation and change. Perhaps a more balanced focus on internal and external factors is warranted. Hannan's (1998) deeply penetrating analysis of age dependence in mortality moves in this direction by addressing issues such as knowledge, learning, and capabilities (see also Pólos and Hannan, 2002); but he, too, neglects organizational culture. The analysis presented here suggests that the study of age dependence in organizational mortality might be productively advanced by examining culture, although such an approach presents challenging methodological issues.

CHAPTER 12

Concluding Remarks

12.1 INTRODUCTION

This book presents the findings from our research program on the maintenance and transmission of culture in formal organizations. The main goal of this program is to examine the factors and conditions that influence the persistence, maintenance, and variation of organizational culture over time. In undertaking this effort, we departed from the traditional focus on cultural content by giving explicit attention to demographic processes in organizations as well as to socialization processes. The result, we believe, provides a fuller and more realistic depiction of the dynamics of cultural systems in organizations.

In this final chapter, we take stock of what has been accomplished, what it means, and where the research program might go next. In the next section, we proceed by briefly summarizing the model and its motivation. We then review the major findings of the research reported in the book, going over the various topics we have addressed one by one. Following that, we shift into a more speculative mode. In speculating, we first explore what we see as some of the more important implications of our work—implications for cultural research, for organization theory, and for management practice. We then point out several possible extensions to the model that seem to us potentially interesting. Finally, we conclude with a brief comment about the role of demography in organizational culture.

12.2 MODEL OVERVIEW

Demographic processes play a big role in cultural transmission and persistence. This is because organizations do not operate in a vacuum; rather, the individuals who populate them—persons whose sets of ideas, beliefs, values, behaviors, and interpretations of organizational events constitute the foundation of organizational culture—regularly enter and leave organizations, sometimes rapidly and in large numbers. Indeed, a remarkable feature of organizations is their ability to maintain their cultural character in the face of high inflows and outflows of organizational members. Our research identifies the conditions under which this occurs and provides insights as to why it does, or does not, happen.

To study the role of demography, we developed a limited synthetic approach to organizational culture by integrating two previous approaches to culture, the content approach and the distributive approach. The content approach, which characterizes most social science research on organizational culture, emphasizes the substance of the culture by attempting to identify its specific features. In contrast, the distributive approach emphasizes patterns of cultural variation across time and space; in other words, it addresses the distribution of cultural content and how this distribution changes over time. Both demographic and socialization processes influence the content and distribution of an organization's culture. Cultural content and its distribution can change depending on the cultural characteristics of people entering and leaving the organization, and may also be modified by socialization forces acting on the members of an organization.

In our limited synthetic approach, we represent cultural content in terms of an individual's enculturation level, a measure of the individual's propensity to embrace the values and norms of a particular organization's culture. This is a very specific conception of cultural content, indicating the degree to which the individual fits management's cultural ideal. We examine the relationship between our enculturation measure and the underlying dimensions of culture important to management that determine the enculturation level, and show that variation in the average cultural distance between individuals on these underlying dimensions is tightly linked to variation in enculturation across the organization. So this measure enables us to study the distribution of cultural content across an organization; in particular, the mean enculturation level for the organization captures the degree to which the culture matches management's cultural preferences, and the standard deviation in enculturation assesses cultural heterogeneity.

The basis for our analysis of culture is a formal mathematical model of cultural transmission in organizations, which incorporates both demographic and socialization processes. Specifically, the model has three components: an organizational entry or hiring process, a socialization process, and an exit or turnover process. Enculturation plays a central role in each process. In the entry process, new employees can be selected with more or less attention to management's cultural preferences, depending on the distribution of enculturation in the candidate pool. In the socialization process, individual enculturation levels can change in response to socialization influences from management and peers; management influence pulls an individual toward the management ideal, and peer influence pulls the individual toward the enculturation levels of coworkers, with the overall degree of change decreasing with an individual's tenure in the organization. Finally, in the exit process, turnover occurs at a rate that combines a base rate and an alienation rate that produces higher turnover for individuals with lower fitness to the organization's culture.

We explored implications of the formal model using computer simulation techniques. Simulation methodology permits us to examine the consequences of the model's behavior in different situations and under different conditions by changing parameter values in the model and by adapting the model's structure to particular problems of interest. Different hiring policies are simulated by changing the parameters controlling the enculturation distribution of the candidate pool and the rate at which vacancies are filled. Socialization conditions are varied by changing the weights controlling the relative degrees of management and peer influence. Variations in turnover processes are simulated by changing the base rate and the strength of the alienation effect. And growth and decline processes are examined by controlling the number of new entrants and by imposing cutbacks on the organization.

12.3 REVIEW OF FINDINGS

Our research program addresses a range of issues involving the effects of cultural transmission processes in organizations. The issues we study possess relevance for understanding organizational culture and for organization theory more generally. In this section, we review the major findings from our work. The findings highlight the utility of our synthetic approach to studying culture, and in particular illustrate the substantial impact of demographic processes on organizational culture.

Organizational Types

We began our analysis by examining the cultural transmission model's behavior for seven stylized organizational types: Japanese-style, American manufacturing, professional, governmental, entrepreneurial, Z-type, and collectivist-democratic. Each type is defined by a constellation of parameter settings designed to capture its core socialization and demographic characteristics. The analysis examines the length of time it takes each type to reach cultural equilibrium and the mean and standard deviation of the enculturation level for the organization at equilibrium. The findings indicate that the model can reproduce basic known cultural differences across organizational types based on their socialization and demographic processes. For example, the most preferred cultures from a managerial perspective emerge in the Japanese, professional, and Z-type organizations and the least preferred in the American manufacturing type. And time to equilibrium is greatest for professional, governmental, and collectivistic-democratic organizations.

Applying the model to these stylized organizational types also produces new insights. Rather than being detrimental to cultural stability, rapid growth and high turnover can actually enhance stability. Rapid growth provides a large influx of new employees, who are more susceptible to socialization. High turnover provides a mechanism whereby less enculturated employees are likely to leave in larger numbers. Both effects illustrate the interplay between demographics (flows of people) and culture.

Organizational Growth and Decline

Understanding how growth and decline affect organizational culture is important to our program because these phenomena underpin much demographic activity. We explore this issue with a series of simulation experiments examining the effects of growth and decline conditions, as well as conditions of no growth.

A commonsense view suggests that growth and decline represent turbulence and therefore create problems for cultural transmission and maintenance. Our findings suggest otherwise. In our analysis, organizations exhibit cultural resilience during periods of growth and decline. Why? Organizations seem to maintain remarkable cultural stability during periods of rapid growth due to the relative ease of socializing new members rather than long-term employees. And enculturation actually increases during periods of decline. This latter finding has been previously observed but attributed to psychological processes driven by emotional responses to difficulties in coping with decline. The model developed here demonstrates that this effect can be obtained simply by considering the demographics of the exit process; even when layoffs are not based on seniority, less enculturated employees are more likely to leave the organization both because of alienation and because shorter-tenured—and therefore less socialized—employees make up a larger proportion of the workforce.

An interesting implication of these findings holds that static or "steady state" organizations, in which the relevant mechanisms are weaker, may actually be less stable culturally. That is, with smaller flows of culturally more malleable workers entering the organization and of less enculturated workers leaving, static organizations may face greater problems of cultural maintenance than either growing or declining organizations.

LOS Heterogeneity in Top Management Teams

Top management team (TMT) tenure, and specifically the length of service (LOS) distribution, has been the focus of much empirical research by organizational demographers. This research ties heterogeneity in the LOS distribution to a variety of organizational outcomes, including turnover, innovation, diversification, and adaptiveness. While a number of theoretical approaches have been used to explain these effects, the common element is that they posit an intervening social process, social integration or cognitive diversity (either implicitly or explicitly), that links LOS heterogeneity to the outcomes of interest. Since organizational culture is generally regarded as consisting of beliefs and social practices (which provide the underpinning for the concepts of social integration and cognitive diversity), we believe that this intervening social process can be usefully represented macroscopically as organizational culture.

Accordingly, we reformulated the central argument of this research tradition as a three-variable causal chain: LOS heterogeneity influences cultural heterogeneity, which in turn affects organizational outcomes. We then used the cultural transmission model to examine the conditions under which the LOS and cultural distributions will be tightly linked, as these researchers assume. We find that, although the relationship between LOS heterogeneity and cultural heterogeneity is generally positive, the strength of the relationship varies substantially depending on the level of cultural selectivity to the TMT, the strength of peer socialization within the team, the turnover level, and the strength of alienation.

Of particular interest is the discovery that entry and exit processes can affect LOS heterogeneity and cultural heterogeneity in an inconsistent manner, a phenomenon we refer to as the disruption effect. The main reason for this inconsistency is that while entry and exit events produce strong discontinuities in measures of LOS heterogeneity in a straightforward manner, their effects on cultural heterogeneity are more subtle, depending on selectivity, socialization, and turnover in complex ways. We suggest that a single measure of LOS heterogeneity does not effectively capture several processes that can influence social integration, including socialization, group cohesiveness, and common historical experiences, and propose tenure-based measures more directly related to these processes. In this analysis, we also uncovered a previously unknown built-in cross-sectional relationship between the standard LOS heterogeneity measure and aggregate turnover rates, given duration-dependence of individual turnover.

Organizational Influence Networks

The basic cultural transmission model assumes that peer influence operates by pulling individual enculturation levels toward the mean enculturation level of all persons in the organization. While we view this as a reasonable simplification of the peer influence process, clearly some coworkers influence an individual more than others. To explore further the peer influence process, we refined the basic model to permit person-to-person influence patterns, drawing on theory and research on social cohesion, influence processes, and group dynamics. In the refined model, the influence of a person on any other person varies depending on their cultural similarity; it can also change over time—change in an individual's enculturation level over time results from the multiple influences of other organizational members. A model of this dynamic cultural influence process allows us to examine both how the influence network changes over time and its implications for mean enculturation levels and for cultural heterogeneity in the organization. We used the model to examine in depth the effects of cohort-based influence processes, in which interpersonal influence is stronger among individuals who enter the organization at about the same time.

The cultural influence network model shows that the influence network evolves over time to a fairly robust configuration. Although entry and turnover can disrupt both enculturation and influence, the network dynamics appear to mitigate this disruption and help to explain the cultural stability of organizations. The influence structure does vary by experimental condition, however, and the most important factors appear to emerge from cohort-dependent processes and turnover. Cohort-based influence tends to strengthen the influence network—promoting cultural stability—and to reduce influence inequality. Turnover plays an important role by providing for a flow of new entrants, a precondition for cohort formation; with low turnover, cohort-based processes have less opportunity to operate.

The structure of the influence network affects both mean enculturation and cultural variability. It has a stabilizing effect on the mean enculturation level, which shows little change over time regardless of size, turnover, selectivity, or cohort processes. But cohort-based influence—and more dispersed influence in general—tends to reduce variation in enculturation.

Counterterrorism Policies

Terrorist networks, especially Al Qaeda, receive great attention these days in policy circles. To explore the possible implications of the cultural influence network model for policies designed to combat terrorist networks, we modified the influence structure of the model by restricting influence links to fit the typical hierarchical cellular structure found in these networks. Specifically, in the modified model, person-to-person influence can only operate between members within a cell and between a cell leader and the next hierarchical level to which the cell leader reports.

We then examined the impact of various counterterrorism policy options on the effectiveness of cells at the operational (lowest) level of the hierarchy. Cell effectiveness was assessed by observing implications for cell enculturation, cell size, cell isolation caused by breaks in the hierarchical chain of command, and the influence of cell leaders.

We considered four policy options. Two options deal with the removal of terrorists from cells. Individual terrorists can be removed incrementally as they are discovered, or full cells can be eliminated once they are identified—for example, through surveillance or infiltration. Two other options deal with strategies to inhibit the filling of vacancies in cells. The terrorist organization can be forced to fill vacancies with less fit replacements, or the replacement process can be delayed. Influencing the replacement process can be achieved by disrupting recruitment and training activities or by tighter border controls and other methods to make it more difficult for new terrorists to join a cell.

On the basis of the model, the most effective counterterrorism policies appear to be incremental removal of terrorists and delaying replacement when vacancies occur. Cell elimination generates little effect on the network as a whole—an intrinsic strength of cellular hierarchies—but, of course, may very well make sense when a terrorist act seems imminent. And no single policy strategy produces consistent effects on all the outcomes we examined. Whatever strategy is pursued, the terrorist network still retains significant capabilities, indicating the resilience of these networks and the difficulties in combating them.

Cultural Integration Following Mergers

The success of a merger often depends on the ability to integrate effectively the two organizations that are merged. One stumbling block to effective integration is cultural incompatibility of the two organizations that merge. While incompatibility involves differences in cultural content, post-merger cultural integration is a function of organizational demography as well as content.

We focused on demographic factors related to post-merger cultural integration and examined their implications for reducing cultural conflict. Our experiments combine an acquiring organization with a target organization that rates poorly on cultural preferences of the acquirer's management, and vary the relative sizes of the merged entities and the growth rate, hiring practices, socialization processes, and turnover rates (including layoff policies) of the post-merger organization, and also consider the effects of cultural inertia in the acquired organization. Our primary interests are in identifying the conditions that affect the cultural recovery of the combined organization, including increases in mean enculturation toward the level of the pre-merger acquiring organization and reductions in cultural heterogeneity, and the speed with which these changes occur.

Our findings show that demographic factors have a major effect on post-merger cultural integration. The strongest effects are associated with selectivity in hiring to the organization after the merger, strong socialization efforts by management, departures of less fit individuals due to high alienation, and a large size for the acquirer relative to the target. The commonly used tactic of laying off individuals from the acquired organization can increase the enculturation mean but has little impact on cultural heterogeneity.

Culture and Organizational Mortality

To facilitate the investigation of the relationship between organizational culture and organizational ecology, we developed a macro version of the cultural transmission model. The macro model is based on the same theoretical foundations as the multilevel model we have explored in detail. But rather than incorporating individuals as agents, it models entry, socialization, and exit processes at the organizational level. The shift in level allows us to specify more easily organizational growth processes as functions of organizational age, size, and culture—an advance over the relatively limited way in which we have previously modeled organizational growth—and to examine the consequences of these growth processes in a more computationally efficient manner.

We used the macro model to investigate culturally influenced organizational growth processes and their implications for organizational mortality. We developed a new growth model by modifying the well-known Gibrat's law for organizational growth to incorporate explicitly demographic and cultural processes in organizations; in this new model, organizational size, age, and cultural heterogeneity drive the stochastic growth process. Organizational mortality occurs when the size of the organization shrinks to zero.

Stinchcombe (1965) anticipated the relationship between cultural heterogeneity and mortality in his classic analysis of the liability of newness. A basic argument of his, as we interpret it, characterizes new organizations as possessing high cultural heterogeneity. Such heterogeneity makes organization problematic and leads to high mortality rates, but mortality should decline with age as the culture becomes more homogeneous. But Stinchcombe's approach basically rests on a cohort and does not consider the dynamics of employee entry and exit.

We find that considering the influence of demographic dynamics on cultural heterogeneity generates a more complex relationship between age, size, growth, and mortality. Our experiments still show age dependence in mortality rates, but the analysis indicates that this is sometimes a spurious relationship, masking the effects of cultural heterogeneity. Organizations that fail to develop homogeneous cultures as they age can continue to experience higher failure rates than those that do. So the extent to which problems caused by interactions among strangers decline with time depends on the flows of people into and out of the organization.

12.4 IMPLICATIONS

As explained in chapter 1, the synthetic approach to organizational culture we use in this book combines content-based and distributive approaches. It calls attention to the importance of demographic processes as well as socialization processes and helps, we believe, to develop a better understanding of cultural transmission in organizations. In this section, we discuss some additional implications of this work for cultural research, for organization theory, and for management practice.

For Cultural Research

We believe that research on organizational culture has been limited by the tendency to focus on cultural content, as argued in chapter 1. The distributional approach to culture calls attention to the advantages of considering demographic processes, and we have shown how demographic activity can strongly influence cultural content. More research attention to the effects of the flows of people into and out of organizations promises to provide a deeper understanding of organizational culture and its change over time.

Ethnographic research on organizational culture has yielded many useful insights, but cultural research, like organizational research in general, can benefit from large-sample studies. A fuller understanding of cultural change also requires longitudinal approaches, which, among other advantages, permit a better assessment of the impact of demographic activity. Both large-sample research and longitudinal research present formidable challenges for observation and measurement (and the difficulty in conducting such research is a primary justification for the use of simulation methodology to explore dynamic and comparative issues). These research designs also create problems of comparability, since relevant cultural content is likely to vary from organization to organization and over time. While there are no easy answers to the problems of observation and measurement, our approach offers one possibility for dealing with the comparability problem: along with measuring cultural content, obtain data on managerial preferences and convert the content measures into measures of enculturation, which can be compared across organizational observations.

Culture likely varies with organizational structure; we conceptualize this variation by envisioning an overarching shared cultural content for an organization, supplemented by additional cultural content elements at the subunit level. Different subunits also are likely to exhibit different demographic patterns. A focus on subunit demographics may be helpful in understanding the development and persistence of subcultures.

In analyses of the simulation model, we assumed that the labor pool from which organizations draw members includes persons with the cultural characteristics preferred by management—although it may be more or less difficult to hire these people, resulting in differential rates of recruitment. In the interest of focusing attention on the basic characteristics of the model, we neglected other constraints on the characteristics of the labor pool. Clearly, however, labor pools exhibit important contextual differences, varying in skill levels, educational levels, and cultural and institutional characteristics. These considerations seem especially important when contemplating international differences in culture transmission. The broader social context impinges on both the selection and the socialization of organizational members. Potential and actual organizational entrants possess cultural characteristics determined at least partially by the primary socialization they receive as they grow and mature in a society (Berger and Luckmann, 1967) and reflect their national cultures (Hofstede, 1980); socialization into an organization's culture occurs through a process of secondary socialization. So the cultural characteristics of the society from which organizations draw their members likely exert a strong influence on the culture of an organization. They also constrain management's ability to influence effectively some cultural dimensions through socialization, since secondary socialization that conflicts with prior primary socialization will likely be ineffective (Berger and Luckmann, 1967).

The synthetic model may also be useful for understanding cultural transmission at the societal level. Demographic processes seem especially salient in organizational settings, but this observation may simply reflect the smaller scale, and hence easier recognition, of such processes in organizations. All cultural systems experience demographic pressures. So we believe that understanding the demography of cultural transmission in organizations can assist in gaining insight into cultural transmission processes more generally. For example, by some accounts the demographic bulge created by the baby boom in the United States facilitated the development of countercultures in the 1960s (Easterlin, 1978, 1987). Also note that in his analysis of how parents name their children, Lieberson

(2000: 55) finds "reasonably strong" evidence that demographic changes in the extended family ("increasing instability, declining size") undermine the continuity of familial naming traditions. As he explains it:

> As in religion, whereby rules restrict choices, traditions requiring that children be named after ancestors tend to minimize new names because parents' choices roughly repeat the names used in the past. The decline of the extended family's influence in society—particularly the increasing distance between ancestors and descendants, declining contact with living ancestors, and reduced knowledge about ancestors—should free parents to ignore the pressures to assign certain names from their parents, grandparents, and other relatives. Of course, the influence of such a factor varies from country to country. (Lieberson, 2000: 50)

For Organization Theory

One of the well-known debates within organization theory concerns the adaptability of organizations. Some theories assume or imply that formal organizations are highly adaptive, while others contend that successful adaptation is rare and problematic, preferring instead an image of organizations as highly inertial. How does organizational culture contribute to inertia, and to what extent does it change in response to other types of organizational changes, or inhibit such changes? Most theories of organizations make strong assumptions about cultural adaptiveness. Clearly, the debate would be sharpened with a more analytical understanding of the dynamics of organizational culture. That is, consideration of the demographics of culture could lead to new ways to think about when organizations will be more or less inertial.

A major focus of organization theory rests with organizational performance. How does organizational culture affect organizational performance? Some theorists contend that the link between culture and performance is weak or nonexistent (e.g., Martin, 1992). Others argue that culture has clear performance implications, and some empirical evidence exists to support this perspective (e.g., Sørensen, 2002a). The cultural transmission model developed here potentially informs this debate by linking cultural characteristics to organizational growth. It predicts a connection between cultural heterogeneity and organizational growth and survival for new and small organizations. Other possible links between culture, growth, strategy, and performance have not yet been pursued. For example, strategies of high cultural selectivity can slow growth and lead to missed opportunities for market expansion and ultimately poorer performance, or conversely keep firms from expanding too quickly. And firms may choose their strategies—for better or worse—depending on the availability of specific cultural characteristics in the labor market. So considerations of culture and demography can conceivably be linked to performance, and a formal model can facilitate analysis of the relationship.

For Management Practice

The management literature on organizational culture focuses on two things. First, it addresses the ways managers can intensively socialize employees, including orientation and training sessions, publicizing and making salient organizational values. Second, it concerns how to visibly reward those who best conform to managerial preferences through pay, promotion, and ceremonies. Our work here points to two other important factors subject to managerial control: the recruitment process and the turnover process. Management can raise the enculturation level of the organization through highly selective recruitment; this tactic involves assessing the cultural fitness of applicants and giving significant weight to fitness as an explicit part of the hiring decision. Turnover can be managed in two ways. First, alienation can be made a stronger factor in turnover, either by encouraging less fit employees to leave voluntarily, or by removing such employees involuntarily if necessary. As with the hiring process, the preconditions for using this tactic include awareness of employee cultural fitness and the will to act on the basis of this criterion. Second, the base turnover rate of the organization can be increased without regard for cultural fitness, as with layoffs and early retirement programs.

Exercising such controls entails costs, however, including greater managerial attention, potentially slower growth, and higher wages to attract and retain more culturally desirable workers. These costs make it important to be aware of conditions under which various levers are likely to result in significant increases in enculturation—and also those conditions under which such efforts can be curtailed without significantly lowering enculturation. As shown in chapter 6, these conditions likely vary by organizational type and growth scenario. Cautious generalization of our findings suggests that the biggest cultural payoff to socialization occurs at low levels of enculturation and when socialization has not previously been a management priority. Obviously, greater selectivity in recruitment produces a larger cultural effect when many employees are brought on board—that is, when the organization grows or experiences high turnover. Promoting fit-based turnover generates the greatest returns in culturally heterogenous organizations and when the recruitment process results in new entrants who have higher fitness than incumbent workers. As for relaxing managerial efforts to manage culture, enculturation appears least likely to suffer during organizational decline and when efforts are expended on all three controllable factors of recruitment, socialization, and turnover (two may be sufficient, and the marginal benefits of the third are small).

The "steady state" or no-growth organization presents a case of special interest, where less opportunity exists to influence culture through managing inflows and outflows. In such circumstances, promoting turnover as a means of enhancing the flow-through of workers may produce payoffs; an early retirement incentive program is a common mechanism for accomplishing this, as is reorganization. Besides providing opportunities for increasing enculturation, this strategy generates the additional benefit of reducing stagnation by providing a flow of new members with fresh or more current approaches to their work. Management also possesses the opportunity to harness the power of cohort-based influence processes to its cultural advantage. An obvious way to do this consists of hiring in "clumps," with special attention to selectivity; cohorts created in this manner reinforce enculturation within the cohort and exert an upward pull on the enculturation of other members of the organization. This strategy may be particularly effective when applied to subunits deemed to be culturally problematic.

A final area with two clear managerial implications arising from our work involves post-merger cultural integration. First, we find a reduction in adverse cultural consequences of merging with a culturally incompatible organization when the target firm is small in size relative to the acquirer. For a relatively large target, management could decide to forgo the merger or, alternatively, if economically feasible, choose to operate it as a semiautonomous division rather than attempt full integration. Second, once a firm is acquired, the most effective way to speed cultural recovery comes from inducing a strong alienation effect—that is, promoting high turnover of less culturally fit persons.

12.5 EXTENSIONS OF THE MODEL

As a tractable starting point in our investigations, we have assumed that management's cultural preferences remain fixed. But organizations experience regime changes, and new leadership may institute different cultural priorities. Consider, for example, the visible leadership change at Texas Instruments (TI) following the unexpected death of CEO Jerry Junkins. The TI board chose a new CEO and gave him a mandate to shift the firm's focus from national defense contracting to consumer electronics, with clear implications for organizational values and social practices. Examining the enculturation consequences of shifts in the cultural priorities on management, and the conditions under which such shifts tend to lead to successful cultural change, would be a natural extension of our model. The method we used to address post-merger cultural integration (chapter 10) provides a possible route to a more general treatment of this phenomenon.

Organizational diversity is another topic to which the model can be applied and extended. Cultural heterogeneity represents one important dimension of diversity. Diversity also includes age and tenure diversity. These issues can be addressed within the current framework of the model, and the analysis of top management teams (chapter 7) illustrates this approach. Other major dimensions of diversity include race and gender diversity. Obviously, these dimensions cannot be changed through socialization, but they can be strongly influenced by demographic processes in organizations, and the model can be adapted to this context. Among other things, race and gender diversity impact the operation of socialization processes and potentially relate to cultural heterogeneity in organizations, which could be addressed with an adaptation of the influence network model (chapter 8).

Cultural transmission models of organizational culture may also lead to a better understanding of population dynamics, beyond simply linking culture to mortality or other performance measures. Culture, demographic processes, and organizational growth intersect with competition in both labor markets and product markets. Indeed, a motivation for developing the macro model of cultural transmission was to facilitate simulation experiments using populations of organizations, each of which is influenced by cultural and demographic processes.

12.6 CONCLUSION

It has long been noted that organizations operate as open systems, and this observation certainly applies to the cultural systems of organizations. Failure to recognize how organizational culture interacts with its environment leads to a limited and even misleading perspective on cultural transmission and maintenance. To develop a better understanding of cultural processes, it is essential to consider the demographic flows of people into and out of the organization, as well as their relationship to internal socialization processes. As we have seen here, the three basic processes of entry, socialization, and exit interact in complex ways that can pose difficulties to understanding their joint effects on organizational culture. The formal model we have developed here allows for examination of these processes and exploration of their implications in a variety of contexts. While we think that this effort has led to a number of insights into the cultural transmission process, we also recognize its limitations and regard it as only a first step toward a better understanding of cultural dynamics in organizations. However small that step, we conclude with confidence that it shows clearly that efforts to learn more about organizational culture cannot afford to neglect demographic processes and their influences on culture.

Notation

Notation Used throughout the Book

i	Individual
t	Time (in simulated months)
t^*	Time elapsed to equilibrium
u_i	Tenure of individual i in organization
$\bar{u}_t$	Mean tenure among persons in organization at t
$\tilde{u}_t$	Median tenure among persons in organization at t
$\sigma_{u,t}$	Standard deviation of tenure among persons in organization at t
$\underline{C}_{i,t}$	Enculturation level (fitness) of individual i at t
$\underline{\bar{C}}_t$	Mean enculturation level among persons in organization at t
$\underline{\bar{C}}_h$	Mean enculturation level of hiring pool
$\bar{C}_e$	Mean enculturation level at equilibrium
$\sigma_{c,t}$	Standard deviation of enculturation in organization at t
$\sigma^2_{c,t}$	Variance of enculturation in organization at t
σ_{ch}	Standard deviation of enculturation in hiring pool
σ_{ce}	Standard deviation of enculturation at equilibrium
N_t	Number of persons in organization at t
V_t	Vacancies in organization at t
$N_{B,t}$	New hires in organization at t
$N_{D,t}$	Number of persons departing organization at t
H_i	Dummy for vacancy filling
r_g	Growth rate of organization
r_r	Recruitment rate of organization
$A_{i,t}$	Socialization-change intensity of i at t
α_{mgt}	Socialization-change parameter associated with management pull
α_{peer}	Socialization-change parameter associated with peers
α_{decay}	Socialization-change parameter associated with decay
e	Error term in socialization function
σ_e	Standard deviation of error term e
$B_{i,t}$	Susceptibility to socialization of i at t
β_0	Susceptibility to socialization parameter
β_1	Susceptibility to socialization parameter
β_2	Susceptibility to socialization parameter
$r_{i,t}$	Departure rate of individual i at t

γ_0 Parameter of departure associated with base turnover factors
γ_1 Parameter of departure rate associated with alienation
E_i Dummy for departing individual
$G(u)$ Stochastic survivor function for events as a function of duration u

NOTATION SPECIFIC TO CHAPTER 3

C_i Enculturation level (fitness) of individual i
c_{ij} Individual's value on underlying content dimension j
m_j Management's ideal score for a person along dimension j
v_{ij} Individual i's score along cultural content dimension j
β_j Weighting of content dimension scores to find C_i
d_{ij} Distance between i and j on the content dimensions
$\bar{d}_n$ Average d_{ij} level among n individuals

NOTATION SPECIFIC TO CHAPTER 7

C_i Enculturation level (fitness) of individual i
$h(u)$ Turnover function based on tenure u
$\hat{\rho}$ Estimated correlation coefficient
LOS   Length of service in organization (tenure)
TMT   Top management team
CV   Coefficient of variation in LOS
CV_{12} Measure of heterogeneity from socialization
u_{last} Measure of heterogeneity from team cohesiveness
u_{olap} Measure of heterogeneity from common experiences

NOTATION SPECIFIC TO CHAPTER 8

$I_{i,t}$ Intensity of cultural change in i from the influence network at t
$S_{ji,t}$ Influence that person j exerts on i at t
N_t Number of persons in organization or group at t
a Weighting parameter inversely associated with individual cultural inertia
$D_{i,t}$ Mean cultural difference for all individuals j associated with i
$W_{ji,t}$ Weight of change in influence of each person j on i
b Parameter associated with weighting factor $W_{ji,t}$
v Disturbance with normal distribution $N(0, 1)$
$\bar{S}_{ji}$ Influence mean
σ_s^2 Influence variance

S_R	Net influence range
S_C	Influence centralization
P_{ji}	Random uniform deviate squared
Q_{ji}	Cohort-based influence score of j on i
θ_1	Weighting parameter used in cohort-based influence score
θ_2	Weighting parameter used in cohort-based influence score

NOTATION SPECIFIC TO CHAPTER 9

$N_{max,t}$	Maximum number of persons in cell at t
a	Weighting parameter inversely associated with individual cultural inertia
b	Parameter associated with weighting factor $W_{ji,t}$
θ_1	Weighting parameter used in cohort-based influence score
θ_2	Weighting parameter used in cohort-based influence score
p_{cell}	Probability of cell elimination
L_k	Lag replacement time in months for level k cell
α_{idecay}	Decay in enculturation $C_{i,t}$ for isolated terrorist
$\sigma_{c\epsilon}$	Standard deviation of cultural change noise term
$\sigma_{s\epsilon}$	Standard deviation of influence change noise term

NOTATION SPECIFIC TO CHAPTER 10

$A_{i,t}^*$	Socialization-change intensity for full inertia condition
$A_{i,t}^{**}$	Socialization-change intensity for proportional inertia condition

NOTATION SPECIFIC TO CHAPTER 11

$\sigma_{c,t}^2$	Variance of enculturation in organization at t
σ_{ce}^2	Variance in enculturation at equilibrium
σ_{cp}^2	Base variance in enculturation of the hiring pool
σ_{cm}^2	Maximum variance in enculturation of the hiring pool
τ	Organizational age
N_τ	Number of persons in organization or group at τ
$N_{B,\tau}$	Number of new members to organization at τ
$N_{D,\tau}$	Number of departing members at τ
N_s	Number of survivors in organization from τ to $\tau + 1$
ϵ	Error term in cultural variance
σ_ϵ^2	Variance in error term ϵ
a'	Constant representing cultural inertia

ε	Stochastic function associated with Gibrat's law
ν	Disturbance with distribution $N(0, 1)$
σ_τ	Standard deviation term in growth function
$_b\sigma_{c,\tau}^2$	Variance in enculturation of new entrants at τ
$_s\sigma_{c,\tau}^2$	Variance in enculturation of survivors at τ
λ_0	Parameter associated with standard deviation of growth
λ_1	Parameter associated with standard deviation of growth
λ_2	Parameter associated with standard deviation of growth
λ_3	Parameter associated with standard deviation of growth
λ_4	Parameter associated with standard deviation of growth

Simulation Parameter Settings

TABLE B.1
Settings for basic types and figure 5.2

	Japan	Amer-ican	Profes-sional	Govern-mental	Entrepre-neurial	Z-type	Collec-tivistic
N_0	100	100	100	100	5	100	100
$\overline{C}_0$	0	0	0	0	0	0	0
$\sigma_{c,0}$	.10	.10	.10	.10	.10	.10	.10
$\tilde{u}_0$	12	12	12	12	12	12	12
$\sigma_{u,0}$	25.9	25.9	25.9	25.9	25.9	25.9	25.9
r_g	.04	.04	.0035	.0035	.08	.04	0
r_r	.70	1.9	.40	1.2	1.2	.91	.70
$\overline{C}_h$	.50	.10	.80	.30	.30	.40	.50
σ_{ch}	.15	.15	.15	.15	.30	.15	.15
α_{mgt}	.80	.08	.08	.08	.40	.50	0
α_{peer}	.18	.90	.90	.90	.58	.48	.98
α_{decay}	.02	.02	.02	.02	.02	.02	.02
σ_e	.10	.10	.10	.10	.10	.10	.10
β_0	.02	.02	.02	.02	.02	.02	.02
β_1	.60	.60	.60	.60	.60	.60	.60
β_2	.30	.30	.30	.30	.30	.30	.30
γ_0	.005	.03	.015	.005	.015	.01	.01
γ_1	.15	.60	.15	.15	.15	.15	.15

TABLE B.2
Settings for figures 5.3–5.6

	Highest	High	Middle	Low	Lowest
r_r^*	2.0	1.14	.70	.35	.10
$\overline{C}_h^*$	1.0	.75	.50	.25	0
α_{mgt}^{**}	.98	.735	.49	.245	0
γ_0	.03	.0225	.015	.0075	0
γ_1	.60	.45	.30	.15	0

Note: All other settings are same as table B.1 except $N(0) = 100$ for entrepreneurial.
$^*\overline{C}_h$ and r_r vary simultaneously in inverse relationship, i.e., highest $\overline{C}_h$ tied to lowest r_r.
$^{**}\alpha_{peer} = .98 - \alpha_{mgt}$.

TABLE B.3
Settings for figure 6.1

	Highest	High	Middle	Low	Lowest
r_g	.02	.01	.0	−.01	−.02

Note: All other settings are same as table B.1 except $N(0) = 100$ for entrepreneurial.

TABLE B.4
Settings for figures 6.2–6.5

	Highest	High	Middle	Low	Lowest
r_r^*	2.0	1.14	.70	.35	.10
$\overline{C}_h^*$	1.0	.75	.50	.25	0
α_{mgt}^{**}	.98	.735	.49	.245	0
γ_0	.03	.0225	.015	.0075	0
γ_1	.60	.45	.30	.15	0
r_g^{***}	.02		0		−.02

Note: All other settings are same as table B.1 except $N(0) = 100$ for entrepreneurial.
$^*\overline{C}_h$ and r_r vary simultaneously in inverse relationship, i.e., highest $\overline{C}_h$ tied to lowest r_r.
$^{**}\alpha_{peer} = .98 - \alpha_{mgt}$.
$^{***}r_g$ varies along with one other parameter.

TABLE B.5
Settings for table 6.1

	Value
r_g	$-.04$
N_0	200

Note: Other settings are same as table B.1.

TABLE B.6
Settings for table 6.2 data

	High	Medium	Low
r_s	.02	0	$-.02$
r_r^*	2.0	.70	.10
$\overline{C}_h^*$	1.0	.50	0
σ_{ch}	.20	.10	.10
α_{mgt}^{**}	.98	.49	0
α_{decay}	.02	.02	0
σ_e	.10	.10	0
β_0^{***}	.02	.02	0
β_1^{***}	.60	.60	0
β_2^{***}	.30	.30	0
γ_0	.03	.015	0
γ_1	.60	.30	0

$^*\overline{C}_h$ and r_r vary simultaneously in inverse relationship, i.e., highest $\overline{C}_h$ tied to lowest r_r.
$^{**}\alpha_{peer} = .98 - \alpha_{mgt}$.
***Varied simultaneously. $B_{i,t} = 1$ with 0 settings.

Table B.7
Settings in TMT runs (chap. 7)

	High	Low
N_0	20	5
$\overline{C}_0$	0	0
$\sigma_{c,0}$	.10	.10
$\tilde{u}_0$	12	12
$\sigma_{u,0}$	25.9	25.9
r_g	0	0
r_r^*	1.9	.40
$\overline{C}_h^*$	.80	.10
σ_{ch}	.15	.15
α_{mgt}^{**}	0	0
α_{peer}^{**}	.98	.18
α_{decay}	.02	.02
σ_e	.10	.10
β_0	.02	.02
β_1	.60	.60
β_2	.30	.30
γ_0	.03	.015
γ_1	.60	.15

Note: Initial C_i for CEO also varies as either unity or $\overline{C}_t$.

$^*\overline{C}_h$ and r_r vary simultaneously in inverse relationship, i.e., highest $\overline{C}_h$ tied to lowest r_r; denominator for socialization change intensity held constant at 1.

TABLE B.8
Variations in network runs (chap. 8)

	High	Medium	Low
$\overline{C}_0$	.50	.50	.50
$\sigma_{c,0}$	.15	.15	.15
γ_1^*	.04	.02	0
γ_1^*	.40	.40	0
$\overline{C}_h$	.70	.50	.30
σ_{ch}	.15	.15	.15
a	.05	.05	.05
b	.075	.075	.075
θ_1	.01	.01	.01
θ_2	.02	.02	.02

Note: N_0 also varies among the values 5, 15, 25, 50.

Note: Cohort condition also varied (random vs. cohort); θ_a and θ_2 are for cohort condition; in non-cohort condition, all S_{ij} drawn from $U(0, 1)$.

$^*\gamma_0$ and γ_1 vary simultaneously.

TABLE B.9
Settings in terrorist runs (chap. 9)

	High	Low
$N_{max,t}$	5	5
$\overline{C}_0$	.80	.80
$\sigma_{c,0}$	.075	.075
α^*_{idecay}	.02	.02
γ_0	.01	.05
γ_1	.15	.15
$\overline{C}_h^{**}$	.80	.50
σ_{ch}^{**}	.15	.075
a	.05	.05
b	.05	.05
$\sigma_{c\epsilon}$	.02	.02
$\sigma_{s\epsilon}$	.02	.02
θ_1	.01	.01
θ_2	.02	.02
p_{cell}	.05	0
L_1	2	2
L_2^{***}	6	3
L_3^{***}	12	6

Note: Cohort condition only.

*For isolated terrorist.

**Varied simultaneously in inverse relationship, i.e., higher $\overline{C}_h$ tied to lower σ_{ch}.

***Varied simultaneously.

TABLE B.10
Pre-merger settings for target (chap. 10)

	High	Medium	Low
N_0	800	200	50
r_g	0	0	0
r_r^*	.693	.693	.693
$\overline{C}_h^*$	.50	.50	.50
α_{mgt}	.49	.49	.49
α_{peer}	.49	.49	.49
γ_0	.015	.015	.015
γ_1	.15	.15	.15

Note: Common merger settings in table B.13 also apply.

*$\overline{C}_h$ and r_r vary simultaneously in inverse relationship, i.e., highest $\overline{C}_h$ tied to lowest r_r.

TABLE B.11
Pre-merger settings for acquirer (chap. 10)

	High	Medium	Low
N_0	800	200	50
r_g	0	0	0
r_r^*	1.61	.693	.223
$\overline{C}_h^*$	.80	.50	.20
α_{mgt}^{**}	.80	.49	.18
γ_0	.015	.015	.015
γ_1	.60	.15	.15

Note: Common merger settings in table B.13 also apply.

*$\overline{C}_h$ and r_r vary simultaneously in inverse relationship, i.e., highest $\overline{C}_h$ tied to lowest r_r.

**$\alpha_{peer} = .98 - \alpha_{mgt}$.

TABLE B.12
Post-merger settings (chap. 10)

	High	Medium	Low
r_g	.04	0	−.04
r_r^*	1.61	.693	.223
$\overline{C}_b^*$	.80	.50	.20
α_{mgt}^{**}	.80	.49	.18
γ_0	.015	.005	.005
γ_1	.60	.15	.15

Note: Common merger settings in table B.13 also apply.

Note: Layoff policy and cultural inertia also varied.

Note: Except for r_g and γ_0, settings were matched with those in table B.11.

$^*\overline{C}_b$ and r_r vary simultaneously in inverse relationship, i.e., highest $\overline{C}_b$ tied to lowest r_r.

$^{**}\alpha_{peer} = .98 - \alpha_{mgt}$.

TABLE B.13
Common merger settings
(chap. 10)

$\overline{C}_0$	0
$\sigma_{u,0}$	.10
$\tilde{u}_0$	12
$\sigma_{u,0}$	25.9
σ_{ch}	.15
α_{decay}	.02
σ_e	.10
β_0	.02
β_1	.60
β_2	.30

TABLE B.14
Settings for macro model (chap. 11)

	High	Low
$\gamma_0{}^*$	.025	.01
$\gamma_1{}^*$	.50	.10
λ_0	.02	.04
λ_1	.15	.15
λ_2	−.004	−.004
λ_3	.05	.05
λ_4	−.20	−.20
a'	.95	.95
σ_ϵ^2	.0001	.0001
σ_{ce}^2	.05	.05
σ_{cp}^{2**}	.25	.10
σ_{cm}^{2**}	.35	.20

$^*\gamma_0$ and γ_1 vary simultaneously in inverse relationship, i.e., higher γ_0 tied to lower γ_1.
$^{**}\sigma_{cp}^2$ and σ_{cm}^2 vary simultaneously.

References

Abegglen, James, and George Stalk. 1985. *Kaisha*. New York: Basic Books.

Al Qaeda. 2001. "Training Manual." Translated document released by the U.S. Department of Justice on December 7, 2001.

Asch, Solomon E. 1951. "Effects of Group Pressure upon the Modification and Distortion of Judgments." In H. Guetzkow (ed.), *Groups, Leadership and Men*, 117–90. Pittsburgh: Carnegie Press.

Atran, Scott. 2003. "Who Wants to Be a Martyr?" *New York Times*, May 5, A23.

Axelrod, Robert. 1997. "The Dissemination of Culture: A Model with Local Convergence and Global Polarization." *Journal of Conflict Resolution* 41:203–26.

Axtell, Robert, Robert Axelrod, Joshua M. Epstein, and Michael D. Cohen. 1996. "Aligning Simulation Models: A Case Study and Results." *Computational and Mathematical Organization Theory* 1:123–41.

Bantel, Karen, and Susan Jackson. 1989. "Top Management and Innovations in Banking: Does the Composition of the Top Team Make a Difference?" *Strategic Management Journal* 10:107–24.

Bantel, K., and M. Wiersema. 1992. "A Comprehensive Model of Top Team Turnover." GSM Working Paper No. ST91004, University of California at Irvine.

Barnard, Chester I. 1938. *The Functions of the Executive*. Cambridge, MA: Harvard University Press.

Baron, James N., M. Diane Burton, and Michael T. Hannan. 1996. "The Road Taken: Origins and Early Evolution of Employment Systems in Emerging Companies." *Industrial and Corporate Change* 5:239–76.

Baron, James N., Michael T. Hannan, and M. Diane Burton. 2001. "Labor Pains: Organizational Change and Employee Turnover in Young, High-Tech Firms." *American Journal of Sociology* 106:960–1012.

Barth, Fredrik. 1987. *Cosmologies in the Making*. Cambridge: Cambridge University Press.

———. 1993. *Balinese Worlds*. Chicago: University of Chicago Press.

Bendor, Jonathan, and Piotr Swistak. 2001. "The Evolution of Norms." *American Journal of Sociology* 106:1493–1545.

Berger, Peter L., and Thomas Luckmann. 1967. *The Social Construction of Reality*. New York: Doubleday.

Blau, Peter M. 1977. "A Macrosociological Theory of Social Structure." *American Journal of Sociology* 83:26–54.

Boeker, Warren. 1997. "Strategic Change: The Influence of Managerial Characteristics and Organizational Growth." *Academy of Management Journal* 40:152–71.

Boone, C., and W. van Olffen. 1997. "The Confusing State of the Art in Top Management Composition Studies: A Theoretical and Empirical Review." *Netherlands Institute of Business Organization and Strategy Research.* Research Memorandum No. 97-11. Maastricht.

Boyd, Robert, and Peter J. Richerson. 1985. *Culture and the Evolutionary Process.* Chicago: University of Chicago Press.

Brenner, Joel Glenn. 1999. *The Emperors of Chocolate: Inside the Secret World of Hershey and Mars.* New York: Random House.

Brumann, Christoph. 1999. "Writing for Culture: Why a Successful Concept Should Not Be Discarded." *Current Anthropology* 40:S1–S13.

Burke, W. Warner, and Peter Jackson. 1991. "Making the SmithKline Beecham Merger Work." *Human Resource Management* 30:69–87.

Burt, Ronald S. 1992. *Structural Holes.* Cambridge, MA: Harvard University Press.

Cameron, Kim, M. U. Kim, and D. Whetten. 1988. "Organizational Effects of Decline and Turbulence." In K. Cameron, R. Sutton, and D. Whetten (eds.), *Readings in Organizational Decline*, 207–25. Cambridge, MA: Ballinger.

Carley, Kathleen. 1991. "A Theory of Group Stability." *American Sociological Review* 56:331–54.

Carley, Kathleen M., and Vanessa Hill. 2001. "Structural Change and Learning within Organizations." In Alessandro Lomi and Erik R. Larsen (eds.), *Dynamics of Organizations: Computational Modeling and Organization Theories*, 63–92. Cambridge, MA: MIT Press/AAAI Press.

Carley, Kathleen M., Ju-Sung Lee, and David Krackhardt. 2001. "Destabilizing Networks." *Connections* 24:79–92.

Carley, Kathleen, and Zhiang Lin. 1997. "Organizational Decision Making and Error in a Dynamic Task Environment." *Journal of Mathematical Sociology* 22:125–50.

Carroll, Glenn R., and Michael T. Hannan. 2000. *The Demography of Corporations and Industries.* Princeton, NJ: Princeton University Press.

Carroll, Glenn R., and J. Richard Harrison. 1994. "On the Historical Efficiency of Competition between Organizational Populations." *American Journal of Sociology* 100:720–49.

———. 1998. "Organizational Demography and Culture: Insights from a Formal Model." *Administrative Science Quarterly* 43:637–67.

———. 2002. "Come Together? The Organizational Dynamics of Post-Merger Cultural Integration." *Simulation Modelling Practice and Theory* 10:349–68.

Cavalli-Sforza, Luca, and Marcus Feldman. 1981. *Cultural Transmission and Evolution.* Princeton, NJ: Princeton University Press.

Chang, Myong-Hun, and Joseph E. Harrington Jr. 2005. "Discovery and Diffusion of Knowledge in an Endogenous Social Network." *American Journal of Sociology* 110:937–76.

Chang, Victoria, Jennifer Chatman, and Glenn R. Carroll. 2001. "Dreyer's Grand Ice Cream (A) and (B)." Stanford Graduate School of Business (Case OB-35), January.

Chatman, Jennifer A. 1991. "Matching People and Organizations: Selection and Socialization in Public Accounting Firms." *Administrative Science Quarterly* 36:459–84.

Chatman, Jennifer A., and Karen Jehn. 1994. "Assessing the Relationship between Industry Characteristics and Organizational Culture: How Different Can You Be?" *Academy of Management Journal* 37:522–53.

Chatman, Jennifer A., Gwendolyn K. Lee, Glenn R. Carroll, and J. Richard Harrison. 2004. "The Influence of Social Networks on Cultural Transmission and Enculturation: An Empirical Investigation." Unpublished manuscript. University of California at Berkeley.

Cohen, Michael D., James G. March, and Johan P. Olsen. 1972. "A Garbage Can Model of Organizational Decision Making." *Administrative Science Quarterly* 17:1–25.

Cole, Robert. 1990. *Strategies for Learning.* Berkeley: University of California Press.

Coleman, James S. 1964. *Introduction to Mathematical Sociology.* Glencoe, IL: Free Press.

———. 1990. *Foundations of Social Theory.* Cambridge, MA: Harvard University Press.

Collins, James C., and Jerry I. Porras. 1994. *Built to Last: Successful Habits of Visionary Companies.* New York: HarperBusiness.

Columbia Accident Investigation Board. 2003. *Report. Vol. 1.* Washington, DC: U.S. Government Printing Office.

Coombs, Clyde H., Robyn M. Dawes, and Amos Tversky. 1970. *Mathematical Psychology.* Englewood Cliffs, NJ: Prentice-Hall.

Cremer, J. 1993. "Corporate Culture and Shared Knowledge." *Industrial and Corporate Change* 2:351–86.

Cyert, Richard M., and James G. March. 1963. *A Behavioral Theory of the Firm.* Englewood Cliffs, NJ: Prentice-Hall.

Deal, Terrence E., and Allan A. Kennedy. 1982. *Corporate Cultures.* Reading, MA: Addison-Wesley.

Decision Support Systems, Inc. 2001. "Hunting the Sleepers: Tracking Al-Qaida's Covert Operations." Document available on-line at http://www.metatempo.com, accessed June 16, 2003.

Delaney, K. J., and D. Woodruff. 2001. "In Europe H-P and Compaq Face Tougher Merger Task." *Wall Street Journal*, September 6.

Denrell, Jerker. 2003. "Vicarious Learning, Under-sampling of Failure, and the Myths of Management." *Organization Science* 14:227–43.

———. 2004. "Random Walks and Sustained Competitive Advantage." *Management Science* 50:922–34.

DiMaggio, Paul. 1997. "Culture and Cognition." *Annual Review of Sociology* 23:263–87.

Duncan, Otis Dudley. 1975. *Introduction to Structural Equation Models.* New York: Academic Press.

Easterlin, Richard A. 1978. "What Will 1984 Be Like? Socioeconomic Implications of Recent Twists in Age Structure." *Demography* 15:397–432.

———. 1987. *Birth and Fortune: The Impact of Numbers on Personal Welfare.* 2nd ed. Chicago: University of Chicago Press.

Elster, Jon. 1989. *The Cement of Society.* New York: Cambridge University Press.

Encyclopedia of World Terrorism. 1997. *Encyclopedia of World Terrorism.* Armonk, NY: M. E. Sharpe.

Endlich, Lisa. 1999. *Goldman Sachs: The Culture of Success.* New York: Simon and Schuster.

Epstein, Joshua, and Robert Axtell. 1996. *Growing Artificial Societies.* Cambridge, MA: MIT Press.

Feder, B. 2000. "Ill-Fated Merger Costs California Universities' Medical Care Centers 176 Million." *San Jose Mercury News*, December 14, 2001.

Feynman, Richard P. 1985. *Surely You're Joking, Mr. Feynman.* New York: Norton.

Finkelstein, Sidney, and Donald C. Hambrick. 1996. *Strategic Leadership.* Minneapolis, MN: West.

Flatt, Sylvia. 1993. "The Innovative Edge: How Top Management Team Demography Makes a Difference." Ph.D. diss., University of California at Berkeley.

Forrester, Jay W. 1971. *World Dynamics.* Cambridge, MA: Wright-Allen.

Frank, Kenneth A., and Kyle Fahrbach. 1999. "Organization Culture as a Complex System: Balance and Information in Models of Influence and Selection." *Organization Science* 10:253–77.

Freeman, John, and Michael T. Hannan. 1975. "Growth and Decline Processes in Organizations." *American Sociological Review* 40:215–28.

French, J. R. P., Jr. 1956. "A Formal Theory of Social Power." *Psychological Review* 63:181–94.

Friedkin, Noah E. 1998. *A Structural Theory of Social Influence.* Cambridge: Cambridge University Press.

Friedkin, Noah E., and Karen S. Cook. 1990. "Peer Group Influence." *Sociological Methods and Research* 19:122–43.

Friedkin, Noah E., and Eugene C. Johnsen. 1990. "Social Influence and Opinions." *Journal of Mathematical Sociology* 15:193–204.

Geertz, H., and C. Geertz. 1964. "Teknonymy in Bali: Parenthood, Age-Grading and Genealogical Amnesia." *Journal of the Royal Anthropological Institute* 94:94–108.

Gerstel, David U. 1982. *Paradise, Incorporated: Synanon.* Novato, CA: Presidio Press.

Gerstner, Louis V., Jr. 2002. *Who Says Elephants Can't Dance: Inside IBM's Historic Turnaround.* New York: HarperBusiness.

Gibbs, Jack P. 1989. "Conceptualization of Terrorism." *American Journal of Sociology* 54:329–40.

Gleick, James. 1992. *Genius: The Life and Science of Richard Feynman.* New York: Pantheon.

Glick, William H., C. C. Miller, and George P. Huber. 1993. "The Import of Upper-Echelon Diversity on Organizational Performance." In G. D. Huber and W. H. Glick (eds.), *Organizational Change and Redesign*, 179–214. New York: Oxford University Press.

Goffman, Erving. 1959. *The Presentation of Self in Everyday Life*. Garden City, NY: Doubleday Anchor.

Goodenough, Ward H. 1957. "Cultural Anthropology and Linguistics." *Monograph Series on Language and Linguistics* 9:167–73. Washington, DC: Georgetown University Press.

———. 1981. *Culture, Language and Society*. Menlo Park, CA: Benjamin/Cummings.

Graunt, John. 1662. *Natural and Political Observations Mentioned in a Following Index, and Made upon the Bills of Mortality*. London: Printed by Tho. Roycroft for John Martin, James Allestry, and Tho. Dicas at the Sign of the Bell in St. Paul's Churchyard.

Haleblian, J., and Sidney Finkelstein. 1992. "The Effects of Top Management Team Size and CEO Dominance on Performance in Turbulent and Stable Environments." Unpublished manuscript, University of Southern California.

Hambrick, Donald C., Theresa Seung Cho, and Ming-Jer Chin. 1996. "The Influence of Top Management Heterogeneity on Firms' Competitive Moves." *Administrative Science Quarterly* 41:659–84.

Hambrick, Donald C., and Phyllis A. Mason. 1984. "Upper Echelons: The Organization as a Reflection of Its Top Managers." *Academy of Management Review* 9:193–206.

Hannan, Michael T. 1992. "Rationality and Robustness in Multilevel Systems." In J. S. Coleman (ed.), *Rational Action in Sociology*, 120–35. Newbury Park, CA: Sage.

———. 1998. "Rethinking Age Dependence in Organizational Mortality." *American Journal of Sociology* 104:85–123.

Hannan, Michael T., and Glenn R. Carroll. 1992. *Dynamics of Organizational Populations*. New York: Oxford University Press.

Hannan, Michael T., and John Freeman. 1984. "Structural Inertia and Organizational Change." *American Sociological Review* 49:149–64.

Hannerz, Ulf. 1992. *Cultural Complexity: Studies in the Social Organization of Meaning*. New York: Columbia University Press.

Harrington, Joseph E., Jr. 1998. "The Social Selection of Flexible and Rigid Agents." *American Economic Review* 88:63–82.

———. 1999. "Rigidity of Social Systems." *Journal of Political Economy* 107:40–64.

Harris, Marvin. 1971. *Culture, Man, and Nature: An Introduction to General Anthropology*. New York: Crowell.

Harrison, J. Richard. 1997. "Dominant Coalition Dynamics: The Politics of Organizational Adaptation and Failure." Paper presented at the International Conference on Computer Simulation and the Social Sciences, Cortona, Italy.

———. 2004. "Models of Growth in Organizational Ecology: A Simulation Assessment." *Industrial and Corporate Change* 13:245–63.

Harrison, J. Richard, and Glenn R. Carroll. 1991. "Keeping the Faith: A Model of Cultural Transmission in Formal Organizations." *Administrative Science Quarterly* 36:552–82.

———. 2001a. "Modeling Culture in Organizations: Formulation and Extension to Ecological Issues." In Alessandro Lomi and Erik R. Larsen (eds.), *Dynamics of Organizations: Computational Modeling and Organization Theories,* 37–62. Cambridge: MIT Press/AAAI Press.

———. 2001b. "Modeling Organizational Culture: Demography and Influence Networks." In J. Chatman, T. Cummings, P. C. Earley, N. Holden, P. Sparrow, and W. Starbuck (eds.), *Handbook of Organizational Culture and Climate,* 185–216. New York: Wiley.

———. 2002. "The Dynamics of Cultural Influence Networks." *Journal of Computational and Mathematical Organization Theory* 8:5–30.

Harrison, J. Richard, Zhiang Lin, Glenn R. Carroll, and Kathleen M. Carley. 2007. "Simulation Modeling in Organizational and Management Research." *Academy of Management Review* (forthcoming).

Harrison, J. Richard, and James G. March. 1984. "Decision Making and Postdecision Surprises." *Administrative Science Quarterly* 29:26–42.

Hoffman, Bruce. 2001. "Change and Continuity in Terrorism." *Studies in Conflict and Terrorism* 24:417–28.

Hofstede, Geert. 1980. *Culture's Consequences.* Beverly Hills, CA: Sage.

Hofstede, Geert, Bram Neuijen, Denise Daval Ohayv, and Geert Sanders. 1990. "Measuring Organizational Cultures: A Qualitative and Quantitative Study across Twenty Cases." *Administrative Science Quarterly* 35:286–316.

Holmstrom, B., and S. N. Kaplan. 2000. "Corporate Governance and Merger Activity in the U.S.: Making Sense of the 80s and 90s." Unpublished manuscript, University of Chicago.

Horgan, John, and Max Taylor. 1997. "The Provisional Irish Republican Army: Command and Functional Structure." *Terrorism and Political Violence* 9:1–32.

Hutchins, Edwin, and Brian Hazlehurst. 1991. "Learning in the Cultural Process." In D. Farmer, C. Langton, S. Rasmussen, and C. Taylor (eds.), *Artificial Life II.* Menlo Park, CA: Addison-Wesley.

Jackson, Susan E., Jeanne F. Brett, V. I. Sessa, D. M. Cooper, J. A. Julin, and K. Peyronnin. 1991. "Some Differences Make a Difference: Individual Dissimilarity and Group Heterogeneity as Correlates of Recruitment, Promotions, and Turnover." *Journal of Applied Psychology* 76:675–89.

Jacobs, R. C., and P. T. Campbell. 1961. "The Perpetuation of an Arbitrary Tradition through Successive Generations of a Laboratory Microculture." *Journal of Abnormal and Social Psychology* 62:644–58.

Jermier, John M., John M. Slocum Jr., Louis W. Fry, and Jeannie Gaines. 1991. "Organizational Subcultures in a Soft Bureaucracy: Resistance behind the Myth and Facade of an Official Culture." *Organization Science* 2:170–94.

Kaplan, S. N., M. L. Mitchell, and K. H. Wruck. 1997. "A Clinical Exploration of Value Creation and Destruction in Acquisitions: Organizational Design, Incentives and Internal Capital Markets." Unpublished manuscript, University of Chicago Graduate School of Business.

Karr, Alphonse. 1849. *Les Guepes.* Paris: M. Levy.

Keck, Sara L. 1997. "Top Management Team Structure: Differential Effects by Environmental Context." *Organization Science* 8:143–56.

Keesing, Roger. 1974. "Theories of Culture." *Annual Review of Anthropology* 3:73–97.

Keyfitz, Nathan. 1977. *Applied Mathematical Demography*. New York: Wiley.

Kiesler, C. A., and S. B. Kiesler. 1969. *Conformity*. Reading, MA: Addison-Wesley.

Kitts, James A. 2004. "Productive Competition? Hybrid Control Systems and the Divergence of Formal and Informal Norms." Unpublished manuscript, University of Washington.

Kitts, James A., and Paul Trowbridge. 2003. "Shape Up or Ship Out: Socialization, Attrition and Organizational Stability." Paper presented at the annual meetings of the American Sociological Association, Atlanta, Georgia.

Klerks, Peter. 2001. "The Network Paradigm Applied to Criminal Organizations: Theoretical Nitpicking or a Relevant Doctrine for Investigators? Recent Developments in the Netherlands." *Connections* 24:53–65.

Koene, B. A., C. Boone, and J. L. Soeters. 1997. "Organizational Factors Influencing Homogeneity and Heterogeneity in Organizational Cultures." In S. A. Sackmann (ed.), *Cultural Complexity in Organizations*, 279–93. Newbury Park, CA: Sage.

Krackhardt, David, and Lyman W. Porter. 1985. "When Friends Leave: A Structural Analysis of the Relationship between Turnover and Stayers' Attitudes." *Administrative Science Quarterly* 30:242–61.

Krebs, Valdis E. 2001. "Mapping Networks of Terrorist Cells." *Connections* 24:43–52.

Kreps, David M. 1990a. "Corporate Culture and Economic Theory." In J. E. Alt and K. A. Shepsle (eds.), *Perspectives on Positive Political Theory*, 90–143. Cambridge: Cambridge University Press.

———. 1990b. *Game Theory and Economic Modelling*. New York: Oxford University Press.

Lager, Fred "Chico." 1994. *Ben & Jerry's: The Inside Scoop*. New York: Crown.

Law, Averill S., and W. David Kelton. 1991. *Simulation Modeling and Analysis*. 2nd ed. New York: McGraw-Hill.

Lawrence, Barbara S. 1997. "The Black Box of Organizational Demography." *Organization Science* 8:1–22.

Lazear, Edward P. 1995. "Corporate Culture and the Diffusion of Values." In H. Siebert (ed.), *Trends in Business Organization*, 89–133. Tubingen: J. C. B. Mohr.

Lee, Jeho, and J. Richard Harrison. 1997. "Innovation and Industry Bifurcation: The Emergence of Strategic Groups." Paper presented at the International Conference on Complex Systems, Nashua, New Hampshire.

Levinthal, Daniel. 1991. "Random Walks and Organizational Mortality." *Administrative Science Quarterly* 36:397–420.

Levitt, Steven D., and Sudhir Alladi Venkatesh. 2000. "An Economic Analysis of a Drug-Selling Gang's Finances." *Quarterly Journal of Economics* 115:755–89.

Lewis, Michael. 1989. *Liar's Poker: Rising through the Wreckage on Wall Street*. New York: Penguin.

Lie, John. 1997. "Sociology of Markets." *Annual Review of Sociology* 23:341–60.

Lieberson, Stanley. 2000. *A Matter of Taste: How Names, Fashions and Cultures Change*. New Haven, CT: Yale University Press.

Lincoln, James R., Mitsuyo Hanada, and Kerry McBride. 1986. "Organizational Structures in Japanese and U.S. Manufacturing." *Administrative Science Quarterly* 31:338–64.

Lincoln, James R., and Arne Kalleberg. 1990. *Culture, Control and Commitment*. Cambridge: Cambridge University Press.

Lomi, Alessandro, and Erik R. Larsen (eds.). 2001. *Dynamics of Organizations: Computation Modeling and Organization Theories*, Cambridge: MIT Press/AAAI Press.

Loomis, Carol J. 2005. "Why Carly's Big Bet Is Failing." *Fortune*, February 7, 50–62.

Louis, Meryl Reis. 1980. "Surprise and Sense Making: What Newcomers Experience in Entering Unfamiliar Organizational Settings." *Administrative Science Quarterly* 25:226–51.

Love, John F. 1995 (1986). *McDonald's: Behind the Arches*. Rev. ed. New York: Bantam.

MacArthur, Robert H. 1972. *Geographical Ecology*. New York: Harper and Row.

Macy, Michael W., and Robert Willer. 2002. "From Factors to Actors: Computational Sociology and Agent-Based Modeling." *Annual Review of Sociology* 28:143–66.

Mangalindan, Mylene. 2004. "Boss Talk: The Grownup at Google—How Eric Schmidt Imposed Better Management Tactics But Didn't Stifle Search Giant." *Wall Street Journal*, March 29, B1.

March, James C., and James G. March. 1977. "Almost Random Careers: The Wisconsin School Superintendency, 1940–1972." *Administrative Science Quarterly* 22:377–409.

March, James G. 1962. "The Business Firm as a Political Coalition." *Journal of Politics* 24:662–78.

———. 1978. "Bounded Rationality, Ambiguity, and the Engineering of Choice." *Bell Journal of Economics* 9:587–608.

———. 1991. "Exploration and Exploitation in Organizational Learning." *Organization Science* 2:71–87.

———. 2001. "Foreword." In Alessandro Lomi and Erik R. Larsen (eds.), *Dynamics of Organizations: Computational Modeling and Organization Theories*, ix–xvi. Cambridge, MA: MIT Press/AAAI Press.

Mark, Noah. 2004. "Cultural Transmission, Disproportionate Prior Exposure, and the Evolution of Cooperation." *American Sociological Review* 67:323–44.

Martin, Joanne. 1992. *Culture in Organizations: Three Perspectives*. New York: Oxford University Press.

———. 2002. *Organizational Culture: Mapping the Terrain*. Newbury Park, CA: Sage.

McCain, Bruce, Charles A. O'Reilly, and Jeffrey Pfeffer. 1983. "The Effects of Departmental Demography on Turnover." *Administrative Science Quarterly* 26:626–41.

McCartney, Scott. 1999. *ENIAC: The Triumphs and Tragedies of the World's First Computer.* New York: Walker.

McKendrick, David G., and Glenn R. Carroll. 2001. "On the Genesis of Organizational Forms: Evidence from the Market for Disk Drive Arrays." *Organization Science* 12:661–82.

McNeil, Kenneth, and James D. Thompson. 1971. "The Regeneration of Social Organizations." *American Sociological Review* 36:624–37.

McPherson, J. Miller, Lynn Smith-Lovin, and James Cook. 2001. "Birds of a Feather: Homophily in Social Networks." *Annual Review of Sociology* 27:415–44.

McWilliams, Gary. 2001. "Computer Megamerger: Will Bigger Be Better?" *Wall Street Journal*, September 5, A14.

Michel, J., and Donald C. Hambrick. 1992. "Diversification Posture and Top Management Team Characteristics." *Academy of Management Journal* 35:9–37.

Mohr, John W. 1998. "Measuring Meaning Structures." *Annual Review of Sociology* 24:345–70.

Murray, Alan. 1989. "Top Management Group Heterogeneity and Firm Performance." *Strategic Management Journal* 10:125–41.

Nelson, Richard R., and Sidney G. Winter. 1982. *An Evolutionary Theory of Economic Change.* Cambridge, MA: Belknap Press of Harvard University Press.

O'Reilly, Charles A., III. 1989. "Corporations, Culture and Committment: Motivational and Social Control in Organizations." *California Management Review* 31 (4):9–25.

O'Reilly, Charles, A., III, and David Caldwell. 1979. "Information Influence as a Determinant of Perceived Task Characteristics and Job Satisfactions." *Journal of Applied Psychology* 64:157–65.

O'Reilly, Charles A. III, and David Caldwell. 1998. "Cypress Semiconductors: Vision, Values, and Killer Software (A) and (B)." Stanford Graduate School of Business (Case HR-8).

O'Reilly, Charles A., III, David F. Caldwell, and William P. Barnett. 1989. "Work Group Demography, Social Integration and Turnover." *Administrative Science Quarterly* 34:21–37.

O'Reilly, Charles A., III, and Jennifer Chatman. 1996. "Culture as Social Control." *Research in Organizational Behavior* 18:157–200.

O'Reilly, Charles A., III, Jennifer Chatman, and David Caldwell. 1991. "People and Organizational Culture: A Q-Sort Approach to Assessing Person-Organization Fit." *Academy of Management Journal* 34:487–516.

O'Reilly, Charles A., III, and Sylvia Flatt. 1986. "Executive Team Demography, Organizational Innovation, and Firm Performance." OBIR Working Paper No. 9, University of California at Berkeley.

O'Reilly, Charles A., III, and Jeffrey Pfeffer. 2000. *Hidden Value: How Great Companies Achieve Extraordinary Results with Ordinary People.* Boston: Harvard Business School Press.

O'Reilly, Charles A. III, Richard C. Snyder, and Joan N. Boothe. 1993. "Effects of Organizational Demography on Organizational Change." In G. D. Huber and W. H. Glick (eds.), *Organizational Change and Redesign*, 147–75. New York: Oxford University Press.

Ott, Steven J. 1989. *The Organizational Culture Perspective*. Pacific Grove, CA: Brooks/Cole.

Ouchi, William G. 1981. *Theory Z*. Reading, MA: Addison-Wesley.

Parsons, Talcott. 1956. "Suggestions for a Sociological Approach to the Theory of Organizations I." *Administrative Science Quarterly* 1:63–85.

Parunak, H. Van Dyke, Robert Savit, and Rick L. Riolo. 1998. "Agent-Based Modeling vs. Equation-Based Modeling: A Case Study and Users' Guide." *Proceedings of Multi-Agent Systems and Agent-Based Simulation*, 10–25. Springer LNAI 1534.

Pascale, Richard T. 1985. "The Paradox of Corporate Culture." *California Management Review* 27 (2):26–41.

Perrow, Charles. 2000. "An Organizational Analysis of Organizational Theory." *Contemporary Sociology* 29:469–76.

Peters, Thomas J. 1978. "Symbols, Patterns and Setting." *Organizational Dynamics* 7:3–23.

Peters, Thomas J., and Robert H. Waterman. 1982. *In Search of Excellence*. New York: Harper and Row.

Petersen, Trond, and Seymour Spilerman. 1990. "Job Quits from an Internal Labor Market." In K. U. Mayer and N. B. Tuma (eds.), *Event History Analysis in Life Course Research*, 69–95. Madison: University of Wisconsin Press.

Pfeffer, Jeffrey. 1981. "Management as Symbolic Action: The Creation and Maintenance of Organizational Paradigms." In L. L. Cummings and B. M. Staw (eds.), *Research in Organizational Behavior*, 3:1–52. Greenwich, CT: JAI Press.

———. 1983. "Organizational Demography." In L. L. Cummings and B. M. Staw (eds.), *Research in Organizational Behavior*, 5:299–357. Greenwich, CT: JAI Press.

Pfeffer, Jeffrey, and Charles A. O'Reilly III. 1987. "Hospital Demography and Turnover among Nurses." *Industrial Relations* 26:158–73.

Podolny, Joel M., and James N. Baron. 1997. "Resources and Relationships: Social Networks and Mobility in the Workplace." *American Sociological Review* 62:673–93.

Pólos, László, and Michael T. Hannan. 2002. "Reasoning with Partial Knowledge." *Sociological Methodology* 32:133–81.

Pólos, László, Michael T. Hannan, and Glenn R. Carroll. 2002. "Foundations of a Theory of Social Forms." *Industrial and Corporate Change* 11:85–115.

Prahalad, C. K., and Gary Hamel. 1990. "The Core Competence of the Corporation." *Harvard Business Review* 68 (3):79–91.

Prichard, James Cowles. 1839. "On the Ethnography of High Asia." *Journal of the Royal Geographical Society of London* 9:192–215.

Pyati, A. 2000. "UCSF/Stanford: Marriage Was Rough; Divorce Is Expensive." *San Francisco Business Times*, April 21, 25.

Ragin, Charles. 1994. *Constructing Social Research: The Unity and Diversity of Method*. Newbury Park, CA: Pine Forge Press.

Repenning, Nelson P. 2001. "Understanding Fire Fighting in New Product Development." *Journal of Product Innovation Management* 18:285–300.

Repenning, Nelson P., and John Sterman. 2002. "Capability Traps and Self-Confirming Attribution Errors in the Dynamics of Process Improvement." *Administrative Science Quarterly* 47:265–95.

Rivkin, Jan W., and Nicolaj Siggelkow. 2003. "Balancing Search and Stability: Interdependence among Elements of Organizational Design." *Management Science* 49:290–311.

Rodgers, T. J. 1990. "No Excuses Management." *Harvard Business Review* 68 (4):84–98.

Rodseth, Lars. 1998. "Distributive Models of Culture." *American Anthropologist* 100:55–69.

Rohwer, Goetz, and Ulrich Potter. 1998. *Transition Data Analysis 6.2:* User's Manual. Technical Report. Ruhr Universitaet Bochum.

Romanelli, Elaine. 1990. "The Evolution of New Organizational Forms." *Annual Review of Sociology* 17:79–104.

Rothenberg, Richard. 2002. "From Whole Cloth: Making Up the Terrorist Network." *Connections* 24:36–42.

Rothschild-Whitt, Joyce. 1979. "The Collectivist Organization." *American Sociological Review* 44:509–27.

Roughgarden, Jonathan. 1979. *The Theory of Population Genetics and Evolutionary Ecology.* New York: Macmillan.

Rousseau, Denise M. 1990. "Quantitative Assessment of Organizational Culture: The Case for Multiple Measures." In B. Schneider (ed.), *Frontiers in Industrial and Organizational Psychology* 3:153–92. San Francisco: Jossey-Bass.

Sackmann, Sonja A. 1992. "Culture and Subcultures: An Analysis of Organizational Knowledge." *Administrative Science Quarterly* 37:140–61.

Saloner, Garth, Andrea Shepard, and Joel M. Podolny. 2001. *Strategic Management.* New York: Wiley.

Sapir, Edward. 1932. "Cultural Anthropology and Psychiatry." *Journal of Abnormal and Social Psychology* 27:229–42.

Schein, Edgar H. 1968. "Organizational Socialization and the Profession of Management." *Industrial Management Review* 9:1–15.

———. 1985. *Organizational Culture and Leadership.* San Francisco: Jossey-Bass.

———. 1992. *Organizational Culture and Leadership.* 2nd ed. San Francisco: Jossey-Bass.

Schneider, Ben. 1987. "The People Make the Place." *Personnel Psychology* 40:437–53.

Schwartz, Theodore. 1978a. "The Size and Shape of a Culture." In F. Barth (ed.), *Scale and Social Organization,* 215–42. Oslo: Universitetsforlaget.

———. 1978b. "Where Is the Culture?" In G. D. Spindler (ed.), *The Making of Psychological Anthropology,* 419–41. Berkeley: University of California Press.

———. 1992. "Anthropology and Psychology: An Unrequited Relationship." In T. Schwartz, G. M. White, and C. A. Lutz (eds.), *New Directions in Psychological Anthropology,* 324–49. Cambridge: Cambridge University Press.

Scott, W. Richard. 1987. *Organizations: Rational, Natural, and Open Systems*. 2nd ed. Englewood Cliffs, NJ: Prentice-Hall.

———. 2003. *Organizations: Rational, Natural, and Open Systems*. 5th ed. Englewood Cliffs, NJ: Prentice-Hall.

Sherif, Muzafir. 1935. "A Study of Some Social Factors in Perception." *Archives of Psychology*, no. 187.

Simmel, Georg. 1906. "The Sociology of Secrecy and of Secret Societies." *American Journal of Sociology* 11:441–98.

Simon, Herbert A. 1962. "The Architecture of Complexity." *Proceedings of the American Philosophical Society* 106:467–82.

Smith, Ken G., K. A. Smith, J. D. Olian, H. P. Sims, D. P. O'Bannon, and J. A. Scully. 1994. "Top Management Team Demography and Process: The Role of Social Integration and Communication." *Administrative Science Quarterly* 39:412–38.

Smircich, Linda. 1983. "Concepts of Culture and Oganizational Analysis." *Administrative Science Quarterly* 28:339–58.

Sørensen, Jesper B. 2000a. "The Ecology of Organizational Demography: Tenure Distributions and Organizational Competition." *Industrial and Corporate Change* 8:713–44.

———. 2000b. "The Longitudinal Effects of Group Tenure Composition and Turnover." *American Sociological Review* 65:298–310.

———. 2002a. "The Strength of Corporate Culture and the Reliability of Firm Performance." *Administrative Science Quarterly* 47:70–91.

———. 2002b. "The Use and Misuse of the Coefficient of Variation in Organizational Demography Research." *Sociological Methods and Research* 30:475–91.

———. 2004. "The Organizational Demography of Racial Employment Segregation." *American Journal of Sociology* 110:626–71.

Sperber, Dan. 1996. *Explaining Culture: A Naturalistic Approach*. Oxford: Blackwell.

Staw, Barry M. 1980. "The Consequences of Turnover." *Journal of Occupational Behavior* 1:253–73.

Stinchcombe, Arthur. 1965. "Social Structure and Organizations." In J. G. March (ed.), *Handbook of Organizations*, 142–93. Chicago: Rand McNally.

Strang, David, and Michael Macy. 2001. "In Search of Excellence: Fads, Success Stories, and Adaptive Emulation." *American Journal of Sociology* 107:147–83.

Strauss, Claudia, and Naomi Quinn. 1997. *A Cognitive Theory of Cultural Meaning*. Cambridge: Cambridge University Press.

Sutton, John. 1997. "Gibrat's Legacy." *Journal of Economic Literature* 35:40–59.

Sutton, Robert. 1988. "Managing Organizational Death." In K. Cameron, R. Sutton, and D. Whetten (eds.), *Readings in Organizational Decline*, 381–96. Cambridge, MA: Ballinger.

Tam, Pui-Wing. 2003. "Merger by Numbers." *Wall Street Journal*, April 28, A1.

Trice, Harrison, and Janice Beyer. 1993. *The Cultures of Work Organizations*. Englewood Cliffs, NJ: Prentice-Hall.

Tucker, David. 2001. "What's New about the New Terrorism and How Dangerous Is It?" *Terrorism and Political Violence* 13:1–14.

Tuma, Nancy Brandon, and Michael T. Hannan. 1984. *Social Dynamics: Models and Methods.* Orlando: Academic Press.

Tushman, Michael A., and Charles A. O'Reilly. 1997. *Winning through Innovation: A Practical Guide to Leading Organizational Change and Renewal.* Boston: Harvard Business School Press.

Tylor, Edward B. 1871. *Primitive Culture.* London: J. Murray.

Ulam, S. M. 1991. *Adventures of a Mathematician.* Berkeley and Los Angeles: University of California Press.

Useem, Michael. 1975. *Protest Movements in America.* Indianapolis: Bobbs-Merrill.

Van den Steen, Eric. 2003. "On the Origin and Evolution of Corporate Culture." Unpublished working paper, MIT. Sloan School.

Vlasic, B., and B. A. Stertz. 2000. *Taken for a Ride: How Daimler-Benz Drove Off with Chrysler.* New York: Morrow.

Wagner, W., Jeffrey Pfeffer, and Charles A. O'Reilly. 1984. "Organizational Demography and Turnover in Top Management Groups." *Administrative Science Quarterly* 29:74–92.

Waldrop, M. Mitchell. 1992. *Complexity: The Emerging Science at the Edge of Order and Chaos.* New York: Simon and Schuster.

Wanous, J. P. 1980. *Organizational Entry.* Reading, MA: Addison-Wesley.

Wasserman, Stanley, and Katherine Faust. 1994. *Social Network Analysis.* Cambridge: Cambridge University Press.

Weber, Max. 1947. *The Theory of Social and Economic Organization.* Edited by A. H. Henderson and T. Parsons. Glencoe, IL: Free Press.

Weber, Roberto A., and Colin F. Camerer. 2003. "Cultural Conflict and Merger Failure: An Experimental Approach." *Management Science* 49:400–415.

Weber, Yaakov. 1996. "Corporate Cultural Fit and Performance in Mergers and Acquisitions." *Human Relations* 40:1181–1202.

Wiersema, Margarthe, and K. Bantel. 1992. "Top Management Team Demography and Corporate Strategic Change." *Academy of Management Journal* 35:91–121.

Wiersema, Margarthe, and Alan Bird. 1993. "Organizational Demography in Japanese Firms: Group Heterogeneity, Individual Dissimilarity and Top Management Team Turnover." *Academy of Management Journal* 36:996–1025.

Williams, Katherine Y., and Charles A. O'Reilly. 1998. "Demography and Diversity in Organizations: A Review of 40 Years of Research." *Research in Organizational Behavior* 20:77–140.

Williams, Molly. 2001. "H-P's Deal for Compaq Has Doubters as Value of Plan Falls to 20.52 Billion," *Wall Street Journal*, September 5, A3.

Wilson, James Q. 1989. *Bureaucracy.* New York: Basic Books.

Wolf, John B. 1978. "Organization and Management Practices of Urban Terrorist Groups." *Terrorism*, 1:169–86.

Index